Praise for Robert Camuto's *Corkscrewed:*
Adventures in the New French Wine Country

Winner of the 2008 Gourmand World Cookbook Awards, Best
Book on French Wines

The French translation of *Corkscrewed* (*Un Américain dans les*
vignes: Une ode amoureuse à la France du bien-vivre) won the 2009
Clos de Vougeot literary prize

"Camuto's lighthearted book is a particularly enjoyable read that
chronicles the author's journey through French wine country in
a scrumptious collection of stories about wine, food, vineyards,
and winemakers." ♀ BETH HISER, *Bloomsbury Review*

"[*Corkscrewed*] inspires thirst and curiosity. . . . Mr. Camuto's
adventures will introduce readers to little-known French wines
. . . and to the passionate individuals that persevere despite the
absence of monetary reward. These may not be the wines that
earn one spurs as a connoisseur, but they certainly may produce
a worthy sense of humility at how much there is to learn. I can't
wait to drink them."
♀ ERIC ASIMOV, *New York Times*, Dining & Wine section

"If you think you would enjoy having a conversation with a
passionate French wine craftsman, dive into Robert Camuto's
delicious new book. I spend a good part of my life underground
in France, and everything Camuto relates of his adventures rings
true. And to those of you tiring of the varietal bandwagon, here's
an escape route." ♀ KERMIT LYNCH, wine importer and author of
Adventures on the Wine Route: A Wine Buyer's Tour of France

"[Camuto's] enthusiasm for underdog grapes, regions and winemakers makes him a pleasant guide along the back roads of France." ♀ THOMAS MATTHEWS, *Wine Spectator*

"If you saw and liked the film *Mondovino*, get this book. Like a collection of love letters to wine, each chapter showcases a winemaker who has carved out a niche for himself amid the encroaching corporate tide, sprawl, or commercialization. In a world of oak chips and cost-benefit analysis, these are the winemakers who must endure, even in beloved France."
♀ MAGGIE SAVARINO DUTTON, *Seattle Weekly*

"Mr. Camuto's writing is precise, entertaining and compelling enough that it should appeal to audiences beyond the normally narrow scope reached by wine books. It reads very much like a collection of short stories that come together to form what is essentially a non-fiction novel. . . . A rare gem in the field of wine literature and a highly recommended read."
♀ DAVID MCDUFF, *McDuff's Food and Wine Trail*

"[Camuto] is a stylish writer with a gift for describing the way his subjects look and think, and express themselves in words and wine. He explains each winemaker's approach and results, also adding a bit of insight about intra-French competition and the export market in the French wine industry today."
♀ CLAIRE WALTER, culinary-colorado.blogspot.com

"Deliciously descriptive, Camuto is informative without being too technical, a serious observer yet humorously light-hearted at times." ♀ JULIA LAUER-CHEENNE, *Lincoln (NE) Journal Star*

PALMENTO

AT TABLE

A SICILIAN WINE ODYSSEY

Robert V. Camuto

University of Nebraska Press | Lincoln and London

Library of Congress Cataloging-
in-Publication Data
Camuto, Robert V.
Palmento: a Sicilian wine odyssey /
Robert V. Camuto.
    p. cm. — (At table)
ISBN 978-0-8032-2813-9 (cloth: alk. paper)
1. Wine and wine making—Italy—
Sicily—Anecdotes. 2. Wineries—Italy—
Sicily—Anecdotes. I. Title. II. Title:
Sicilian wine odyssey. III. Series:
At table series.
TP559.I8C275 2010
641.2'209458—dc22
2010001694

Set in Dante by Shirley Thornton
Designed by Nathan Putens.

In Memoriam

Luigi Camuto

1898 (Bronte) – 1938 (New York)

and for my parents

To the hope that

Sicily remains

an island

"LOOK HERE, CYCLOPS," said I, "you have been eating a great deal of man's flesh, so take this and drink some wine, that you may see what kind of liquor we had on board my ship. I was bringing it to you as a drink-offering, in the hope that you would take compassion upon me and further me on my way home, whereas all you do is to go on ramping and raving most intolerably. You ought to be ashamed yourself; how can you expect people to come see you any more if you treat them in this way?"

He then took the cup and drank. He was so delighted with the taste of the wine that he begged me for another bowl full. "Be so kind," he said, "as to give me some more, and tell me your name at once. I want to make you a present that you will be glad to have. We have wine even in this country, for our soil grows grapes and the sun ripens them, but this drinks like nectar and ambrosia all in one." — HOMER, *The Odyssey*

THEN ONE OF THEM ASKED me what those Italian volunteers were really coming to do in Sicily. "They are coming to teach us good manners," I replied in English. "But they won't succeed, because we think we are gods." — GIUSEPPE TOMASI DI LAMPEDUSA, *Il Gattopardo* (*The Leopard*)

Contents

Illustrations

Acknowledgments

IN MY TRAVELS ACROSS SICILY, I have been touched by the generosity and warmth of many Sicilians. I want to thank all the winemakers and families cited in this book for their help and hospitality. Among those who generously have given days of their time and helped with research contacts so that I should better understand the island they love: Giusto Occhipinti and Titta Cilia of COS, Alessio Planeta, Marco and Sebastiano De Bartoli, the entire Tasca d'Almerita family, Frank Cornelissen, Ciro Biondi, and Alberto Aiello Graci.

I can think of no barman with a better appreciation of wine than Sandro Dibella of Solicchiata. I feel privileged to have tasted the straight-from-the-heart home cooking of Angela and Rosa Aura Occhipinti. In this project's early stages, I received inspiration and encouragement from many, including Provence winemaker and Sicilian-at-heart Raimond de Villeneuve de Flayosc. In the later stages before going to print, the manuscript was proofread by my friends and fellow wine adventurers Ken McNeill, Art Nelson, and John Forsyth, who offered comments and corrections that are greatly appreciated. I want to thank all my friends and family who have listened to my stories and encouraged me to share them. And I want to thank my wife, Gilda, and son, Dantino, for their patience and for making me homesick whenever I am away.

Finally, I want to thank all those who have courageously worked to make Sicily free, including Letizia Battaglia; all those who have spoken out against the Mafia; and the anti-Mafia groups such as Libera Terra and Addiopizzo. They have created a climate of expression for all—including many of the voices in this book.

Introduction

I WENT TO SICILY IN the winter of 2008 to explore and write about an emerging wine scene. What I discovered in more than a year of travels to the island was more than a fascinating, teeming wine frontier; I found something close to my own heartbeat.

On a trip to Sicily years earlier, I'd sensed that I had landed on *terra santa*. It is a feeling that has only grown as I've come to know this island: from the anarchic street markets of old Palermo, to the morning stillness of the vineyards and lava flows of Mount Etna, to the vast grain-covered hinterlands that turn from vibrant Scottish green in spring to a nearly colorless brown under a scorching summer sun. Despite the legacies of corruption, emigration, violence, and efforts to obliterate its patrimony or scar its nature, something sacred persists here: a natural, familial way of life tied to the farmlands, forests, and seas of what Sicilians call their "continent."

This book was inspired by a personal milestone. The approach of my fiftieth birthday produced one of those moments when you ask, "If this year were my last, how would I spend it?" And so I headed south from my home in Mediterranean France to a land that was more feral, lawless, random, contradictory, and therefore more profoundly Mediterranean. I suppose the fact that my grandfather was born in Bronte (and died in New York when my father was an infant) has something to do with the visceral attraction, although I know people with no Sicilian blood who have similar emotions.

Goethe wrote in the eighteenth century, "To have seen Italy without having seen Sicily is not to have seen Italy at all, for Sicily is the clue to everything."

That statement now seems truer than ever. Modernity seems to have enriched swaths of mainland Italy materially, but robbed something of its soul. Sicily, however, seems to have so far resisted the forces that transform places into replicas of everywhere else. The traditions that form its identity are intact: a fervent pagan-like adherence to religious symbols, a profound commitment to the extended family above all, the obligation to break or ignore rules imposed by the state, and the correct belief that Sicily's natural bounty and cuisines make the rest of the world seem pale and wanting.

The story of Sicilian wine is a long one: Homer mocked it; Pliny the Elder exalted it; Arab Muslim conquerors probably more than tolerated it. The British merchant John Woodhouse "discovered" it in the sherry-like wine of Marsala at the end of the eighteenth century. And the French and Italians coveted Sicilian wine when the phylloxera parasite ravaged their vineyards at the end of the nineteenth century. Today the vestiges of that last golden age are the *palmenti*—traditional stone wineries with massive wood lever presses that for the most part lie abandoned across winegrowing Sicily. Made obsolete by newer technology or deemed illegal for commercial use by modern European regulations, the old structures have been given over to brambles and the elements or recycled into *agriturismo* bed-and-breakfasts or modern wineries.

Sicily has long been Italy's biggest grower of wine grapes. What is new is that in our shrinking world with an appetite for authenticity, Sicilian *terroirs* and their indigenous wine grapes are valued far from Sicily's shores—from the rich red Nero d'Avola that spread from southeastern Sicily to the elegant Nerello Mascalese resembling Pinot Noir or Nebbiolo on the slopes of Mount Etna, along with white grapes such as Carricante, Catarratto, Grecanico, Inzolia, Zibibbo (Muscat of Alexandria), and many more.

The rediscovery of Sicilian *terroirs* is accompanied by a boom of smaller-scale quality wine production. In 1990 the number of commercial Sicilian wine producers was little more than three dozen; today the number is approaching three hundred—including "foreigners" from the Italian peninsula and beyond as well as European celebrities, but mostly new generations of Sicilians who chose to stay rather than find opportunity elsewhere. Much of this change has to do with greater forces in society. Following decades of Mafia wars and assassinations culminating in the 1992 killings of Palermo prosecutors Giovanni Falcone and Paolo Borsellino, the Sicilian people and an aggressive anti-Mafia movement seem to have pushed the mob underground or off the island. The result is a new sense of openness to the world and what may be Sicily's first entrepreneurial class: after millennia of domination by outsiders, feudal land ownership, poverty, and criminality, Sicily is growing its first generations that—in the modern sense of the word—can be said to be "free."

I am not a wine critic but a writer who sees in wine metaphors for us all. Wine to me is food (physical and spiritual), an expression of humanity and of nature and that zone where the two merge into something larger. In this communion of life forces, I know of no place richer than Sicily—no place at this moment that seems to have more to say.

TYRRHENIAN
SEA

Salina

N

Palermo

Trapani

San Giuseppe Jato

Messina

Randazzo
Solicchiata
Bronte
Linguaglossa

Marsala

Santa
Margherita
di Belice

Corleone

Regaleali

Mount Etna

Menfi

Sambuca
di Sicilia

Catania

IONIAN
SEA

Agrigento

MEDITERRANEAN
SEA

Siracusa

Vittoria
Ragusa

Pantelleria

Scoglitti

Noto

Ispica

Pachino

0   5   100 km

0   25   100 mi

PALMENTO

Winter

I

Benvenuti in Sicilia

I HAD ARRIVED IN SICILY only a few hours earlier, and on the drive to dinner I would break more laws than I had violated during any prior twenty minutes of my life. Indeed, I could always say that I was an innocent *straniero* merely following a lawless guide in Valeria, the waif with the brick-sized monogrammed Dolce & Gabbana belt buckle and the ever-singing *telefonino*, who greeted me at Azienda Agricola cos, which I'd chosen as my first stop in Sicily for all noble reasons. I was here because—more than two and a half decades after its founding by a group of university friends—cos had become a thriving symbol of the new Sicily. Its wines were fashionably sipped in cosmopolitan capitals the world over, and cos was considered on the cutting edge of the growing and wholesome natural wine movement. Indigenous grape varietals were farmed biodynamically (using herbal tea treatments and a few practices that resembled alchemy tied to the phases of the moon) and wines were produced with naturally occurring yeasts found in grapes and with minimal added sulfur (sulfites). More than that—burnishing cos's authenticity credentials—the winery had been fermenting some of its wines not in wood barrels or steel or cement vats but in clay amphorae, a process reminiscent of the Greeks who had first settled Sicily; and therefore it elevated my role here to something like an epicurean archaeologist.

Of course, I wouldn't have to explain my behavior to anyone, because this was Sicily. And in Sicily, life's little laws and sense of order—let's call them "constraints"—tend to have a need to be not so much broken as simply ignored. I had spent a couple of hours driving from the new, sleek, glass and lava stone Catania airport across the Sicilian countryside, and I felt as though I were the only person on the road enslaved by inconveniences such as wearing a seat belt and observing the lanes marked on the pavement. As a bright afternoon sun and cornflower blue sky faded to night, I'd driven through the randomness of olive groves and stands of eucalyptus that abutted cinderblock housing complexes and junkyards. I'd passed through seas of densely packed citrus trees—arranged with no apparent design and now weighted down with blood-red oranges that dropped into the road only to be splattered by speeding traffic.

It was night when I pulled up cos's entry road outside Vittoria, and with the help of dim entry lights I could make out the mix of old and new buildings that formed the cos winery and *agriturismo* where I would be spending the next couple of nights. Sitting at right angles at the end of the drive lined with olive trees and lavender was a pair of centuries-old buildings with pale pistachio shutters and tiled roofs. In the taller of the two buildings—a two-story villa with pretty stone balconies and iron balustrades—I noticed the glow of office lights and human activity.

Inside the door of the office was Valeria, a sprite of a woman in her twenties standing talking into her *telefonino* as her free hand fluttered and waved, with her fingers signing their own soliloquy. She recognized me with a raised eyebrow and a quick nod and went back to her business. Her blonde-and-brown-streaked hair was pulled back in a tight ponytail, and she wore a current version of the Italian youth fashion uniform: baggy pants with enough pockets to move multiple *telefonini* every waking hour of the day, hooded sweatshirt, flat sneakers, and that polished steel belt buckle.

"*Ciao, ciao, ciao,*" she said into the phone what seemed more than a dozen times.

"*Va bene?*" she asked, and introduced herself. I shook her out-stretched hand and skipped the details about being lost on my first evening at the wheel in the Sicilian interior. "*Va bene,*" I responded. Valeria and a woman colleague, who'd appeared next to her, began discussing the most pressing matter that evening: my dinner.

The nearby pizzeria was closed. But there was a seafood restaurant about twenty minutes away in Scoglitti where one eats well, they said. I asked if getting there was complicated.

"*No, è facile*"—easy. Valeria said this with such confidence I almost believed her. She volunteered to draw out the route. To make things even easier, she said, I could follow her to the restaurant around eight, as she lived nearby. She showed me to my room across the courtyard and up a flight of stairs.

An hour later, I found Valeria in the office, where she gave me a hand-drawn map—a series of circles, lines, and arrows. She went over the directions slowly. It all meant nothing to me.

"*Va bene,*" I said.

Valeria must have picked up something tentative in my voice, because she looked me in the eye and asked if I was sure I understood. I responded with a *non-è-problema* shrug. Valeria grabbed her *telefonino* and the car keys that dangled from a long cord, and thus began my first lesson in how to drive like a Sicilian.

Which is where the lawbreaking started.

Valeria climbed into her little dust-covered Ford and I followed her to the end of the drive. She rocketed onto the main road, her wheels a cloud of dust from the drive. I was shifting through all gears on my gearbox and racing the RPMs just to keep up with her. Without slowing, she whipped through one roundabout and then another—and as I followed in pursuit, the G-forces made me realize how empty my stomach was. A straightaway provided an opportunity for her to push the accelerator to the floor, hurling her little car into the night—and within inches of the back bumper of another vehicle that rather inconsiderately seemed to be driving at a legal speed.

Her car veered left over the solid white line in the center of the road, and I followed. We blew through a stop sign, careened through a roundabout, and made the little car engines whine. Was the traffic light we just went through *technically* red? Valeria was breaking even more laws than I: peering ahead into her car, I noticed the driver's seat belt hanging neglected and limp, while Valeria cradled her *telefonino* to her ear.

We entered the little well-lit village of Scoglitti and turned off onto a small piazza. Valeria popped out of her car and motioned for me to park in an empty space in a line of cars set at an angle to the curb.

But, I said, protesting, I didn't know the Italian for "crosswalk," and I pointed to the white stripes on the street where Valeria wanted me to park.

"*Va bene*," she said with such self-assuredness it made me feel like a dope for caring about such trivialities. And off she tore into the provincial night.

I parked in the crosswalk and stood outside the car for a few minutes to see if anyone would mind. There were few people on the street. A pair of local police wearing white caps and carrying matching leather satchels that looked full of parking tickets walked right past me and into a corner bar.

Va bene.

Thanks to Valeria's driving, I was early for dinner. So I took a walk around Scoglitti, crossing a brightly lit plaza with groups of old men discussing things the old-fashioned way: with their mouths, their faces, and their hands—not a single *telefonino* in sight. I followed the signs to the port—for Scoglitti sits on the southeastern coast of Sicily facing North Africa. The waterfront with its seawall promenade and stone benches was deserted. The *gelaterie, pizzerie*, and seafront condos were shuttered for winter. A few dozen fishing and pleasure boats bobbed in the harbor.

I walked back to where I had parked and climbed the flight of stairs that led to Sakalleo. Pushing open the door, I stood in a small entryway. There was a desk with a small cash register and, off to the right, a kitchen with a pair of women in white aprons busily chopping while chirping in Italian. I could smell onions and garlic simmering in olive oil, the scent of freshly cut lemons, and the vapors of salty boiling pasta water.

A woman of maybe fifty with curly, light brown hair showed me a table in a corner of one of four rooms lit by fluorescent wall torches—a good sign, as some of the best meals I've eaten in Italy have been in family restaurants lit as brightly as operating blocks. On the walls were photographs of scenes from the same fishing boat. As I would later learn, the boat—also named *Sakalleo*—was the commercial boat of the restaurant owner Pasquale Ferrara, who saved the best of his catch for his restaurant. The woman who greeted me was Pina Strano, who had been one of three partners running cos before she left to marry Pasquale and join him at the restaurant.

Sakalleo seemed ready for business. A young man and woman in blue jeans and sweaters were busily putting finishing touches on the bright blue and gold table settings. But for whom? There were no other customers in sight and it was already 8:30 on a Monday night.

I was hungry. I hadn't eaten anything all day except for some shoe-leather prosciutto at the Rome airport. I sat waiting for a menu to arrive. Instead, the young woman came up to me and asked in a soft voice, *"Crudo va bene?"*

The question was if I wanted some raw seafood to start. For instead of a menu, Sakalleo poses its guests a series of yes/no questions. To nearly all those questions, I repeated about the only two words I'd pronounced since I'd arrived on the island: *"Va bene."*

The Sicilian wine list was short and to the point. Though Sicily produces mostly white wines—made chiefly from native Catarratto vines planted on the western half of the island—here in southeastern Sicily I was in red country. The island's dominant red grape is hearty Nero d'Avola—literally, the black grape of Avola—named for the port town on the island's Ionian coast about seventy miles from where I sat. I chose a bottle of cos wine from the local appellation Cerasuolo di Vittoria, a ruby-colored blend that balances the deep-purple tannic heft of Nero d'Avola with the lighter, cherry-colored, and more acidic local Frappato. The wine came in cos's signature old-fashioned short, stubby bottles and was served with a small glass made for drinking rather than for savoring aromas. This yin-yang blend—like most Cerasuolos I've since enjoyed—was not the world's most deeply complex wine, but it was surely one of the most easygoing. It was the kind of wine that lets you think you could drink it all day while you *ciao-ciao*-ed into your telephone and parked illegally.

The first of the *crudi* arrived—a pair of raw marinated langoustines and a few prawns in lemon and oil accompanied by a small portion of *merluzzo* (cod) seasoned with garlic and pepper flakes. More than *bene*, the seafood was so finely delicate as to hardly need chewing. Each morsel softened my heart as it slid, dripping its marinade, down my throat. To find fresher I would have had to put on a wet suit. When the first dish was gone, I broke the first of many pieces of bread to mop up the sauce. I followed with another mouthful of wine, which seemed weightless and melded perfectly with the flavors on my plate.

As I reclined against the back of my chair, a muscular man of about sixty, in a blue pin-striped suit and a loosened pink tie with a fat knot, strutted into the room like he owned the place. This man, with his ruddy complexion and a fat radish of a nose, walked over to me, glanced at my polished clean plate, and then looked me in the eye. He lifted a hand out for me to shake. It was as thick and fleshy as a slab of pancetta. *"Buona sera,"* he said softly, the voice churning gravel. As it turned out, he *did own the place*. This was Ferrara.

The young woman returned to sweep away the dish and cutlery and in less than a minute returned with another—this time grilled squid accompanied by a small patty she referred to as *"am-booor-gar di seppia"* (cuttlefish "hamburger"). A third plate, lightly fried baby squid in lemon, was followed by a fourth, a small piece of perfectly grilled, tender swordfish, and a fifth, octopus drizzled with olive oil.

Even before the arrival of the sixth dish—sweet steamed mussels—Sakalleo had earned a place in my personal pantheon of most remarkable restaurant meals ever eaten. It was a short list of restaurant experiences that I created in the early 1980s when I first began traveling to Italy and France as an adult. Yet in recent years—despite those two countries being the places where I spent most of my time and where I'd eaten my way through dozens of Michelin stars—the list had few new additions. The most inspiring food, I've learned, comes in simple packages without the self-consciousness that accompanies critics' stars. Sakalleo was turning out to be an orgy of the sea in an impossibly plain brown wrapper: not so much comfort cuisine as it was comfort itself.

How was it possible, I wondered, that I remained the only client, even on a Monday night in off-season? The answer to that question came sometime after nine as groups began filing in. Sicilians, I would learn, like to eat in numbers and late. A dozen people in business suits—including one woman who appeared to be laughing and at ease in her singularity—took a table that filled one of the side rooms. An equally large table began filling up another room. Next to me sat two young couples—the women with streaks of fluorescent hair and oversized earrings, and the men sprouting short upright spikes of black hair and styling gel.

Everyone was greeted by Ferrara with the minimum of a handshake. Most of the women and some of the men, apparently depending on their familiarity, got slow cheek-brushing kisses on each side. And everyone, regardless of whether they merited handshakes or paternal embraces, got the same food I did, though at the big tables the portions were served on heaping platters and passed around family-style.

When the young woman returned to my table, she uttered three words that nearly made we weep with appreciation.

"*Pasta va bene?*" she asked me as deadpan as she asked all the other questions. I let out an enthusiastic affirmation. And as she turned away I thought I saw something vaguely resembling a smile pull at the ends of her mouth.

About ten minutes later she returned to the table with a bowl of spaghetti cooked al dente and covered ever so lightly with a transparent white wine sauce flecked with pieces of pink crab. This was pasta as it was meant to be eaten but so rarely is outside of Italy: the noodles and the sauce in a perfect harmony of flavors, texture, and—as the Italian chefs like to say, particularly in Sicily—*emozioni* (emotions). This symbiotic dance of pasta and sauce is one of the most subtle arrangements I know of and not easy to master; in most places outside Italy the sauce gets overthought, overburdened, overserved, or overseasoned while the pasta itself is neglected. Perhaps it should stand to reason that pasta is understood on an instinctive level in Sicily, now widely accepted as the place that pasta as we know it was introduced by Arabs more than a thousand years ago.

I finished every last strand. Then I watched as the bowl disappeared and another was set before me—this one a plate of chickpeas tossed in a wine and seafood sauce. The aromas drifted up from the plate into my brain's pleasure center, beckoning. I fell back in my chair as helpless and supple as a baby squid. From this vantage I watched one of the simplest dramatic gestures I've ever seen.

Ferrara stood in the middle of the room, after making a lap of handshakes and kisses. It was going on 10 p.m. on a Monday night in winter in the Sicilian provinces, and the place was now packed. He casually looked around him and let his pinstripe jacket slip off his shoulders and down his arms. He took the jacket in one hand, then transferred it to the other, holding it by its collar between thumb and forefinger out in front of him.

As if on cue, the young woman server swept by and removed the jacket from its perch. Ferrara then began methodically rolling up his sleeves, and the woman returned on cue and handed him a burgundy apron, which he slipped over his head onto his wide shoulders with the air of a knight putting on his armor for the trip to Jerusalem. But Ferrara wasn't voyaging to the Holy Land. He was on his way to the kitchen.

I methodically finished the second plate of pasta and watched as the platters of food came out from the kitchen to locals who seemed to regard it all as a normal part of life. This is but one of Sicily's many paradoxes: that people who live with a diet of daily confusion and services at times not much better than the Third World take for granted that they should eat so much better than we modern mortals. Ferrara came out of the kitchen in his apron, carrying a thin plastic supermarket bag that he brought to the table of business suits. Discreetly, he opened the bag to the man at the head of the table. I caught a glimpse of a tail and fins as Pasquale showed a fish from his daily catch.

Then the young woman appeared again, cleared my plate, and chirped, *"Secondo va bene?"*

Did I want a main course? Was this a joke?

Of course it was not a joke—and I succumbed after I learned that the *secondo* was not very big and would only add five euros to my bill. Before she left the table, she looked at the crumbs on the tablecloth and scolded that if I was getting full, I should not eat so much bread.

I poured the last of the Cerasuolo and drank—the wine seemed to leave something I thought I recognized as appetite in its wake. Then out came a platter that made my insides cry out for help: a mixed grill dominated by fresh crustaceans of various sizes and colors grilled in their shells with their heads and tentacles intact, scented with a hint of herbs and lemon. There were large pink *mazzancolle* (large Mediterranean prawns), smaller deeper-red prawns (known as *gamberelli*), and shrimp (*gamberetti*), as well as a pair of *scampi* (langoustines).

I ate my way though about half of the dish and then gave up. As delicate and delicious as it all was, I could go no further. I collapsed into the chair, feeling the sudden urge for a long nap. The woman—observing that I'd stopped eating and that I wore the lost look of a boiled octopus—asked what was wrong.

The word *basta* spontaneously erupted from somewhere deep in my gut.

She again scolded me for leaving so much on the plate.

It was after ten and there wasn't a seat left in the house. I asked for an espresso but was told the restaurant had none. Ferrara, I figured, was truly an artist who did not want to muddle his message or the sublime odors coming from his kitchen by serving coffee: *You want an espresso, go to a bar.* So instead, I took a shot of strong, cold, and sweet Limoncello to help me navigate the dark and lawless path to bed.

2

Romancing the Amphorae

I AWOKE THE NEXT MORNING to the sound of roosters clearing their throats and the rumble of the occasional truck out on the provincial road. From my room window, I looked out at the architecture that was the new COS winery. Rising up from the plain at the other end of a parcel of vine rows was a collection of old stone and new masonry lit up by an incisive morning sun. In the center of the group of buildings was a square, two-story tower, red as the dirt between the vines and set on an arched base of yellow stone. Behind the winery, off in the distance, was the low brooding profile of the Iblei Mountains.

I followed the steps down into a courtyard and entered the tall nineteenth-century *palmento* that now served as COS's dining and reception area. An old stone basin for foot-stomping grapes ran along a wall at the back of the room, slanting toward fermenting pits into which the juice and skins had once flowed. Scattered throughout the room under the tall timbered roof were a few wood tables, a baby grand piano, and three fat red sofas grouped around the tall hearth in which burned a crackling, whistling fire.

At one long table there was a single place set for breakfast, and in front of it a platter of plump Sicilian pastries decorated with candied fruit—and no doubt filled with almond paste, nut creams, and sweetened ricotta. After the previous night's feast, I was not seduced. I picked a blood orange out of a wood bowl. Gloria, a Serbian émigré and housekeeper in charge of breakfast, brought coffee and, in a display of maternal instinct, asked why I was not eating.

At about nine I was greeted by Giambattista Cilia, one of cos's two partners. At fifty, "Titta" was about the furthest thing I expected from a Sicilian *vignaiolo* (winegrower). He was fair-skinned with white hair shaved close to his head, and he wore a preppy uniform of a new red sweater over a pressed cotton shirt. He spoke a measured, unexcitable Italian, his sentences finishing in his lower vocal range.

I knew the outlines of cos's story, which Titta filled in during the early part of the morning. The letters c-o-s are an acronym of the last names of Titta (Cilia) and two friends—Giusto Occhipinti and Pinuccia Strano. The three friends from their high school days all finished their university studies in Palermo in 1980 and began to make wine as something of a game that started with Titta's father, Giuseppe.

Giuseppe Cilia, the descendant of a line of Vittoria winemakers, was a ripe sixty-six years old at the time when he noticed that his son and his university friends had nothing to do. Titta and Giusto were scheduled to start architectural school, and Pinuccia, medical school—all in late fall, which was months away.

So Giuseppe gave his son a graduation present of about two metric tons of Nero d'Avola. The three men made their wine under Giuseppe's guidance in the *palmento* that belonged to Titta's family. They stomped grapes with their feet, shoveled skins and juice into old cement fermenting vats, and later used an antique hand wine press to fill one old large oak cask. When the wine was deemed finished the following year, it was a bombastic, concentrated cocktail with an alcohol level of 16 percent. Giuseppe pronounced the wine *buono* and suggested that the new winemakers bottle and try to sell it in Palermo.

My father, Titta said, "liked wine that went . . ." Here Titta's Italian dropped off as he mimed with the fingers of his right hand—running them from his mouth, down his throat to his chest, and then in the area of his stomach, he made a fist and punched the air: "Boom!"

A wineshop in Palermo bought out the stock and sold it—about 1,400 bottles—though the proprietor suggested making the wine less explosive by using grapes that were less ripe. Every year for five years, Giuseppe doubled the amount of grapes he gave to Titta and his partners.

By the time the cos trio had finished their advanced studies in 1985, they were ready to invest in equipment and vineyards. Pinuccia, however, turned over his portion of the partnership to his sister Pina, who stayed on for the following decade before she quit to marry Pasquale Ferrara and join him at Sakalleo.

For nearly three decades cos has helped restore Vittoria winemaking, which had seen a hundred years of decline since its heyday in the nineteenth century. Wine had been produced here since antiquity, but it was in the early seventeenth century with the founding of Vittoria that the local wine known as Cerasuolo took on greater importance. At that time Vittoria Colonna, countess of Modica, donated land to the first colonists on the condition that they cultivate vines. Over the next two centuries, Cerasuolo came to be shipped to South America and southern Italy for drinking and to northern Italy and France as *vino di taglio* (cutting wine), used to give a potent boost of high alcohol and color to wines from cooler climes. When the phylloxera pestilence ravaged mainland Europe in the late nineteenth century, this provided a temporary boon to Sicily that lasted decades—until phylloxera later attacked Sicily's vines.

Other events conspired to all but destroy Vittoria winemaking: waves of emigration to the United States, two world wars, and global wine crises. By the 1950s, winegrowing in Vittoria had been abandoned by most landowners and *contadini* (farmers), who pulled out their vines to cultivate citrus and other crops and left their *palmenti* to the elements.

In 1973 the Italian government's efforts to resuscitate its wine regions touched Vittoria, which was added to the Italian appellation or DOC (for Denominazione di Origine Controllata) system. Thirty-two years later, in 2005, with another impressive-sounding stroke of law, Italy made Cerasuolo di Vittoria the only Sicilian winegrowing area with the highest appellation standard of DOCG (Denominazione di Origine Controllata et Garantita). The cherry-colored fragrant wine is composed of 50 to 70 percent Nero d'Avola and completed with Frappato. The twenty-first century has produced a boom: the number of winemakers bottling their own Cerasuolo tripled from six in the year 2000 to eighteen by the beginning of 2008.

There were two things that brought me to COS. First was the wine's reputation for natural integrity. From the start they rejected chemicals in the vineyards and additives in the wine, using only indigenous yeasts found on grape skins for fermentation. In recent years they had converted all of their fifty-four acres of vineyards to beyond-organic biodynamic agriculture, the holistic—and increasingly fashionable throughout the wine world—method of soil restoration tied to the lunar calendar prescribed by the Austrian philosopher Rudolf Steiner in the 1920s, and using elements such as cow dung buried in horns in the vineyards and herbal teas for the vines.

The second thing that appealed to me about COS was its appetite for experimentation. The first distinctively shaped, stubby bottles of COS wine I'd stumbled onto in a wineshop in northern Italy were a Cerasuolo di Vittoria called Pithos. The wine was made entirely in terra-cotta amphorae—a notion that evoked Dionysian rites and images of toga-wearing ancients dancing up to their thighs in grapes. I saved the bottles and opened the first with friends at dinner. Expecting to find something inside as profound and rich and down-to-earth as a Sicilian *contadino*, I was underwhelmed by the contents, which seemed as nervous as a Roman driver at rush hour. The second bottle of the same vintage, opened months later, had the same limpid pinot color but was much more relaxed; it smelled as deep as unearthed fossils and tasted long and fresh. It was terrific. This was an experience that has repeated itself over a few years: one bottle from a case might taste unremarkable, while another from the same case tasted in a different time of year will be gorgeous. Of course, all wines evolve in the bottle and there can be variation from one to the next, but I'd never experienced this degree of change in wine. I sensed there was something different and more temperamental about this wine and the way it showed its moods. I was ambivalent, but fascinated.

Months later—after I began traveling regularly to Sicily—I was having dinner at a trattoria in Palermo and struck up a conversation with a lawyer and regular client at an adjoining table, who seemed to have eaten and drunk his way across the island. When the topic turned to Pithos, he shook his head.

"It's not meant to be drunk," he said, and then lifting a hand and twirling it above his head, he added, *"Non e il vino. E la poesia."* ("It's not wine. It's poetry.")

TITTA'S PARTNER, GIUSTO, ENTERED THE room like a blast of air, singing into his *telefonino*. Also fifty at the time, Giusto is darker, more typically Sicilian-looking than Titta. He has a prominent Mediterranean beak and olive skin, and his graying hair looks windblown even when there is no wind. He wore a thermal vest, a print cotton scarf, and light tan construction boots. Animated and in perpetual motion, Giusto is a Sicilian version of the colorful Holmes to Titta's sober Watson; his vocal range roller-coasters through dramatic highs and lows, and he frequently completes his sentences with the linguistic shortcut "blah, blah, blah."

After saying our greetings, Giusto—hands flapping and speaking faster than an Italian soccer commentator—covered some pressing but incomprehensible-to-me business with his partner. The three of us were set to go up to the new winery, but just as we left the building, Giusto's *telefonino* launched into a high-pitched aria and he excused himself, disappearing in a cloud of *ciaos* and operatic Italian. This odd couple of personalities seemed an unlikely formula for the successful partnership that was cos.

As Titta and I walked up the dirt road under a warm morning sun, I asked about the typical division of winery responsibilities: who oversaw the winemaking, and who, the vineyards—not to mention sales and business. Titta said there was no such structure; they both did a bit of everything. "When something important comes up, we talk," he said.

The red soil, recently moistened by rain, seemed as light as cake and was carpeted with weeds, clover, and wildflowers. The Vittoria plain faces southward and gently drops from the Iblei Mountains toward the swath of Mediterranean known locally as the Mare d'Africa. A relentless afternoon summer sun tempered by cool evenings, and ample winter rains coupled with drying winds that blow from the Iblei, make for a climate in which winegrowing is not difficult.

"Here, everybody is organic, though they may not call themselves organic," Titta said with a proud Sicilian shrug. Although Sicily is Italy's largest producer of organic grapes, I was sure he was exaggerating. Titta went on to say there was no need for manmade chemicals in paradise. "Sicily really is organic."

About a dozen workers in plaster-covered clothes moved about the site, parts of which were still under construction, evidenced by the orange plastic conduit that sprouted like weeds from the holes in ground and walls. We walked through the archway of the tower and into a courtyard. To our right were the stone walls of an old *palmento*; to the left was the new winery—a long white building with shuttered doors painted Mediterranean blue, its roof covered with solar electricity-generating panels.

We entered through a set of those doors and looked down into the great open subterranean court of the winery. Below us were twenty immense cement fermenting tanks—each holding 2,500 gallons of wine—aligned in two rows, painted in white and blue to match the building and fitted with electronic climate-controlled systems.

We walked down a flight of stairs through this court, then took another staircase further below ground. The vast cellar was supported by a line of thick stone arches, built to support the hundreds of tons of cement and wine above our heads. Like much of Sicily, the Vittoria plain lies in a high-risk zone for earthquakes like the one that leveled the nearby provincial capital of Ragusa in 1693.

"The same old story—Africa pushing up into Europe," Titta said, pressing the fingertips of his two hands against each other to illustrate. For that reason, he said, the winery was built with a flexible earthquake-resistant structure designed to bend with the earth without releasing floods of Nero d'Avola.

Under the arches were several immense new 3,000-liter Slovenian oak casks positioned on their sides on wood supports and fitted with steel spouts. Off in a corner on the ground lay a dozen much smaller 225-liter French oak *barriques*. These two types of oak barrels tell a lot about the story of winemaking in Italy in the last quarter century. Traditionally, wine from Vittoria—as in many other regions across the Italian peninsula—was aged in *botti*, the larger Slovenian casks that allowed minimum exposure to air through the porous oak. But in the 1990s fine winemakers, seeking to appeal to an international marketplace, critics, and Americans who had developed a taste for the familiar roasted oak flavor in wines, mimicked the practice of Bordeaux by raising wine in *barriques* typically for a year or longer. The smaller size of the Bordeaux *barriques* meant more wood flavor—particularly when new oak barrels were used—because there was simply more wood surface per gallon of wine. In the new millennium, however, wood burnout had taken hold. Oak became a pejorative—synonymous with wine manipulation and "international-style" wines with no sense of identity. More and more wine importers and wine lovers were demanding authentic *terroir* wines that reflected the place and year in which the grapes were grown and the wine made.

cos once had hundreds of *barriques*, used chiefly to mellow wine made from Nero d'Avola before it went to bottle or was blended with Frappato. Now the winery had all but abandoned the *barriques* and had returned to the traditional *botti*, which mellowed the Nero d'Avola's stout tannic personality while imparting less perceptible traces of oak.

With the 2008 vintage, Titta pronounced, all the *barriques* would be gone and all cos wines would pass at least some time in cos's new container of choice: clay amphorae. We walked upstairs and Titta led me across the courtyard to the old stone building. I followed him through a doorway and down a couple of stone stairs. In a matter of seconds, it seemed we had gone back centuries in time. Here, within the damp stone walls in a floor of sand gravel, were buried 101 amphorae. These terra-cotta vessels—400 liters apiece—showed only a few inches of red clay above the ground. Covering the mouth of each amphora was a stainless steel lid clamped to the outer rim. In the center of each lid was a hole with a plastic bung.

The place smelled more like wine than any wine cellar I'd ever been in: a marriage of fermenting fruit and damp earth. It is in this pit that cos made its Pithos—the Greek word for clay storage jar or amphora. In modern red winemaking, grapes are fermented in steel or cement and then pressed in a matter of weeks. Then they are returned to similar neutral containers or put in barrels to undergo a later secondary (or malolactic) fermentation. Pithos, however, is a repudiation of modern winemaking: grapes are simply crushed and left in the amphorae up to seven months before the must is removed and pressed.

I looked at the necks of the amphorae sticking out of the ground. Though the forms were identical, each one had a different patina. Some had remained true to their original reddish clay color. Some were stained black or deep green with mold, others were streaked white, and still others were dripping wine-colored tears. Titta found a pair of wineglasses and a glass wine thief, and we spent the next twenty minutes walking amid the amphorae and tasting the wines inside. Each amphora was numbered in chalk on its neck, and Titta played a game asking me to "pick a number." He would then go to that amphora, pull out the bung, and draw out the contents with the thief.

The wines from the two varietals that made up Cerasuolo di Vittoria were fermented separately. The Nero d'Avola samples were a deep purple and smelled of minerals and earth, and they had a tannic kick. The Frappato had the lighter color of a cherry soda and tasted like a melon that had been cut on a summer morning. Yet not only did the wines from the two varietals contrast, the wine from each amphora tasted different from the next—even when made from the same grapes.

cos had become the largest user of amphorae in Italian winemaking. I wondered what exactly that meant. Technically speaking, the appeal of both wood and clay is their porous qualities that allow for a small exchange of oxygen. Untreated terra-cotta, while more porous than oak, might impart less of its own flavor to the wine. Was this a wine revolution in the making? Was there science here? Or was it, as the man in the Palermo restaurant had claimed, pure poetry?

Objective truth in this world is an elusive goal. In the world of wine it is rare. In Sicily it might be impossible. Before my return to Sicily, I had reread *Il Gattopardo (The Leopard)*, the sole novel by the late Sicilian prince Giuseppe Tomasi di Lampedusa, which in the half century since its publication had come to be viewed on the island as something close to a third testament of the Bible. My favorite sentence from the book is one that explains the Mediterranean difficulty of truth in Sicily:

> Nowhere has truth so short a life as in Sicily; a fact has scarcely happened five minutes before its genuine kernel has vanished, been camouflaged, embellished, disfigured, squashed, annihilated by imagination and self-interest; shame, fear, generosity, malice, opportunism, charity, all the passions, good as well as evil, fling themselves onto the fact and tear it to pieces; very soon it has vanished altogether.

At one point Giusto arrived and joined us. He spoke of how he grew tired of aging wine in barrels. He railed against industrial winemaking and the tricking of wine to standardize its flavors. "Oak is a form of mascara, cosmetic surgery," he said. "Vanilla, toasting, and blah, blah, blah . . ." Neither amphorae nor wood barrels do miracles, Giusto went on. "There is no magic material that will transform a banal wine into a great one." But, he said, the qualities that come from the wine made in amphorae "are all from the grapes."

I had the feeling that the amphora pit was to Giusto and Titta as much an aesthetic statement as a winemaking *choice*. The amphora pit seemed to complete an image of cos that was quintessentially and emotionally Italian: daring yet simple, modern yet primitive. Like those stubby bottles cos reproduced from a century-old original, and like everything else at cos, the amphorae looked fantastic.

The roots of cos amphora winemaking were in fact far from

Sicily. On a trip to Friuli after the Vinitaly wine show in Verona in 2000, Titta and Giusto visited Josko Gravner, the radically natural, moon-following neo-*contadino* winemaker. In 2001 Gravner began fermenting his white wines in huge 2,500-liter amphorae imported from the Caucusus in the Republic of Georgia and lined with beeswax. In 2000 Gravner was still in the experimentation phase and served his Sicilian visitors a taste of wine made in amphorae from Ribolla, a varietal with ancient Greek roots.

"I tasted that wine, and it was unknown territory," Giusto remembered. "It was a primordial wine."

Gravner's wine amphorae also touched something in their Sicilian hearts. Though Gravner was experimenting on the border near Slovenia, amphorae had been popularized by the ancient Greeks, the first colonizers of Sicily. Could there be any vessel more Sicilian than the amphora?

"I said to myself, 'Why didn't I think of that?'" Titta recounted. "We talked about it all the way home in the car, and by the time we got back it was decided that we would make wine in amphorae."

The following year, Giusto and Titta did a test. They ordered three amphorae (commonly used for decoration or plantings)—one each from Sicily, Tunisia, and Spain—in which they made wine from Nero d'Avola. The result: "The amphora from Sicily made vinegar. The amphora from Tunisia produced an anonymous wine. The amphora from Spain is the only one that produced a positive result." Starting with the next harvest, cos started vinifying Pithos in Spanish amphorae.

Giusto went to get a tasting glass for himself, and when he reappeared he was with two older men who were introduced to me as *avvocati* (lawyers). One of the lawyers was tall, dark-haired, and bespectacled; the other was short, white-haired, with a cropped moustache. Titta greeted them with cheek-brushing kisses.

Giusto used the wine thief to withdraw samples from different amphorae. There were now five of us in the cellar with three glasses, but in a gesture that seemed as much a rite of Sicilian brotherhood as about a lack of stemware, each glass was filled with a sample and made its rounds tasted by all five of us.

The *avvocati* pronounced the winery *bellissimo*, the wine *buono*. Then the mustachioed one asked Giusto more about the amphorae.

"We live in a world that is becoming more and more superficial," Giusto said somewhat obtusely, adding something about technology and standardization, and finishing with "blah, blah, blah."

"Wine is a memory of the year. And the amphora is a form of stimulation for the wine," Giusto said. He spoke of the inverted pyramid form of the amphora, its bloated belly resembling a pregnant woman's. His hands were painting canvases in the air. The amphora, Giusto said to the *avvocati*, was a way of trapping *energia cosmica*.

With this mention of cosmic energy, I could see the interest of the *avvocati* wane. It was lunchtime, after all. "*Bene*," the mustachioed *avvocato* said, taking Giusto by the arm and turning to the door. The men bade their ceremonious Sicilian farewells with another round of cheek kissing, and Giusto and Titta and I walked back across the property.

Giusto asked if I minded if we did not go to a restaurant for lunch but stayed at COS where his sister would cook. It was a polite question that a Sicilian would only ask a foreigner, who could be forgiven for not knowing that some of the world's best home cooks can be found in Sicily. Fine gastronomic restaurants are a recent phenomenon; traditionally, the restaurant in Sicily was a somewhat paler alternative to a home-cooked meal.

The room of the old *palmento* where I'd taken my breakfast was filled with the aromas and sounds of grilling meats, delicate sauces, and veiled mysteries being prepared by Giusto's sister Angela, who runs the kitchen. Giusto poured glasses of COS's white wine called Ramí, a simple, fruity, fresh blend of Inzolia and Grecanico grapes. Then he poured some COS olive oil from a can into a small dish, and we sponged it up with pieces of bread. The recently pressed oil was still electric green; it had the fleshy taste of a fresh pressing with a spicy after-burn in the throat.

Angela, who shares many of her brother's features and wore her dark gray–streaked hair cropped at the neck, first brought out plates with small mounds of oven-baked ricotta set on lemon leaves, and powdered with black and red crushed pepper. Accompanying the cheese were small pieces of grilled pancetta (unsmoked bacon) and a few dry-cured black olives on the side. When we finished this course and complimented Angela, more of the baked cheese and pancetta were passed around.

Giusto talked about his travels to America and specifically California, where he said he drove from San Francisco to Los Angeles.

"Beautiful," he told his partner confidently; "you can do it in three hours."

I said that it would take most non-Italians at least twice that amount of time.

"Four hours at the most!" Giusto protested. "I did it twice."

For the second course, Angela brought out handmade tagliatelle in a pale fragrant tomato sauce on which we sprinkled grated *caciocavallo*, the semi-hard cheese made for centuries in Sicily and southern Italy and often used as a table cheese. The tomatoes, which had been canned from the garden and cooked to the point that they were just beginning to fall apart, were some of the sweetest I've tasted.

The white wine drained, we moved on to reds: 2006 Pithos Cerasuolo di Vittoria, as well as cos's traditional Cerasuolo de Vittoria, fermented in cement and raised in large wood *botti*. We drank them with a course of delicately spiced *involtini*—little rolls of veal with a bread and herb stuffing accompanied by grilled fennel.

After soaking up the ambience and smells of the amphora pit, I was prepared to prefer the Pithos. Never mind that the winemakers of antiquity were known to use techniques that would make most of us gag—preserving wine with seawater and then sweetening it with honey—I wanted to believe in the ability of amphorae to turn grapes into not just poetry but poetic wine.

I started with the traditional Cerasuolo—it was medium-bodied, well-structured, a delicious blend of Nero d'Avola and Frappato with all the harmony of Lennon and McCartney. Then came the Pithos—the color was half a shade lighter. I closed my eyes and smelled earth and the promising aroma of a horse barn. I tilted the glass back to let the ancient wisdom of the Mediterranean roll down my tongue. I tasted: there was a light initial burst of something, and then . . . and then . . . it seemed to fizzle out on the tongue.

As the meal went on, the traditional Cerasuolo seemed to grow tastier, more complex, and the Pithos still seemed flat. Angela's cooking alone had put us in a state close to euphoria that rendered us nearly silent. Who wanted to start judging wines against each other? I wasn't asked for my opinion, so I didn't give it.

For dessert Angela brought each of us a pair of *cannulicchi*—bite-sized cannoli—decorated with small morsels of candied orange. Giusto left the table and returned with large tulip-shaped glasses and pulled out a small dark-colored bottle of 1986 Marsala Superiore by Marco De Bartoli.

Marsala and cannoli—both Sicilian inventions with their storied pasts. Cannoli—"tubes" of pastry filled with sweetened ricotta—were originally associated with winter carnival feasts around Palermo. Centuries later they would become associated with both cinematic and real organized crime. The famous quote from *The Godfather*, "Leave the gun. Take the cannoli," is a statement of priorities if there ever was one. Just a week after my trip to cos, the Sicilian governor, Salvatore Cuffaro, was convicted and given a five-year sentence for aiding and abetting individual mafiosi. Because he was not convicted of the more serious charge of collusion, Cuffaro celebrated. He was shown in a widely circulated photograph handing out cannoli to his aides, but he insisted that it was a well-wisher who brought him the treats. Nevertheless, amid cannoli-fueled public anger, Cuffaro resigned eight days later.

The cannoli we ate that day were *cannoli*—the real thing and not the cloying knockoffs that have proliferated off the island in other places like the United States. The filling was lightly sweetened fresh ricotta made from fresh whole sheep's milk. It was from another universe than most of the cannoli I remembered from my youth around New York, which were filled with industrial "cannoli cream" that did not even resemble cheese.

Marsala—named by conquering Muslims as *Marsa-Allah* (Allah's port)—is both a port town at Sicily's southwestern tip that stretches out toward Tunisia and a fortified wine similar to port or sherry. The English merchant John Woodhouse "discovered" the wine of Marsala in 1773 after a storm forced his ship to land in the port. He liked what he tasted and sent a ship full of local white wine back to England—infused with brandy to protect it on the voyage. His countrymen demanded more and more over the generations. Then, for most of the twentieth century, Marsala degraded into an industrial cooking wine and cannoli flavoring.

Since 1980 Marco De Bartoli had been the undisputed maestro of fine Marsala wines. But I'd never tasted De Bartoli's Marsala, nor, in fact, any fine Marsala. Giusto poured the golden-amber liquid into the glasses.

"*Che colore,*" remarked Angela, who took a glass with us.

"*Madonna!*" chimed Titta.

We stuck our noses in our glasses. It smelled as warm and complex as a village bakery on a spring morning. It tasted sweet but at the same time ancient as an old church missal, and it seemed it could last in the mouth for hours.

THAT AFTERNOON TITTA AND I took a drive in his new four-wheel-drive truck. We stopped at a vineyard where a small crew was busily trimming the winter vines of the previous season's growth, walked through a cos olive grove of centuries-old trees with their stubby twisted trunks, and then pulled into Titta's family's old *palmento*, now part of cos. Titta got out of the truck to unlock a wooden gate and then drove into a narrow courtyard between two rustic stone farm buildings. Titta explained the logic of this winery, now more than a century and a half old: The building with the southern exposure in the courtyard was naturally warmer and used for fermenting and pressing; the building with the northern exposure was used for raising and storing wine.

Inside were a couple of rooms cluttered with old bottles, boxes, barrels, winery equipment, and wood basket presses. This was where the cos partners had made their first vintages—wading in grape must in cement fermentation tanks buried in the floor. Dominating the main room was the long, fat wood beam of a lever press held up on one end by a human-sized wooden screw at a 30° angle. Sicilian *palmento* wines were traditionally left to ferment only forty-eight hours before they were pressed. The grape skins were gathered into piles, wrapped in hemp rope, and pressed by the crushing weight of the beam lowered onto them.

"Pliny described the same system two thousand years ago," Titta said, pausing and staring at the press as if to admire the beauty of the thought. We walked to the other side of the courtyard, where there were rooms with sand floors on which lay now-abandoned *barriques*.

"Soon there will be amphorae here," he said. "There will be amphorae everywhere."

ON MY SECOND DAY at COS, the most pressing matter on the agenda was lunch. It would not be just any lunch but lunch with Marco De Bartoli, who was en route from Marsala to a business meeting on the eastern edge of the island. Among Sicily's new generations of winemakers, De Bartoli is nothing short of iconic. He was born (on his mother's side) into one of Sicily's largest Marsala houses, Pellegrino, but broke away from the family business in the late 1970s to start his own small production of something that seemed anachronistic: quality Marsala.

"In 1980 when we started, to speak of quality wine in Sicily was to speak of nothing," said Giusto, sitting by the fire on that cloud-covered morning. "Thirty years ago there was no real wine culture outside of France. It was Marco who started the renaissance of Sicilian wine."

In their early winemaking days, the COS partners were inspired by lone, quality winemakers, such as Angelo Gaja in the Piedmont and De Bartoli, who was introduced to them by their Palermo wine seller. It was De Bartoli who convinced them that wine should be an expression of tradition and nature.

"Marco is the soul of Sicily," Giusto effused. "He is crazy, of course, but he has a heart . . ."—here Giusto put his hand on his chest for emphasis—". . . of a *chevalier*."

Around noon Giusto generously put together a tasting of every Pithos cos made, rummaging in an adjacent wine storage room to produce bottles that went back to the first experiments with amphorae in 2001. Giusto opened the bottles and set them out on one end of the long dining table—a liquid history of cos and its amphorae. Up until this point I had remained intrigued but confused about the amphorae and their effect on winemaking; this tasting, I assumed, would somehow clear things up.

The first wine was the 2001 experiment from a Sicilian amphora. The wine was a burnt-orange color; it smelled like a blanket that has spent too much time in a leaky attic; and it tasted like a wine that was decades older than it was—tired to the point of falling apart. The same experimental vintage from the Spanish amphora was less dilapidated—more wholly wine. And with every subsequent year there seemed to be a progression of quality. Yet as much as I wanted to believe in the alchemy of amphorae, I wasn't convinced that the technique was the future of Sicilian winemaking.

Then I tasted the Pithos 2005. Like the 2006 I'd tasted the day before, it was horsey—only more intensely so. I closed my eyes and sniffed and I saw the foothills of the Iblei, fields of golden wheat ready for harvest, stands of cypress trees and olives, and the smoke from a small fire in the distance. I sipped and the stuff danced across the tongue. The wine had it all: fruit, staying power, elegance. It was a wine that seemed to come from a place and time long before *telefonini*.

We again tasted the 2006, which fell flat as it did the previous day. What was it with these wines? They seemed quirkier, more erratic, less stable than cos's traditionally made wines. But they could also be beautiful. (I bought a case of 2006 Pithos for my cellar at home to taste from time to time, and I was underwhelmed until five months later, when I opened a bottle and found inside a wine that was lush and complex and that reached up and grabbed you by the nose.)

The only thing the tasting had convinced me of was that amphora-produced wine was less than reliable. Poetry indeed. I tried to convey this to Giusto in our common language, which was French (he spoke no English, and while my Italian comprehension was good,

my speaking was not yet at the point where I could express nuance).
I said that I thought the difference between the other wines and
the Pithos wines was like the difference between architecture and
music. COS traditional wines were solid, structured, and substantial: architecture, I said. The Pithos wines were intangible, variable,
fleeting: music.

When Titta arrived, Giusto was happy to share my critique, adding hand gestures.

"Architecture is beautiful, but with time it disappears," Giusto
said in Italian, mangling my thought. "But music . . ." He held up
his hand. His fingers moved as though stroking the wings of a but-
terfly. ". . . Music is lasting."

"*Bello*," Titta nodded meaningfully.

I said that I'd meant something closer to the opposite. Giusto
ignored my protests. He had made up his mind, and he was on the
side of music. At least twice more that day he recounted this interpretation, each time adding a layer of Baroque ornamentation until
he arrived at *"la musica è eterna"* ("music is eternal").

I thought of what Lampedusa had written about truth in Sicily,
and there seemed a certain logic to this interaction. Through thousands
of years, it was the Sicilians who decided what to throw away and
what to keep from foreign rulers, invaders, traders, and visitors, and
they formed a culture that way. Giusto had decided that music was
more durable than stone and so it would stay that way.

WHEN DE BARTOLI ARRIVED—about 2:30 in the afternoon—he strode
into the room like a general returning from battle, his head held
erect, the line of his imperial nose perpendicular to the earth. A long
colorful striped scarf was draped around his neck; an unlit cigar that
looked like a piece of kindling wood dangled from his lips. He was
dressed casually in jeans and a zip-up sweater that covered his upper
body built like a wine cask.

At sixty-three, his rugged, handsome features were just starting
to melt, and his close-cropped hair was faded white. But his light
eyes betrayed a boy's mischievousness. Following behind him was a

young, taller man, thirty years old, handsome, clean-cut, "preppy"-looking—De Bartoli's son Sebastiano.

The De Bartolis were greeted like family; there were kisses with Giusto and Titta and warm hugs from Angela. From the kitchen came the smells of butter, meat, and boiling salt water ready for the making of pasta.

De Bartoli installed himself at his seat at the head of the table, and everyone else spread out to the sides. I sat to De Bartoli's left, Giusto to his right. In a matter of minutes, Angela delivered plates of ricotta-filled tortelli pasta drizzled in butter and olive oil. Giusto sang out, *"buon appetito."* I noticed that both he and De Bartoli crossed themselves before lifting their forks.

De Bartoli explained to me in French that his grandmother, who was from Bordeaux and came to Sicily with her family during the beginning of the Marsala trade, spoke French and didn't want her offspring to learn English.

"Now, my son . . . ," De Bartoli told the table in Italian. He gave Sebastiano a look that only a father can give—simultaneously mocking and proud. "He studied his English at Cambridge." He pronounced the word "Cambridge" with the most exaggerated lofty BBC-English accent he could muster.

De Bartoli then proceeded to rail against industrial wine producers, Japanese wine buyers, and the high prices being paid for wine that was nothing short of *merda* (shit)—pronounced *"merrrr-daaaa."*

"This is how I speak," he said as he turned to me. "This is the language I speak."

"I am always angry with the Italian producers—especially the Sicilian producers. In Italy today there are many wine producers. But what are most of them, really? They are administrators or industrialists. Very few are *vignaioli.*"

We passed around bottles of cos wines and cleaned the rest of the tortelli from the platter. Then Angela brought out a course of chicken scaloppine cooked with cos oranges.

We tasted. We chewed. Angela hovered, just long enough to see that the cooking was working its magic.

"Ninety percent of the wine Sicily produces is *merda*," De Bartoli continued, repeating, "*Merrrrrrrr-daaaa.*"

News was exchanged about mutual acquaintances. Then the maestro turned back to me, put down his fork, and in his gravelly voice summarized centuries of Sicilian history.

"The nobles who came to govern Sicily were the stupidest in the world," he said. "They did nothing for Sicily . . . the delinquents who we call the Mafia—who have nothing to do with the real Mafia, which was a system to protect the people—many are in prison. But today we have a new Mafia in Italy . . ."

De Bartoli finished chewing and his eyes flashed. "This new Mafia is called *lo stato Italiano!*" (the Italian government).

There were knowing nods around the table. Wine flowed.

"What is the Mafia today? It is Bush," Giusto said of the then president of the United States. He shrugged and described the whole Iraq war as a battle for turf and rackets (oil) between Mafia dons (Bush, Saddam).

There were more knowing nods as the scaloppine made its last lap.

For the next course, Angela brought out a Sicilian seasonal specialty that is as disorienting to most Western palates as it is evocative: a bright-colored orange salad made from blood oranges, new onions, and black olives, seasoned with parsley, salt, and pepper and tossed with green olive oil. In Sicilian cooking, oranges have a special place—used in pastas, seafood marinades, and the sweet, acidic, salty, spicy orange salad. When done right it is a dish that can change your life. I had been in Sicily only three days, and three memorable meals made me question how I had eaten up until that moment. Now the orange salad made me ponder how I would live the rest of my days.

"Where but in Sicily would they think to make such a dish from oranges?" De Bartoli sang. "I have traveled the world. I have seen it all and drunk it all. And I can say without chauvinism, that the *terroir* of Sicily is the grandest of the world. We are not a region . . ." He paused and held up his right index finger to bellow, "*Siamo un continente*" ("We are a continent").

De Bartoli's *telefonino* chimed; he pulled it from his pants pocket. And before answering it, his face lit up like a child's as he announced, "I hope this is a woman!" He spoke into the phone; business was discussed, briefly, in a low voice. And when the call ended, De Bartoli explained that it related to another of his passions—vintage sports cars—which I would learn about later.

There were more courses—cold pork in gelatin followed by baked ricotta—and more wines. Titta brought out a 1970 Cerasuolo di Vittoria from his deceased father's old stock. For a wine that is generally thought best drunk young, this old Cerasuolo was strikingly, thoroughly alive. Then Sebastiano opened a bottle of Bukkuram, De Bartoli's late-harvest *passito* made from sun-dried grapes on the island of Pantelleria. It was nearly as dark as cola, and it smelled of dry stone and wildflowers just before death. Though it was served at room temperature, it wasn't sticky but long and polished.

As the afternoon faded into evening, De Bartoli explained that his desire had been to make wines "as the English found them in the nineteenth century." What I'd tasted had been convincing.

At the end of the meal, Angela—out of her apron and smartly dressed in a dark wool sweater and skirt—made a triumphant appearance at the table. I asked about the orange salad, and she shared some tips such as only adding salt at the last minute. Then she took an orange from a bowl and a knife from the table and, standing next to De Bartoli, demonstrated how to peel an orange for the salad. She held the fruit and turned it, removing first the peel, then slicing in between the sections to remove the flesh from the inner membranes.

She set the orange down. Her hands were wet with juice and scented with orange skin. De Bartoli took her hands in his and turned them over—back and front—and bowing his head, he covered them with kisses.

3

Stranieri

THE FIRST WINEMAKER I MET in Solicchiata was Pippo the mechanic—though at the time, I didn't know he made wine. I learned about the wine later, a few days after he greeted me with the suspicious gaze I imagined was normally reserved for an Italian tax collector.

I'd climbed to the haunches of Mount Etna by car, taking the road from the sea through small farms, olive groves, and vineyards pinned to the hillsides on black terraces of stacked lava stone and passing through towns paved and ornamented with that same stuff that had been spewed from on high.

Solicchiata nestles at an elevation of about 700 meters—a point where the air just begins to thin and Etna's summit looms. On that first day, the mountaintop exhaled a long plume of white smoke into an otherwise perfect blue sky.

Etna's north face is veined with *sciara*, lava fields left from the mountain's periodic eruptions. Once the rivers of lava cool, shrines are erected, prayers are said, and life continues. It is a fatalistic landscape—shaped by the hand of God or the gods that every so often remind humans of their smallness. The Greeks believed Etna was the entry to the Underworld and the homes of Vulcan, Cyclops, and the hundred-headed monster Typhon. At the most desolate point of winter, the vines and fruit trees are silently bare, but the damp, black, sandy soil is teeming with life, pushing up a constant crop of clover and wildflowers. Fennel-like ferula sprouts from roadsides, and the first yellow flowers of *ginestra* (broom plants) color the terraces and *sciara*.

The most surprising first impression you take away from Etna is how little notice the locals seem to give a volcano that could swallow up their world in minutes.

Pippo the mechanic crossed the road and approached my car. I had pulled up in front of his shop on the road that cuts through town and called out to him, asking in broken Italian if he could tell me how to get to the winery of Frank Cornelissen—adding for emphasis *"il belga pazzo"* ("the crazy Belgian").

Pippo listened, resting his hands on the hips of his coveralls. He narrowed his eyes and asked who I was. He looked at the passenger seat of the rental Fiat Panda where there were papers scattered along with a camera. With his thumb and forefinger he twirled the end of his fat moustache. He seemed about to say something when a woman's voice cried out over the din of the garage—not an everyday shriek, but the scream of someone about to be murdered.

Pippo wheeled around to see the source of the death warning: a round fiftyish woman in a peasant smock and rubber boots and holding a pair of pruning shears. She stood at the edge of her garden—perched behind the mechanic's shop—gesticulating wildly as if miming an operatic solo of her own bloody end. Her gaze was riveted on a woman in a white Fiat at whom she unloaded what seemed to be an aria of insults and accusations of treachery.

I looked closer to figure out what the woman in the Fiat had done to become the object of such a torrent. It seemed that her crime was to dare to stop her car in such a way as to block Pippo's neighbor's entryway.

Pippo called out to the madwoman, signaling with an easy voice and a patting gesture of the hand for her to calm down as he crossed the road in her direction. This, of course, had the opposite effect, pushing the opera diva into a higher register and prompting her to brandish the shears at Pippo. I had no idea what she was saying in her mix of guttural Italian and Sicilian, but I guessed she was not wishing well either on Pippo, his mechanics, and their entire family lines or on the Fiat driver, who ended the morning's drama by shaking her head and putt-putting out of the drive.

Pippo turned back to me, walking up to the open driver's window. He might have simply told me that Frank's winery was a couple hundred meters up the road on the left. But he did not. Instead, he reached a blackened hand into his coveralls and withdrew a cell phone, then thumbed a few buttons.

"I'm calling him," Pippo informed me.

He put the phone to his ear, listened, waited—looking furtively at those papers on the seat next to me.

"He doesn't answer," Pippo shrugged.

We exchanged arrivedercis and I continued driving to the edge of town, where I found Frank myself.

Frank Cornelissen was the first winemaker I visited on Etna because I suspected he might be close to insane—in every positive sense of the word. Why else would a middle-aged northern European choose to plant himself there and make wine from vineyards that had been neglected or abandoned by the locals for most of a century? Why else would anyone choose to scratch out a life with little help on land so perilously placed within spitting distance of one of the world's most active volcanoes?

Frank was one of the first *stranieri* (foreigners) to venture up the north face of Etna in 2001 to begin making reds dominated by the local grape, Nerello Mascalese, along with its cousin Nerello Cappuccio, which are capable of producing the sort of elegance that had some believing this frontier was a hidden Barolo or Burgundy. Other *stranieri* and Sicilians would follow—some because the market was telling them to go. But Frank apparently listened to other voices. A former mountain climber, he had come to Etna because he believed it was one spot in the world where you could make a wine entirely free of all chemicals, additives, and modernity both in the vineyards and in the winery. He had come, it seemed—to borrow a mountaineering cliché—to *be the mountain*.

Among fellow winemakers—even those who regard him as extreme—Frank is generally respected as a perfectionist, a guy who insists on doing all the work most other winemakers pay someone to do for them. Among hard-core wine purists in northern Europe and Japan, Frank has developed what could be called a fan base for a minuscule production of about 10,000 bottles of wine per year. His top wine, cheekily called Magma, is made from the fruit of high-altitude vineyards, some of which were never touched by the phylloxera pestilence that ravaged most of Europe in the late nineteenth century. After the grapes are crushed by foot, they are fermented in amphorae buried in lava sand, pressed after seven months, and left there to age "until several full cosmic cycles have passed" (around eighteen months). The unfiltered, unsulfured wine—both white and red—is placed in Burgundy-style bottles hand-painted by Frank in Japanese calligraphy. The cult nectar sells for around $200 a bottle around the world (the inaugural release was 515 bottles for the planet), and Frank insists the high price of Magma subsidizes his cheaper wines that he sells from his door starting at the equivalent of about $10.

Cornelissen's wines tend to elicit strong reactions. British wine writer Jancis Robinson once described them as a "walk defiantly on the wild side." Some Sicilian winemakers from other parts of the island have called them undrinkable. Some of his first wines in particular had problems with stability and oxidation; I once witnessed the horror of restaurant diners in Linguaglossa when the wine from a bottle of Magma they ordered poured out the color of Coca-Cola. In recent vintages I have found more of the weirdly wonderful than the weird. Giovanni Melita, a local antiquarian whose father brokered "strong Sicilian wines" for shipping from the port at Riposto, told me, "I love Frank's wines because they are exactly like the wines my father had fifty years ago."

Winemakers were beating a path in Cornelissen's footsteps—higher and higher up the north face of Etna. Andrea Franchetti, the Roman impresario from a South Carolina textile fortune and founder of Tuscany's Tenuta di Trinoro, had arrived at the same time as Frank. The Italian American importer Marc (known on the mountain as Marco) de Grazia followed, as did winemakers from Tuscany and central Italy along with the larger-scale Sicilian winemaking families Planeta and Tasca d'Almerita. More and more players, pioneers, and dreamers wanted a piece of the mountain that had been abandoned by so many in the modern age for the easier, machine-friendly flat plains of western Sicily —or for a life elsewhere.

As I pulled up to the Cornelissen winery—a series of small buildings connected by alleyways, courtyards, and abandoned stables—Frank was helping a trucker finish loading his lorry with cases of wine. Spotting the lone Belgian in Solicchiata was about as difficult as picking out a Nordic ice fisherman at a Greek wedding. His shock of silvery-white hair stood, tousled, atop sharp features softened by a sandy beard. Frank was a wraith of a man in his mid-forties, wearing work pants that sagged off his frame.

Frank finished his business with the trucker, speaking perfect Italian, and then he turned and greeted me in American English with barely a hint of a European accent.

When I explained my encounter with the mechanic, he laughed. "Here, we're on an island within an island," he said. "Everybody's knows everybody else's business."

I followed Frank back through an alley to a large, flat concrete terrace looking up the forested slopes of Etna. Filling much of the terrace were large plastic vats—chest high, about two yards across, and covered with taut plastic tarps. These were, in fact, the vats in which Frank fermented his base wine—Rosso del Contadino (Peasant Red)—under an open sky, exposed to the elements and occasional blasts of volcanic ash.

A younger man named Giuseppe—Frank's one full-time employee at the time—in a white T-shirt, jeans, and rubber boots, was pulling with all his weight on the long iron ratchet of an old wooden basket press. With each tug, more deep-purple juice splashed out from the base of the press into a knee-high plastic vat.

Giuseppe strained one more time against the ratchet, squeezing out the last of the juice. He unwound the pressing block from the upright screw and began to disassemble the sides of the wood press, in which sat a cake of pressed grape pomace. Frank, meanwhile, took a piece of thick rubber hosing, stuck one end in the low vat with the freshly pressed wine, and climbed a stepladder, putting the other end in the round dinner-plate-sized opening of a tall 5,000-liter plastic container. The hose was connected to a hand pump resembling a car jack, and Frank used it to suck the wine from the smaller receptacle to the larger one. It was all going fine until a hose broke free and splattered wine over the terrace floor, while Frank scurried around cursing in about three or four languages under his breath.

Later that week, after the wine in the large plastic vats was all pressed, Frank would siphon the pressed wine through a hose that would travel down the alley, turn left for a few yards along the side of the road, and then bank left again through a series of weathered wood doors into Frank's cellars, where the wine would be stored for the better part of a year in amphorae sunken to their necks in lava sand.

After cleaning up the mess, Frank showed me his cramped cellars. They were spotlessly clean—the walls were painted white, and the raised floors that held the amphorae were glossy red. The amphorae were topped with lava stone or glass lids fitted with bungholes. Unlike the partners at cos, Frank had coated the insides of these Spanish amphorae with resinous paint to limit oxidation of the contents.

"I am not so convinced about the quality of clay vessels," Frank said in his characteristic flat monotone. "I think if you know what you're doing you can make wine in anything . . . plastic, it doesn't matter."

These sounded like the words of a fool or a prophet, I figured. Frank seemed to toss thousands of years of winemaking experimentation out the window. Here on the mythic soil where he had come to look the volcano in the face, he had grown disillusioned with amphorae. He had found his next new thing: polycarbonate buckets worked just fine.

We walked a few more yards up the road to an alley entrance through an iron gate fastened shut with a wood twig. I followed Frank up a stairway where Lupo, his Siberian husky, greeted him. He kicked off his rubber boots and entered the small apartment that served as his home and as the administrative center of his wine business. Dominating the room was a pine slab table for no more than five people. Light streamed in from a pair of glass doors that led onto a small terrace with a view of Etna—its peak now obscured by a ring of clouds. A small woodstove provided the only heat. On two walls were pine shelves crammed with music CDs, computer equipment, and dozens of now empty wine bottles from some of Italy's and France's most renowned appellations: Barolo, Châteauneuf-du-Pape, Vosne-Romanée, Savennières.

Out of the small kitchen stepped a Japanese woman—not much older than thirty—who smiled and shook my hand, introducing herself as Aki. Frank went out the door again to fetch some wine for lunch, and Aki, Frank's lady friend visiting him from Japan, set the table with cloth napkins and tin cutlery. Giuseppe appeared at the door, removing his work boots and entering in stocking feet, followed by Frank. The four of us—one local and three *stranieri*—sat down to a lunch that began with caponata, the ubiquitous cold Sicilian side dish made from a base of cooked eggplant and celery folded into a sweet and sour tomato-onion sauce, and in this case seasoned with capers and olives.

The wine that Frank poured into our glasses was called white but was anything but that. It was labeled MunJebel Bianco from 2006—the name derived from Etna's Italian moniker, Mongibello (a combination of two words meaning "mountain": the Latin *mons* and the Arabic *gebel*). The color was burnt orange as murky as unfiltered fruit juice—which, essentially, it was. White wines are typically made from white grapes that are immediately pressed into juice before fermentation. But Cornelissen made his only white—from the Sicilian varietals Grecanico, Coda di Volpe, Catarratto, and Carricante—no differently than he made his reds: skins were left to ferment with the juice, which imparted the rustic dark color.

"It's really a red wine that happens to be made with grapes that are a different color," Frank offered.

It smelled like cut ripe apricots, and it tasted richer and more whole than any white wine I'd ever tasted. It was delicious and at the same time disconcertingly unrefined, aboriginal. It was the wine of someone who had left the trail and wandered off on his own. From drinking it I knew that Frank had thought about things more than the rest of us. Perhaps too much.

"The only thing I want to do is make a direct product from grapes, and to lead a simple life," Frank said, tearing a piece of bread and resting his elbows on the tabletop. "I prefer to make an authentic product that is a little rough in its presence than to make a more refined product that needs help to be refined."

I nodded, chewed, drank. I imagined Frank howling at the full moon with his wolf dog.

"Humans are by nature fucked up," he continued. "We have evolved into a world that is so man-made. That is something I want to step away from."

In the world of winemaking, Frank is singular—an adherent to no ideology but his own. He added no sulfur to his wines to protect them from oxidation, a risk taken by only the most extreme natural wine-makers. But even more edgy, he uses no sulfur to treat his vines and has rarely used Bordeaux mixture (copper sulfate), both considered organic treatments against fungal diseases and rot—though it should be noted that Etna is a natural source for sulfurous volcanic gasses.

Like biodynamic practitioners, Frank often worked according to the cycles of the moon and had experimented with herbal treatments on his vines, but in his view any treatment at all meant something in the vineyard was out of balance. A couple of days later I would ask Giuseppe about the guiding philosophy of Frank's agriculture, attempting to attach a label. *"Biologico?"* ("Organic?") I asked. *"Bio-dinamico?"* ("Biodynamic?") *"No,"* Giuseppe laughed. *"Frank-o-logico. Frank-o-dinamico!"*

Leaning over in his chair, Frank took a small log of cut olive wood from a basket, opened the iron door of the woodstove, and fed the wood to the flames. Frank seemed as consistent as only a madman can be, yet I found his mad logic oddly seductive.

"Let's be honest," Frank said, taking the piece of bread he'd been holding and wiping up the last of the caponata sauce from his plate. "I drive a car. I don't go around on a mule. But I think we need to do things that make sense. I think a golden rule is that if you make your life as difficult as possible you will make beautiful things."

He smiled with something I took for irony, and added, "You know, I think the Arabs have it right when they go on pilgrimages and beat themselves."

Giuseppe and Aki seemed not to take notice of anything Frank was saying, as they spoke no English. In fact, Frank communicated with Aki in a mix of Italian and his rudimentary Japanese. Aki disappeared into the kitchen and came out minutes later with a big dish of ferrazzuoli—long, double-barreled noodles tossed with *broccolini*, Frank's olive oil, and an aged local cheese.

The pasta made its rounds. Following Frank's self-flagellation remark, I imagined the long whips of ferrazzuoli, cooked al dente, as ideal for flogging.

Frank poured some of his MunJebel 3 red (the numbers signifying different bottlings from different vineyards) from 2005. Like the white MunJebel made in the amphorae Frank disavows, it was light in color like a murky Pinot Noir. It too seemed like a wine from another time: a rustic combination of black earth, fruit, and rocks that tasted as though it were made by a man who indeed rode on a mule. Perhaps the most startling thing about it was how long and fresh it was in the mouth despite an alcohol level over 15 percent.

Over the wine and whips of pasta, Frank recounted the arc of his life that had led him to this spot. Born in the rural north of Belgium, his father was a NATO fighter pilot who collected fine wines in his travels; his mother was a teacher at a hotel-restaurant school. Family life revolved around one meal at the end of the week.

"Sunday lunch was holy," he remembered. While his mother cooked, he and his father went into the kitchen to smell and taste the beginnings of the meal and then plunged into the cellar to select wines.

At fourteen years old, Frank used his savings to buy his first case of wine: a mixed case from Domaine de la Romanée-Conti, now the most expensive and prized wine in the world. (An early 1970s case of DRC that cost Frank the equivalent of a couple hundred dollars would today cost tens of thousands.)

After studying language at the university level, Frank quit to go mountain climbing, and he worked as a distributor for a Japanese outdoor equipment company. Then, in the mid-1990s, Frank rode the wheel of fortune of day trading in futures and options. At the end of the decade, when the markets collapsed, he lost everything— including his house and his restored vintage Porsche.

Frank returned to wine, working as a distributor in Belgium, which led him to the door of the renowned Barolo maker Elio Grasso. The thought of making his own wine had entered Frank's mind, and Grasso, a former banker, tried to discourage him.

"He told me, 'You have to bust your ass ten hours a day, every day. If you don't have trouble with the weather, you have trouble with the workers. If you don't have trouble with the workers, you have trouble with the tractor.' But the more he busted my ass—the more he pushed me into it," Frank said. "I'd climbed enough mountains to know that the greatest rewards come from the most desperate situations."

Aki brought out a round of espressos and biscotti, which were quickly downed. The men stood and returned to the winery works. Giuseppe returned to wrestling with his wine press. Frank put a blue baseball-style cap on his head and climbed into his Russian-made two-door diesel truck with faded, mud-splattered red paint. I climbed into the passenger seat. Behind the two of us was a compartment loaded with chain saws and other equipment. I don't know if the vehicle ever *had* seat belts—I didn't see any. As we rode along the main road away from Solicchiata back the way I'd come that morning, I asked Frank why he'd chosen to come to Sicily.

"Actually, I didn't choose Sicily," he responded quickly. "I chose Etna."

Etna's north face appealed to him for several reasons. Most

important, he wanted to be able to plant whole nongrafted vines. Since the phylloxera outbreak destroyed most of Europe's vineyards in the nineteenth century, vines have typically been planted on phylloxera-resistant American rootstock. The sandy soils of many of Etna's vineyards, however, resisted phylloxera, and the mountain was one of the few places in Europe with vineyards of nongrafted vines. The other factors were the combination of environmental traits for making elegant aromatic wines: hot days and cool nights, altitude, bright sunshine, and a long vegetative cycle that pushed the harvest back to October or November, weeks or months after most of Europe.

"Etna is crazy," Frank said. "It's an area much more related to the north than the south."

Frank bought his first vineyards here in 2001 and, with no formal wine training, began experimenting. "I've made some off wines," he said candidly. The grapes that went into one of his early vintages of Rosso del Contadino was so infected with botrytis (a good thing known as "noble rot" when it appears on *white* wine grapes that make Sauternes and other great sweet and off-dry whites) that the red wine turned brown and funky with oxidation. "It was a wine lost in the Twilight Zone. But my Japanese importer came and tasted it and said, 'I love it, you should put that in bottles,' so I sold it. Now I have these freaks who come and want to buy my Contadino 2003. But I don't want to make that shit. I didn't make a wine that year . . . I made a statement without knowing it."

Frank pulled his truck north, down a country road that led onto a dirt track. We crossed a small river and climbed a road severely broken and scarred by rain and the elements. At times the truck lurched slowly, dipping, rocking with the terrain. Pressed up against the door, I hung on to the roof handle as my insides churned like a washing machine.

Frank pointed through the flat windshield at the low terraced hills of this zone, or *contrada*, known as Ciapparotto, covered not with vines but with brush and bramble and ferula and occasional patches of olive trees. "All these hills were once planted with vines,"

Frank said, adding that in the 1970s, fires and the collapse of the wine market all but destroyed the terraces. We came to another crest in the hilltop and a vista of olive trees—low-cut with healthy, pendulous branches. "I bought five hundred trees here," he said. "Nobody wants the land because nobody wants to work this hard anymore. It's too remote. If you don't have a four-by-four, you're up shit's creek."

Frank turned the truck around in a small clearing where a young man and woman stood next to a rusted iron and wood trailer. The couple had dark eyes and round, open faces. Their work clothes were streaked with black, oily juice and powdered with the dust that falls from olive trees when their branches are combed and struck for their fruit. Maria Rosa and her brother, Santino, worked for Frank on his land. And this day they were picking plump black olives as big as dates. That weekend, Frank would load a week's worth of olives onto the trailer and take them to a local mill, where they would be mechanically pressed in a method that had been almost entirely replaced by modern centrifugal presses across oil-producing Europe. In this traditional method the olives are crushed into a paste that would in turn be spread onto mats (Frank meticulously insisted on using his own mats so as to keep his production chemical free) and then put on a hydraulic press that would squeeze out green, hearty olive oil.

Leaving this clearing was more difficult than arriving, as the load to be hauled was significantly greater. The trailer was loaded with crates of olives and a motorized rake for combing the olive branches. Then Frank hitched the trailer to his truck. He opened the truck's tailgate and spread a folded tarp across the tool crates. Santino crawled into the back compartment and lay across the tools; Maria Rosa squeezed in between me and the gearbox. I slammed my door shut and we ambled, with trailer in tow, back down the hill. But rather than going back through Linguaglossa, Frank took a northerly road through towns that hung to the lowest hills of Etna above the Alcantara River Valley, formed between Etna's haunches and the low ridges of the facing Peloritani Mountains.

The afternoon light began to fade as Frank's load struggled uphill, approaching Castiglione di Sicilia, a medieval town perched on a spur overlooking the valley and topped by a strategically positioned Norman castle.

"What we do now is nothing compared to what was done in the past," Frank said, pushing the accelerator of the truck to the floor as we crept up the hill. "Fifty years ago people worked fourteen hours a day."

"If you don't have flexibility and creativity in Sicily," he added, "you're not going to make it."

Up close, Castiglione is a maze of buildings spanning centuries—all clinging to rock and stacked on each other. It is a patchwork of peeling masonry in Mediterranean shades of green and yellow accented by half the town's linens and undergarments hung out to dry. We seemed to be crawling up narrow stone streets through medieval archways; weathered men wearing flat *coppola* caps waved at Frank's familiar face.

Frank explained in English the strategic importance of Castiglione as a customs station suspended over the pass that led to Palermo. Santino, who was lying quiet behind us, recognized his town's name and suddenly called out over the whine of the engine and the rattling of the frame and its load, *"I re di Castiglione"* ("The kings of Castiglione").

Frank laughed, mimicking Santino in a mocking singsong Sicilian: *"I re di Castiglione . . . i re di Castiglione,* and look at it now—it's dead, *morto!"*

Santino continued on about the lost *"re di Castiglione,"* laughing. Frank laughed back, mocking the imaginary kings. Everyone was laughing now. Frank deposited Santino and Maria Rosa in their neighborhood, saying he would be back the following morning at daybreak to pick them up.

It was night when we got back to Frank's winery. Giuseppe was still pressing wine—now under the glare of a mercury vapor light. Frank still had hours of work to do, pumping the wine, bagging the skins and seeds pressed that afternoon, and hosing down the terrace and the equipment before it all became a vinegar factory.

As Frank shoveled the pomace (to be taken to a distillery for grappa) into bags steadied by Giuseppe, he talked about women.

First there was his wife—ex-wife, that is—the Bulgarian ballerina, who came with him here to Etna and left after a month. He shrugged: "Obviously in Solicchiata, there's not much of a dance scene."

Then there was his girlfriend Yoko, who stayed on as a partner in the winery for a few years before they separated and she moved back to Japan. Aki, he said, would be leaving in a few days.

"Finding yourself a woman who wants to live this sort of life, it's not around the corner," Frank said, pushing the shovel into a pile heavy with black grape skins. "It's not even in Sicily anymore."

I NEEDED TO FIND a place to sleep, and Frank knew of an apartment cottage nearby that rented by the night. I followed Frank's truck to the edge of town, down side streets lined with small family gardens and olive trees.

He directed me to park in front of an old stone cottage. Frank rang a buzzer outside a two-story building that was split into several apartments. An old, grizzled man with white hair and a close-cropped moustache stuck his head out the window and, after giving us a sign, came down a staircase on the side of the building and greeted us.

Signor Purello, Frank told me, made wine—a fact of which I made a mental note. Sig. Purello walked with a bent gait to the cottage and used a key to open the door. Inside was a simple apartment: a kitchen was followed by two bedrooms—the first of which had a pair of children's beds, and the second which had one larger bed. At the end of it all was a bathroom.

"Va bene," I said. It was fine, except it was freddo—as cold as a walk-in refrigerator.

Sig. Purello held up his hand to signal "no worries." We walked into the kids' room and he pointed to a metal propane heater. He went over to it, turned a knob on the propane bottle in back, and then turned the switch on top of the heater and waited. Nothing happened. He bent down to put his ear to the heater, then stood up and reported there was no more gas.

He would have to change the bottle. I took this opportunity to ask Sig. Purello if I might move the heater to the other room with the larger bed. Sig. Purello gave me an odd, questioning look and asked, "Why?" I was only one person, no? It would be comfortable here, he said, pointing to one of the kid's beds. Christ looked down over the head of the bed from his cross. At the side of the bed—covering a piece of the cracked tile floor—was a small rug with a smiling Mickey Mouse. There was no arguing—this would be comfortable.

Frank left to return to the winery, and Sig. Purello fetched another twenty-liter gas bottle and a couple of wrenches. After fiddling for a few minutes, he had connected the new bottle, turned the ignition switch on the top of the heater, and . . . nothing. Sig. Purello turned the switch again and again and again. After about twenty tries and no reaction, I asked, *"Va bene?"*

"Si, si!" he assured me so confidently I felt impatient for asking.

Another twenty rhythmic twists of the switch by Sig. Purello still produced not a breath of heat.

On about the forty-first try, the heater coughed, and in the instant of a split second, flames shot out of its mouth only to die instantly in a "poof." Now Sig. Purello seemed to be getting somewhere. He continued to turn the switch—each time slower and more methodical than the last. Finally, on about the fiftieth try, the gas gently ignited and the heater coils began to glow.

Sig. Purello stood and smiled into my face with a look of vindication. Then he gave me a serious look and said that before I went to sleep (he mimed the verb *dormire* by tilting his head onto his hands and closing his eyes), I must *spegnere* (turn off) the heater. He pointed to the off position.

"But it's not cold at night?" I managed in Italian.

"No, no, va bene," he said, pointing to the thick polyester cover on the kid's bed emblazoned with a cartoon graphic of a jockey racing a white horse. Then he repeated the whole mimed routine about my turning off the heater when I went to sleep. He added that if I didn't do this it would make me *mal di testa*. I wondered if he really meant I'd get a headache, or if the carbon monoxide would kill me.

Later that evening I returned to Frank's home and winery. We went through his cellars with the amphorae—Frank wearing a red knit wool cap that made him look like a mad Himalayan elf. We tasted his most expensive wines—Magma—that sold in nearby Linguaglossa wineshops for 99 euros, about four times as much as other high-quality bottlings in the area.

Using a glass wine thief, Frank withdrew a sampling of what he said he would call his Magma Riserva 2006. The red wine was made from the grapes of a single plot of high-elevation vines north of town in a *contrada* called Barbabecchi Soprano. After renting the vineyards for two years, Frank had purchased about thirteen acres—planted as far back as the end of the nineteenth century—with a young winemaker from Catania, Alberto Aiello Graci, who bottled his wine under his label, Graci.

The wine lined the rim of the glass with an orange ring. For the second time that day, I tasted something beyond the realm of my experience. It hit the center of the tongue and exploded—a hint of sweetness was followed by a blast of 16 percent alcohol, not unlike a fine sherry.

Months later when I spoke about this experience with Alessio Planeta, the winemaker from the most important wine-producing family in modern Sicily, he was incredulous at the idea of Cornelissen wines selling at what were among the top prices in all of Italy.

"Did you like it?" he asked.

I barely got out the word "interesting" before Alessio fired back, "That's because you didn't pay for it!" He laughed heartily. He had a point. While I've bought and enjoyed Frank's lesser wines, how could I rationalize spending Magma prices on something I didn't quite recognize as wine?

Over a dinner of chickpea soup and a dry-cured ham of free-roaming black pig from the Nebrodi Mountains, we tasted more wines—some delicious and some just odd. And for the next few hours, Frank complained about the Italian bureaucracy and administration, the phone company, taxes, and just about everything else associated with doing business in Italy. In fact, he said in order not to have to deal with the state wine bureaucracy, he was going to declassify all his wines starting with the next vintage, removing them from the DOC Etna classification and simply calling them *vino da tavola*—table wine.

Yet at the same time, Frank said, the lack of a workable system made Sicily all the more human. "People don't expect anything from the government, so if you need something, you have to call on your neighbor, who has a cousin . . . and that's how people get things done."

I returned to my cottage, turned off the heat as Sig. Purello had warned, and climbed into bed. A couple of hours later I awoke, my muscles frozen by cold and damp, and my bladder straining to release a torrent of Magma. I lay there wondering whether I should try to hold back the flow or risk freezing on the way to the toilet. After contemplating this long enough, I jumped from out of the covers, ran over to my duffel bag, put on a sweater, and ran to the bathroom. After a quick emptying of the bladder, I ran back to climb under the covers and wait for morning.

At sunrise I went to the heater—which started on the second click of the switch—and sprinted to the bathroom, where I warmed my flesh under a modest stream of tepid water. Then I ran back to the bedroom shivering, huddling on the Mickey Mouse rug in front of the flames while I dried myself off. After I dressed, I rang the Purello doorbell. Signora Purello stuck her head out the window—her husband was gone and wouldn't be back until noon, she said.

I told her I had an emergency and unexpectedly had to leave.

"But I thought it was two nights!" she called down in Italian.

I shrugged. When she came down, I gave her the key, paid her the daily rental of 25 euros, and drove off toward Linguaglossa, where I would find breakfast and check into a heated hotel by the side of one of Sicily's only golf courses. I had no intention of ever tasting her husband's wine.

BY NINE O'CLOCK, WHEN I passed by Frank's winery, he had been working for hours and had already made the round trip to Ciapparotto. We got into his truck and headed west of town and then climbed up Etna through vineyards and lava fields.

Leaving paved road behind, the truck strained, heaving and shimmying its way up a dirt ravine until we came upon a theater of vine-covered terraces planted at the edge of a forest. This was Barbabecchi Soprano, the *contrada* that produced the Magma Riserva wine I'd drunk the night before.

The terraces' dry walls—built from stacked lava stone—followed the contours of the mountainside and were often broken and overtaken by brambles. Century-old stubs of vines were planted in irregular rows, traditionally goblet-trained into small bushes the Italians refer to as *alberello* (literally, "little tree"). Each—yet to be trimmed of last year's shoots—had its own wooden tutor that would support the vegetation and fruit in the coming growing season.

Frank listed the work ahead of him. Part of the vineyard had been burned by a fire the previous summer. Other areas had been dug up by cows or pigs left to graze there. He would fix the walls, move earth, and replant damaged vines. And at the top of the land now covered with forest and resting at an elevation of 1,000 meters (or about 3,280 feet toward the summit of nearly 11,000 feet), he planned to clear land for a new vineyard.

Because the land lay in the state-administered Etna Park, extensive permits and red tape would normally be required to bring in heavy equipment to dig on the side of the mountain. "I would have to file a thousand pieces of paper and wait forever," Frank said. "Instead, I spoke to the forest rangers last summer. They know me and know I'm a naturalist. I told them what I needed to do. They told me, 'Do it after October—we won't be here.'"

In that moment I realized the transformative power of Etna. Frank had come in search of something I'd never know. The mountain had taken the pilgrim and turned him into her willing servant. Somewhere along the way, stained by the land and the volcano's breath, Frank Cornelissen had become Sicilian.

THE NEXT STRANGER I WENT TO meet on Etna was an American—more mainstream than Frank but someone whose life had followed a similar circuitous and magnetic path to the mountain.

From Solicchiata I continued west on the road to Randazzo, turning north and following the small signs for Tenuta delle Terre Nere (literally, "Estate of the Black Soils") across what was a low plateau of vineyards to a building that stood out impressively from the drab gray farmhouses of these parts.

The two-story winery was covered in pink masonry and trimmed with black cut lava stone around its arched windows and tall arched wood doors. Out front, a half-dozen workers were busy trimming dormant, twisted old vines in advance of the growing season. To the right there was a small courtyard enclosed by an old *palmento* and other farm buildings.

Marco de Grazia's newly built winery was stocked with large steel tanks, and the inside walls were coated with fresh white paint. In a light-filled second-floor office, I found de Grazia speaking Italian into his cell phone as he stood at a work table in front of a picture window filled with a view of Etna.

At fifty-five, he was a man with presence, accentuated by a Roman nose and curly brown hair. He wore a red North Face jacket (the brand that was *de rigeur* among some oenophiles on the north face of Etna) that met a pair of khakis at the base of an epicurean's paunch.

On the wall facing de Grazia was a long map of Burgundy's Côte d'Or. When de Grazia greeted me, he slipped into English accented with what sounded like an unhurried California delivery.

"I've been working in wine for almost thirty years and . . . I . . . am . . . sick . . . of . . . the . . . bullshit," he enunciated each word as he sat and slid the phone into a jacket pocket. It was a statement that, naturally, put my bullshit detector on red alert.

De Grazia may not be a household name, but in the last few decades he'd done as much as anyone to Italianize American wine-drinking habits. He was born in Washington DC—his mother a painter-sculptor, and his father, Sebastian, a historian and political philosopher (awarded the 1990 Pulitzer Prize for his biography, *Machiavelli in Hell*). Schooled in Rome and Florence, as a young man de Grazia bounced between two continents and universities in the 1970s, graduating at twenty-eight years old with a degree in comparative literature from the University of California at Berkeley.

At Berkeley, de Grazia's life took a turn that began in a wineshop. De Grazia had grown to know and love local Italian wines, but in America he found mostly mediocre imports from Italy. De Grazia invited Berkeley wineshop owner Joel Butler (now a Master of Wine and wine educator in California) to dinner to taste some of his personal stock. Impressed, Butler urged de Grazia to return to Italy to scout quality Tuscan and Piedmont wines for export to the United States. De Grazia built a thriving business that boomed with the 1985 vintage of Brunello di Montalcino and Barolo.

De Grazia's brother, Iano (short for Sebastiano), joined the business, and Marco became a leading partner with a handful of Italian friends in Argentina's Altos Las Formicas wine estate in the 1990s.

After years of traveling to Sicily, de Grazia said, "Little by little I got attracted to Etna. There was nothing here. The terraces were abandoned. But when I came and tasted even the farmers' wines, you could tell that the wines were different: they didn't taste anything like the wines from the south; they were not baked.

"When I chose a place to make wine, after helping other people make wine, I wanted to choose a place that had the same nobility as Barolo or Burgundy. Of course when you taste the wines next to each other they are different, but they have the same mother as Burgundy and Barolo."

In 2002, on the heels of a divorce and the death of his father, de Grazia bought his first Etna vineyards. Over the next few years, he handed over operation of the wine export business to his brother, bought the old *palmento* next door, and built a new winery. He owns about thirty-eight acres on Etna, which are cultivated organically to make Nerello reds.

Etna is, in de Grazia's words, "the Burgundy of the Mediterranean." And why not? A few years earlier he'd told a glossy magazine that Italy's Campania region was "the new Piedmont." De Grazia had built a successful career in finding the next new thing. "It's what I like to do," de Grazia told me: "discover wine and bring it out of its black hole."

Bringing wines to the forefront of the American market hadn't been without controversy, for as much as de Grazia changed American wine-drinking habits, he also altered Italian winemaking. In Barolo and the Piedmont, coming into the modern world meant the replacement of traditional large *botti* with smaller, more oak-imparting French *barriques*—a part of recent history that some traditionalists blame on de Grazia.

On Etna, de Grazia has used a different strategy, undertaking a mapping project of his and other local vineyards in the belief that the area has at least twenty-five different *crus*—vineyard locations that because of geology, soil, altitude, and microclimes give extraordinary and varying results. One of those *crus* happens to be the vineyard right in front of his winery where more than an acre is planted with pre-phylloxera vines—a vague label referring to old vines that predate phylloxera blight as well as their ungrafted descendants.

"Solicchiata to Randazzo was the Côte d'Or of Sicily," de Grazia said, squeezing his metaphor as though it were grape skins in a press to extract all he could. "The problem is that for the last century, nobody's done anything here."

De Grazia spoke of the oenological school established in Catania in the nineteenth century and how Etna shipped thousands of barrels of wine every month from the port at Riposto—a period that ended with the relatively late arrival of phylloxera at the tail end of the nineteenth century. Yet with more drama and conspiratorial accusation than I've heard from any Sicilian, de Grazia pinned the decline of Sicilian winemaking on the policies of northerners from the Piedmont who unified Italy under a kingdom in 1861.

"The golden period ended with the double blow of phylloxera and the unification of Italy," he said. "The unity of Italy despoiled the south."

At one point that morning, a couple of men from Catania arrived for de Grazia. The taller man, wearing a sweater and glasses, had come to talk about a contract to maintain the sailboat de Grazia was considering purchasing and docking in Catania. His friend, a shorter man in a leather jacket with a shaved, shiny head, was a Catania wine merchant.

While they talked business, I explored de Grazia's cellar—housed in the rustic *palmento*—with his cellar master, Francesco Mazzola, an older, quiet, but harried-looking man.

Mazzola explained that Terre Nere wines are aged eighteen months in mostly used Bordeaux *barriques*, larger Burgundy barrels, and some larger Austrian barrels up to 3,000 liters.

We tasted our way through a series of red wines—mostly from the 2006 vintage. Although de Grazia makes a limited amount of white wine from an assemblage of local varietals, nearly all of the 100,000 bottles produced annually are red. We started with de Grazia's generic Nerello Mascalese and continued with the *crus* de Grazia was now mapping.

Each bank of barrels, stacked on top of each other, contained a different vineyard, and with our tasting glasses we climbed the flanks of the mountain—from the vineyard known as Calderara Sottana (600 meters) up another 100 meters to Feudo di Mezzo and then to Guardiola at 900 meters.

I tried to put de Grazia's Burgundy talk out of my mind. The wines were bolder than fine Burgundies, somewhat easier drinking than Barolos. After Frank's wines, de Grazia's reds tasted familiarly tame. Yet they were strikingly different from each other. The Feudo di Mezzo was expressive, floral, and spicy—a bit long on the licorice-woody flavors. The Guardiola was deeper and at the same time more nervous and smelled of hay. We finished by tasting from a *barrique* of wine from the pre-phylloxera plot in front of the winery—a wine that de Grazia labeled La Vigna di Don Peppino for the old *contadino* who helped work the plot. It appeared lighter in the glass—pink at the edges—but it was by far the most powerful of de Grazia's wines: tannic, with a mineral edge, and high in alcohol (15 percent), and it left the inside of my mouth feeling as dry as if it had been rinsed with the Sicilian summer countryside. I searched with my taste buds for traces of the infamous de Grazia oak imprint, but found none. The stuff tasted as though it could have been resting in stone. I swallowed, and in its wake it seemed to leave a path for hunger.

As I emerged into the daylight, de Grazia was talking with his visitors in the courtyard. It was afternoon, the sun was high, and the man with the shaved head held his stomach and asked de Grazia if he had any bread and olive oil to hold him over for the drive back to Catania.

De Grazia's answer was typically Sicilian: he invited us all to stay for lunch.

We crossed the courtyard and continued through the open doorway of the old farmhouse into de Grazia's kitchen—a bachelor's kitchen in the center of which was a rectangular table piled with bread, fruit, paper bags, bottles of olive oil, water, wine, and other unidentifiable liquids. The kitchen opened onto a small apartment that looked as though it might be inhabited by a college freshman. There was a living room with a couch, television, and acoustic guitar, and a bedroom with a mattress on the tile floor and an open suitcase whose contents were spilling over.

De Grazia liked to cook. We, the guests, cleared openings in the clutter of the table as de Grazia lit a fire under a pot of pasta water and set out a mortadella (from a local butcher whose grapes de Grazia vinified), a fresh loaf of country bread, and local olive oil. The bald-headed man cut off slices of the sausage, which we ate with our fingers. De Grazia opened a bottle of Etna red produced by Cottanera, a modern winery that grew out of a family farm in Castiglione more than a decade earlier. We saluted, drank, and dipped bread in the oil.

De Grazia served tube pasta mixed with his own jarred sauce made from ricotta and fresh spinach. We ate, drank, and spoke in Italian about what was of most interest to the men: boats, wine, women.

After lunch, the men left for Catania. De Grazia and I stood outside, and an old hunched man resembling Sig. Purello wearing a *coppola* cap drove up and stepped out of his Fiat. "Do they sell wine here?" he asked in an accent heavily sauced with Sicilian.

He explained that he was from Messina and wanted to buy wine before returning—a tradition that has kept some of Etna's small wine production alive for decades. De Grazia, like many Etna producers, sold excess wine not used in his bottlings in bulk—filling jugs of local customers who showed up at his door.

"*Si*," de Grazia beamed, "*buoni vini*."

He went around the corner and reappeared with Mazzola, who took the man inside the cellar. De Grazia's cell phone rang and he vanished.

What seemed like two minutes later—barely enough time to throw a couple of ounces of wine down his throat—the old Sicilian came out of the cellar alone and headed for his car.

"*Che fa?*" I asked, wanting to know why he was running off so quickly.

The man turned his head left and right, making sure no one else was in earshot. He scrunched his nose and lips and said in a near whisper, "*Amaro*" ("Bitter").

Burgundy under the volcano might have been the mantra of the foreigners, but at that moment it didn't seem to concern this old man in search of something red and easy to fill his trunk with. I thought about stopping him to talk, but he moved too quickly—disappearing up the drive of black earth.

FRIDAY EVENINGS IN SOLICCHIATA mean the social event of the week: a wine tasting at Bar Sandro Dibella. This is not a bar in which I expected to find a wine tasting. There are no sommeliers, smartly dressed clients, works of art, or anything for that matter that could be construed as being designed to good taste. Sandro's is a wine tasting that could only happen at the edge of the world, Sicily.

The bar is typical of thousands of local joints all over Italy. The exterior is framed by a pair of gold-colored aluminum entry doors and two faded yellow awnings that tell you nothing about the place—one reads CAVE OX, the other SNACK BAR. Inside it is the usual setup: the small Formica and stainless steel bar around which about four people can stand resting their elbows, the mirrored wall behind the bar with shelves of liquor bottles, the video arcade games, the industrial-sized espresso machine, shelves of bagged snacks, candy bars and gum, and a freezer of prepackaged colorful ice creams.

But once your eyes adjust to the jaundiced fluorescent light, you notice what makes the place different: the shelves that wind around the main barroom are lined with hundreds of empty wine bottles from all over Italy, France, and beyond—Tuscany to Bordeaux, Friuli to the Loire Valley, the Tyrol to Japan (Sake), and, of course, Barolo to Burgundy. Every week, Sandro, some Etna winemakers, and a group of locals tastes something new, leaving behind the empties as their record.

When I arrived that Friday evening, there were about ten people in the bar, including Pippo the mechanic. Behind the bar stood Sandro, a big fleshy man around thirty with a broad smile, a shaved head, and wide-open light eyes that don't seem to blink. One of Sandro's big hands waved me over to the bar while the other poured a glass of white wine from the featured winery of the night—Cantine Russo, the family winery of Pippo the mechanic's cousin, Vincenzo Russo.

As more people filled the place, Sandro's father put coals in a small rusted barbecue grill outside on the curb and lit them afire. Sandro's mother brought out plates of appetizers and set them on the barrel that serves as a countertop in the middle of the bar floor. In most places on earth this bar food would be considered delicacies: bruschetta toasts topped with eggplant and mozzarella, new green cracked olives, sun-dried tomatoes in oil, grilled fennel, and *broccolini*.

Frank helped Sandro organize these tastings, and I asked Sandro where Frank was.

"We never wait for Frank. Frank is *Sicilianizzato* ("Sicilianized")," he laughed. "He is never on time."

Then Sandro added over the growing din in the bar, "Frank is *bravo*. A little different from how we do things here, but *buono*."

"*Buono*," echoed Pippo, coming up behind me. He had changed out of his coveralls into slacks and a beige overcoat. His hair was neatly slicked back and his white hands—scrubbed of the shop grease after a week's work—held a large tulip-shaped glass. He no longer eyed me with suspicion as we saluted with his cousin's fresh white wine.

Pippo said something to Sandro, who then produced from behind the bar a tall green bottle that wore only a strip of masking tape. On it was marked "Brunetto" (Pippo's last name) and "2007." This was Pippo's new wine from the fall harvest just months earlier. Sandro took out a trio of fresh glasses, poured Pippo's wine in it, and we saluted again.

The wine was straightforward and uncomplicated. There was no Côte d'Or. No Barolo. No *cru*. No philosophy. No statement. Just simple deep fruit wine that probably would have pleased the old-timer at de Grazia's winery that afternoon. Brunetto 2007 seemed an honest wine. With a few sips I thought I could recognize what kind of mechanic Pippo was: the kind who could tune an old engine not with a computer or gauges but by putting an ear to it and listening.

Pippo explained how he had come to make wine: *"Sono nato in vino"*—he was born into it. His father had tended the high-altitude vines in Barbabecchi Soprano that now partly belonged to Frank.

"Ma ha bevuto tutto," Sandro said, putting his thumb to his lips as he joked that Pippo the Baby drank all the wine.

Frank arrived after nine with Aki and a pair of guests—the French Loire Valley winemaker Patrick Desplats of the small organic Domaine des Griottes and his wife, Claire. There were more than twenty people in the place at this time—Brandon the American from Catania, a Dutch couple, Italians, Sicilians. Sandro's father came in from the street with a tray of just-off-the-grill sausages flavored with fennel seeds and stuffed with fresh scallions and cheese. Sandro took these sausages, folded them in fat sections of cut bread, wrapped them in napkins, and passed them around.

We drank Pippo's cousin's wines. It was a moment without class or pretense or nation or the "bullshit" of the world of wine—a feeling of freedom I have experienced on Sicily more than anywhere else. It was Friday night in Solicchiata and we were all Sicilian.

Spring

4

Planet Planeta

DISCOUNTING THE BOTTLES OF FRUITY Corvo red and white that seemed to be everywhere in my youth—in New York Italian restaurants and family gatherings—the first Sicilian wines I enjoyed were on mainland Italy. A few years ago, in traveling through winegrowing regions above the knee of Italy's boot, I was more than surprised to find Sicily represented on wine lists—from seaside summer terraces in Tuscany to trattorias in Lombardy to chic restaurants in the Veneto. I was amazed that in fiercely provincial Italy, Sicily had somehow made the cut. Italians—including northerners—were actually drinking Sicilian wine. More often than not, the wine was Planeta.

What—or who—I wondered, is a Planeta?

In fact, it's impossible to consider Sicilian wine in the twenty-first century without Planeta. That is not to say that Planeta produces the most singularly profound wines from Sicily—nor, for that matter, the most *Sicilian* wines. Yet in the last twenty years, no one has been more effective in showing the world that Sicily and its vines have something important to express.

Planeta is three wineries across Sicily, about a thousand acres of vineyards, and many more hundreds of acres of wheat, tomatoes, and other produce. It is a palazzo in Palermo and a second one in the farming community of Menfi on Sicily's southwestern coast. Above all, Planeta is a family. Wine writers have been tempted to compare Sicily with California and liken the Planetas to the Mondavis. But while both families profoundly changed wine in different parts of the globe, the Mondavis lost their empire through partnerships in the larger corporate world of American capitalism. In contrast, Planeta has remained both a family and a family enterprise in the true Sicilian sense—not only a clan, but their own world.

Every world has a sun, and the brilliant star of Planeta is Diego, the inexhaustible patriarch who nurtured Planeta wines from nothing to a producer of 2.5 million bottles distributed annually in sixty countries.

To get to the world of Planeta, I followed Alessio Planeta—Planeta's chief winemaker and therefore the Planeta closest to his uncle Diego in family wine hierarchy—along his Monday morning commute. The drive began in Palermo at the Palazzo Planeta, an old palace with numerous family apartments built at the edge of the old city. After jockeying for half an hour through the free-for-all that is Palermo Monday morning traffic, we took the highway that cuts through the mountainous interior of western Sicily to the Belice Valley—vibrant green with grasses and wheat and colored with the first spring poppies—and arrived at the hilly vineyards of Sambuca di Sicilia.

Here on the chalky plain between the 1950s-era manmade Lake Aráncio and the nearby wooded low mountains is the Planeta's Ulmo estate of more than 200 acres of vines and olive groves—hermetically silent except for the darting and chattering of swallows. About a hundred yards down a dirt road toward the lake is the modern winery used by the Planetas to make some of their best white wines; further on by the edge of the lake is the outline of the ruin of an Arab castle. The building we'd stopped in front of—the farmhouse owned by the Planetas since the 1600s—doesn't look like a house at all. Rather, it is a small fort that once served as stables and as a secure resting spot for horse travelers on the Palermo-Sciacca highway. Viewed from its outer walls, it is a block of featureless pink and beige mortar bleached by the sun and blackened by rain. The thick masses of walls are broken only by openings for small barred windows and narrow slits with about enough room for the barrel of a shotgun. A few meters away from the outer walls is a low spring-fed trough of a fountain—long enough to quench the thirsts of half a dozen horses and their riders at the same time.

A rising white sun cast sharp shadows on the worn cobblestones and the stubby grasses pushing up between them. Dismounting his four-wheel drive and stepping into a light breeze that seemed constant in the valley, Alessio remarked that the farmhouse provided refuge from highway outlaws, including the legendary 1940s Sicilian separatist Salvatore Giuliano, whose life was romanticized by local lore and in Mario Puzo's novel *The Sicilian* (1984).

"Giuliano was made out to be a kind of Robin Hood, but he wasn't," Alessio said, as if to correct the record. "He was totally a bandit. A cousin of my father was kidnapped by him and was in a cave for two months."

Alessio Planeta—like most of his fifteen cousins who collectively own the Planeta estates—speaks multiple languages, including English, and does not look classically southern Italian. His gray-green eyes, soft features, and long, fair face seem to reflect the family's ancestral home of Catalonia, Spain. With his blue blazer and horn-rimmed glasses set on a pointed nose, Alessio looks more like a Continental engineer than a Sicilian *vignaiolo*. At forty-one, he was at the head of six Planeta cousins directly involved in the Planeta wine business, including his brother, Santi, who runs Italian distribution, and Diego's half-English daughter, Francesca, who lives in Milan and oversees international marketing.

I followed Alessio through a thick wood door that led into the courtyard of the farmhouse, and from there we proceeded through another doorway into what were once Ulmo's stables. They were now transformed into a large, elegant country room with irregular, mud-colored terra-cotta floors, arches that held up a tall wood-ribbed ceiling, and a decor of dark wood antiques and colonial-era paintings.

Alessio led me over to a picture in the corner of the room. A grainy black-and-white photo blown up to poster size, it showed hundreds of leather-skinned peasants on mules around the building where we now stood. The image (except for the Italian flags and the fact that it was a photograph) could have been made anytime in the last five hundred years. But this photo was taken on May 1, 1948, a postwar May Day when workers across Sicily were pressing for land reform and enforcement of Italian laws regulating tenant farming. Since the time of the Romans, much of Sicily had been carved up into large landholdings, or *latifundi*, and up through the first half of the twentieth century, Sicily resembled a feudal state.

The Planetas lost little land in the postwar reform era, and like other families that have since kept their lands, they have done so by remaining close to it.

"My grandfather and father did agriculture not in the Sicilian aristocratic way," Alessio said. "They did it in a modern way. And to be modern in Sicily was not easy—you can't imagine."

In the postwar years, most winegrowers in southwestern Sicily were still growing grapes for production of Marsala. But when the collapse of Marsala prices in the 1950s shivered through the grape-growing market, many producers looked to alternative crops. Alessio's grandfather Vito had a different idea—that winegrowers should make their own local wines; and in 1958 he helped found the Settesoli cooperative, named after an estate in *The Leopard*. In 1972 Diego Planeta became president of Settesoli (a post he still holds) and later led the cooperative through bottling its first wines.

In the early 1980s Diego approached Alessio with an idea that would change the course of the Planetas' and Sicilian winegrowing. Alessio was an agronomy student in Palermo, and Diego was named president of Sicily's Istituto Regionale delle Vite e del Vino (Institute of Vines and Wine). At the time, Sicily produced lakes of bulk wine—90 percent of it white wine from highly productive Catarratto and Trebbiano grapes. (In 2008 it was about two-thirds white.) Sicily's reputation had been depressed by Mafia violence and assassinations.

"Sicily in the 1980s was . . ." Alessio began, pausing. "I won't say Iran, but it was bad."

He sat at a wood table, his back to a small window that framed a view of an olive grove and a vineyard that sloped toward the lake.

"In 1984 this farm was completely wild. There were cows in this building where we are now. And Diego asked me, 'What do you think about planting this area with different kinds of grape varieties—to try something new?'"

The following year, the Planetas planted more than 100 acres with dozens of types of varietal clones at Ulmo: Sicilian grapes such as Nero d'Avola and white Grecanico and Inzolia. They also began planting non-native international varietals such as Chardonnay, Riesling, Cabernet Sauvignon, and Merlot. In the years that followed, the Planetas did tests by vinifying small quantities at Settesoli and the rustic winery at cos, where Alessio worked as an apprentice. "The Chardonnay and Grecanico were promising," Alessio remembered. "The Merlot and Cabernet were gorgeous."

Ulmo was an open laboratory. The Planetas brought in oenologists from the north to consult, but most seemed to be confounded by Sicily's hot, arid climate. Then in 1989 Diego flew to Australia and recruited a Piemontese oenologist, Carlo Corino, who had worked for more than a decade at the Montrose Group and who had helped transform wine in Australia's Mudgee region. "Diego," Alessio said, "made him an offer he couldn't refuse."

Corino, who had brought Old World traditions to Australia, brought modern winemaking techniques back to Sicily and Italy. Corino favored low yields of ripe fruit in the vineyards, along with modern winery techniques to extract maximum flavor. He also favored the use of Bordeaux *barriques* for fermenting Chardonnay and aging reds.

"Carlo had experience in hot climates. He also had the culture of wine in his blood and the respect of tradition," Alessio said.

In Corino's obituaries in 2007, his collaboration with Planeta was credited with transforming Sicilian wine. But in 1995—before the Planetas' first commercial harvest—Corino departed Sicily for Tuscany, leaving Alessio as Planeta's chief winemaker. The following year, Planeta released three single varietal wines: oak-fermented Chardonnay as well as oak-raised reds from Cabernet and Merlot. Planeta was making a bold statement—that Sicily could produce modern wines as good as anything from the New World, if not better. "It was a shock to the market," Alessio said. "It was new, new, new."

As I listened to Alessio, I felt torn. The longer I live in Europe and travel from one end to another, the more I appreciate local wines that reflect tradition and their sense of place. I generally have a problem with "new, new, new" and would argue that the last thing the world needs is a new Chardonnay. Yet at the same time I respect the Planetas and the trail they have blazed, even if at times the path hasn't seemed very Sicilian. Planeta's friendly wines and smart packaging broke through the snob barrier to the north and made wines from Sicily seem safe—chic, even. A decade earlier, fashionable northerners would rather have been seen strolling downtown in kitchen smocks than ordering Sicilian wine. The change was due in large part to Planeta.

Planeta followed its success with international wines by going local—moving across the island on a mission of discovering Sicilian soils and grapes. Planeta's first expansion outside the Menfi area was to buy vineyards in Vittoria and later to produce Cerasuolo di Vittoria.

Alessio remembered a family dinner in 1998: "We said, 'Why don't we grow in this way so that in some years we could cover all of Sicily?' In each place the project was to buy vineyards and make local wines."

That year Planeta bought more than 140 acres of farmland in Noto and later built another winery to produce both Moscato di Noto and its red called Santa Cecilia, made from Nero d'Avola. Two new wineries were built for a new headquarters on the family farm, La Dispensa, outside Menfi. In 2007 Planeta began production in Menfi of one of the rare Sicilian rosés. And Planeta's latest project was planting vineyards on the north face of Etna in the high-altitude *contrada* of Sciara Nuova—not with the Nerellos that dominate the landscape, but with white Carricante as well as Riesling.

International and Sicilian, market-driven by necessity (all those mouths to feed), and contrarian in spirit, Planeta is literally all over the map of Sicilian winemaking. In the vineyards of La Dispensa, the Planetas grow the Campania varietal Fiano for their white wine called Cometa. On a high plateau above Ulmo, Alessio was experimenting with Pinot Noir.

They are an old family attached to the land and partners in Italy's Slow Food movement, but at the same time they reject many Old World traditions. In the winery, technology trumps chance: Selected yeasts are deployed (rather than relying on yeasts naturally present on grape skins), temperatures are controlled, and tanks are filled with inert gas to prevent oxidation. The Planetas irrigate vineyards to make it through hot summers and practice a sustainable agriculture that permits them to chemically treat plants and soils when deemed necessary.

"We are too big to be organic," Alessio said. Diego later told me he thought of organics as "the stupidest thing" (a remark that Alessio later excused as the reflection of a generation born into a Sicily with severe malaria—wiped out only after decades of spraying DDT).

After a walk down to the winery, through vines pushing out their first buds of spring, and a drive through the high-plateau vineyards where the soils seemed to change color every 100 meters, we returned to Ulmo. Inside the large room was a table covered by a white cloth, and on it there was a ceramic bowl filled with fresh sheep's milk ricotta. The cheese, Alessio explained, is prepared at a local farm and is ready daily at 11 a.m. By my calculation that meant it was less than two hours old. We spooned it warm and wet onto plates and then poured some light emerald Planeta olive oil on top with salt and pepper. The young white wines we drank at lunch were good, fresh, and easygoing, if not very distinctive. The ricotta was the opposite: I could taste the animal scents of the sheep and the land on which they grazed. I can still conjure the flavors in my mind—preserved there like the faded wall photo at the edge of the room.

ALESSIO JETTED OFF TO ROME that afternoon for a classical music concert sponsored by Planeta. That evening his brother, Santi, and his cousin Chiara picked me up at my hotel by the sea for dinner. A ten-minute drive up some dark country roads brought us to the gates of the house where Diego Planeta, now divorced, lived alone. This old Planeta house—which, like much else around Menfi, had been "in the family a long time"—sat at the end of the dirt drive shrouded by densely packed eucalyptus and palm trees. As Santi parked his truck, we were greeted by three large, white, energetic Maremma sheepdogs.

Diego stood in his doorway—a compact man and a picture of elegance. He wore khaki pants and soft brown-leather loafers and a light sweater over a crisp pink shirt. His eyes shone with intensity, studying his visitor over a substantial beak that points like an index finger. The top of his head was buffed, slightly freckled; the remaining hair above his ears was neatly slicked back. He seemed to move with the understated ease of a man who is used to being listened to.

Diego waved us up a wood staircase into a sitting room with deep, dark leather couches set around a fireplace in which a fire burned. As Santi poured glasses of Spumante, Diego seemed distracted. He explained that he had been watching the television news and was concerned about worsening political violence in Bosnia, where he had recently invested in land—for, in addition to guiding the Settesoli wine cooperative and building the Planeta wine business, Diego also had built a network of commercial fruit and vegetable nurseries in Sicily, the Italian Marche, France, and now Bosnia. The nurseries produced one hundred million plants per year on selected rootstalks for European growers: tomatoes, peppers, cucumbers, melons, eggplant, and more.

It doesn't take more than a few moments of talking produce with Diego to lead him to indict the food distribution systems in Europe and the United States, which—owing to my presence—he referred to (in perfect English) as "your country." Nor does it take more than a few moments to notice the way this slight dapper man fills the room and the way the younger Planetas listen to him with reverence and amusement.

"The most important plants—tomatoes—are a disaster," Diego began. "The small producers and the old varieties are going away. The clients only want to buy tomatoes that last—that have a long shelf life. That is why tomatoes you find in the supermarket in Northern Europe or *your country* have no taste."

Diego was sprawled on a couch, one leg tucked under the knee, letting his right hand wave as if by its own will as he continued: "The consumer gets what he wants, and if he wants to eat rubbish he gets rubbish!"

There was something very New World—very *my country*—about Diego's restlessness, his worldview, and his entrepreneurial instincts. As a young man he'd dropped out of agronomy school ("It was too slow") in order to work. While most Italians his age were settling into their pensions, Diego joked about retiring. Yet when it came to essentials like tomatoes, he was as Old World as it gets—an uncompromising parochial Sicilian. He proudly told how the Planeta farm in Vittoria produced old-fashioned stewed tomatoes—fifteen hundred jars of them every year—to be distributed to family members. It was reassuring to learn that the Planetas, with their business success, still knew how to measure wealth in real luxuries like fresh ricotta or eating your own tomatoes, and that these values were being passed down the bloodline.

Somehow the discussion of tomatoes led to a critique of the inferior diet in the world's largest economy—*my country*. "I was in *your country* last week," Diego shook his head. "I was sitting in the Atlanta airport for hours, and I looked around at the people there. They were so large and strange-looking. I said to myself, 'Do you suppose I can see one normal human being?' And you know, I did not see one normal human being!"

Diego himself conforms to no standard of normalcy, and that is part of his petulant charm. He is as brilliant as he is tactless and freely dispenses insults to whole sections of the planet—no place more than Sicily. He is a man of his own making who seems impatient with humanity, time itself, and his own mortality. His observations and actions have had more influence on Sicilian winemaking than anyone's. And that is what brought me to his door: to hear Diego's take on the last half century of Sicilian wine—and to tap the vision inside that shiny crown.

He came of age in the 1950s, a period of revolution for Sicily and the Italian south. Land reform forced landowners to sell off parts of their estates for redistribution (though the program was hampered by bureaucratic inertia, trickery, and corruption). At the same time, agricultural industrialization transformed the way farming had been done for centuries.

"On this island nothing had changed from the year 900 when the Arabs arrived until 1950! And then everything changed! Before 1950 it was a period when all the landowner had to do was sit and wait for the workers to do the work." Diego reached for a pistachio from a bowl on the table, cracked one open, and popped the nut into his mouth.

"At that time the value of wheat and cheese was so high, life was easy. In 1950 the price of a kilo of wheat was the equivalent of 10 euro cents, and the cost of a day of labor in agriculture was 25 cents. Last year the price of a kilo of wheat was 12 cents, and the cost of one day of labor was 70 euros!"

That sort of math, Diego said, meant that landholding families had to adapt and modernize or lose their land. As for wine, he said, "That, is a story typical of Sicily." Diego explained that after the war, most Sicilian wine grape production went to Marsala cooperatives. But by the end of the 1950s, Marsala was in crisis as Italians took up new Americanized drinking habits including whiskey and Coca-Cola. "When Marsala collapsed, everything collapsed with it," he said.

The creation of the European Economic Community in 1957 provided temporary relief to Sicily—favoring European winegrowers and wine producers over North Africans. But over the next twenty years, production of wine grew into a glut. Resettled *pieds noirs* in France added or replanted seas of vineyards in southern France. Prices dropped, and by the mid-1970s French Mediterranean winegrowers were rioting and destroyed hundreds of thousands of gallons of imported Italian wine. The crisis was calmed with a political bandage in the form of European subsidies to distill excess wine production into alcohol for industry—a policy that floated Europe's winegrowing south for more than a decade.

"From 1977 to 1990, what the community was paying for a liter of wine was higher than the market value," Diego said. "For myself as a grower who wanted to survive, I could never believe this system would go on forever."

"Not only that," he said, a smile creasing his face, "the idea of producing grapes to destroy them was not very exciting."

As subsidies dried up, Diego said, Sicilian wine was approaching another crisis—as a big-volume producer in a world that didn't need cheap wine. It took Planeta, cos, and a handful of other quality producers to show the way forward.

"The mentality of Sicily is: 'Why change when everything here is perfect?' Some people thought the subsidies would never end. In Sicily people say, 'All our problems come from somewhere else, from the north.' It's all rubbish. Sicilians love to play the part of the victim."

"Look," Diego sat up and leaned closer to me, clasping his hands between his knees. "I've traveled a lot and I can tell you that farmers throughout the whole world don't like to change. But you combine that with Sicily, and it's . . . ideal!"

Daniele, the Planeta winery's chef, came to the top of the stairs to call us to dinner and we followed him downstairs. Diego's modest dining room was lit by table candles and on the walls was a pair of oversize Roman School paintings perhaps as old as *my country*. The oils depicted a fantasy world of crumbled Roman ruins by the sea: In one, fishermen struggled with their nets in the shallows while up on shore a small group of aristocrats in plumed hats and petticoats was gathered around a small sun-blackened man. I stared at the picture trying to figure out its narrative. Who were these powdered, pampered people? What were they doing there? Buying fish?

Diego came up from behind me, slapped a hand on my shoulder, and said in sotto voce, "Anything I've done is not because I have any vision. I just traveled, read, and talked to people. That's all. I traveled and I said, 'Why not?'"

We sat down to dinner, Diego at the head of the table and me to his right. Daniele, a slight man with elfin features who made his way to Italy from his native British Columbia, sat with us. He served a starter of fresh marinated anchovies with a light fennel sauce. Santi poured from a bottle of Planeta Alastro 1996, a blend of native Grecanico and Chardonnay. When released, it was sold as a wine to last four to five years, but now more than twice that age, it still tasted fresh, floral.

As we ate, Diego picked up where he had left off, sketching the landscape of local wine at the beginning of the 1980s when the Settesoli cooperative began to bottle its wines.

"Our wines were not varieties that could age. Wines from here were completely oxidized," he said as he put down his fork. "Now 99 percent of Sicilians would be against what I am about to say. But how can you select anything here? How does a farmer select anything? He talks to his neighbor. And his neighbor tells him to use a certain variety because it is productive and produces big grape bunches—everything we don't want in wine today! Also, the easier a wine oxidized, the better it was for Marsala. It was a mess. We had to start from zero."

In the early 1980s Diego began to experiment with international grape varietals, not only to prove what he believed Sicilian *terroirs* were capable of but also to challenge local thinking.

Diego lifted his glass and paused to speak. "The big problem on the island is everyone would say, 'My Catarratto is the best in the world.' Oh really? How do you know it is the best in the world? Have you ever challenged it?"

With no school for oenology on Sicily, the Settesoli cooperative brought in oenologists from northern Italy, who Diego said "had tremendous knowledge of their areas but no idea how to get anything from our grapes . . . the result was totally anonymous wines with no character." Diego said, "I was sick and tired of oenologists coming from the north, who had no feeling and no love for the south." He told how he heard of a Piemontese (Corino) who was doing great things in Australia and flew to find him there.

"Uncle, you didn't want to do like a Sicilian and wait for him to come to you?" Santi said, laying on a countrified Sicilian accent over his Italian. Diego and Chiara laughed.

"Carlo was the man who gave the right interpretation to our *terroirs*," Diego went on. "He came in 1989. In 1985 when we planted Chardonnay—everybody said we were crazy. Everyone said, 'You will pick grapes in July, it is so hot here . . . you will destroy the flavor and aromas of Chardonnay.' But Carlo came and looked at the hillside and said, 'Take all the rest out—keep the Chardonnay.' And in fact the Chardonnay became the flagship wine."

As dishes were cleared from the table, Diego announced, "Everybody thinks Sicily is so hot . . . it's not as hot as Bordeaux!"

Daniele brought out the main course: grouper served on a bed of grilled artichokes and tomatoes. Santi set out two more Planeta whites from 2001—a bottle of Cometa made from Fiano and a bottle of Chardonnay. The first wine was soft in the mouth—less minerally than other Fianos I enjoyed on the grape's home turf in Campania, but deliciously floral and fruity. An image popped into my head of freshly washed feather pillows hanging out to dry. It was one Planeta wine I'd drunk that conjured a place, though I was not sure what that place was.

The Chardonnay was harder to figure out. It was a pretty Italian Chardonnay. But what, I wondered, is an Italian Chardonnay? Not as complex as a Burgundy Chardonnay. Certainly not as cloying as most of the New World Chardonnays I've encountered. But there was a detectable wood scent; and was that pineapple I was picking up in the glass?

"It is so easy to make good wine in Sicily. The question is 'How can you be so brave as to make bad wine?'" Diego asked. "We are spoiled. Everything is so easy," he went on in what could have been a passage right out of *Il Gattopardo*. "We have the sun. So much of everything . . . it is like we are sleeping."

Diego scrutinized the wines in front of him, and added, "But now it's their problem—I am going to retire." The statement produced a hearty round of laughter.

I poured myself another glass of Cometa, which with every sip felt more inspirational. I wondered out loud about the next generation of Planeta wines. In a very short time, Planeta had made some very good, reliable wines at reasonable to modestly expensive prices. But, I asked, where was it going? When would Planeta make a truly great Sicilian wine?

Diego leaned back in his chair, sitting upright. You could see his thoughts shine in his eyes before he spoke.

"I tell them all the time," he said, "You can have a wine region that can be popular and successful for a time. But you can never have a wine that will be great for all time unless it can age for a hundred years or more!"

There was a moment of silence. Then Santi protested in Italian, and Chiara followed. There was some discussion. Some "let's be reasonable, uncle." Some negotiation.

"Okay, okay," Diego corrected himself. "You cannot have a wine that will be successful for all time unless it can age fifty years—minimum."

More silence.

Diego believed that the place his family would make that wine was at the opposite end of Sicily on Etna. Not the red wine being pursued by most of the newer players on the mountain, but a white wine from Sicilian grapes.

"I think on Etna you can make a white wine that will age for a long, long time," he said. "They may invest a fortune there. Of course it is for them not for me. I am retiring . . ."

I sensed that Diego would probably be involved in his family's winemaking for a long time—even long after he went to his grave.

"In the next ten years, I think Sicily should start with a completely new project," Diego said, leaning toward me. "We have the chance in Sicily to say something that stays in the books of wine knowledge for all time."

I was waiting for the revelation. Diego stood and said, "I will tell you when I return."

He shuffled to the door and went outside; when he reappeared a few minutes later, he carried a bottle of aged Marsala and a lit cigar. The candles on the table had burned down. I could hear the hooting of owls in the trees outside the door. He set the Marsala on the table and it made its round.

"The thing in Sicily that we have the chance to say is this," he picked up where he had left off. "Here in Sicily there are three thousand or four thousand different grape varieties that need to be tested and selected. This is Sicily's enormous potential."

Diego was saying that thousands of years of cultivation mixed with wild vines had resulted in thousands of unnamed clones, hybrids, and mutations often lumped together under broad categorical names. In Italy, for example, Francese was a name for Cabernet Sauvignon; in Sicilian dialect *Francisi* was a name used for anything that looked foreign or remotely French. He was proposing the sort of study and categorization and cloning that had been done in France on popular varietals from Cabernet Sauvignon to Pinot Noir.

We sipped Marsala and listened to the owls while Diego drew on his cigar—contemplating the something *more* to Sicily and its wines that had yet to be unearthed.

"In Sicily we have been drinking wine for five thousand years," he proclaimed with authority, "and in the four hundred years that the Arabs administered the island, they were drinking wine and making love and forgetting about Mohammed!"

"So you see," Diego said turning to his guest, "Sicily has a lot to offer the world."

THE FOLLOWING MORNING CHIARA drove me out to Planeta's olive groves—thousands of low silvery green trees blanketing hillsides that fell to the sea.

She is a willowy woman, then thirty-five, with chestnut-streaked hair, fair skin, and freckles. She is so pensively calm she hardly seems Sicilian. So passive she hardly seems a Planeta. When she speaks, her words are neither matter-of-fact like Alessio's, nor sardonic like Diego's, but weighted with melancholy.

As we drove to Menfi in her dusty station wagon strewn with

groceries and clothes and odds and ends, the olive stands and vine-yard plots and apricot and orange groves gave way to concrete. And Chiara observed parts of town that still lay in ruins—piles of rubble and buildings abandoned to weeds and nature—from the 1968 earthquake that left hundreds dead and tens of thousands of people homeless in the Belice Valley. She complained that, more than twenty-five years after the earthquake in the early 1990s, families were still living in "temporary" emergency military barracks. But when asked why, she used her whole frame to sigh, and holding the steering wheel with both hands, she shook her head.

In Menfi she parked in front of Casa Planeta, once the family's fifty-eight-room palazzo that was so badly damaged in the earthquake the Planetas (who at the time could not afford the repair work) even-tually donated it to the town. Forty years after the earthquake, Casa Planeta was at the end of a long renovation by local and regional governments to turn it into an "Enoteca de Terre Sicane," a center for Sicilian wine and agriculture. We entered through a courtyard of old square stone tiles where a bougainvillea with a trunk the size of an ancient oak tree rose up to the second story and dangled its blossoms over our heads. We walked through a tall room being built as a wine bar, then we continued around the ground floor. There was fresh paint, furniture for conference rooms covered in plastic, and stainless steel professional kitchens. There were more rooms for a bookshop and a gallery for Planeta's sponsored collection of international art.

Dust covered every surface but there was no sign of activity, just the man from the city government who had let us in. We climbed the marble staircase and toured the rooms of the second floor, and when we returned downstairs the man from the city said confidently that the building would open soon.

We stepped out into the sun. Across the street was an old church—its windows and doors walled shut. After the man from the city drove off, Chiara expressed doubts—perhaps the Casa Planeta would open as planned, she said, perhaps it would not.

"In Sicily we always know when things begin," she sighed. "But we don't know when they'll end."

That afternoon after lunch with Alessio and Santi at Planeta's base of operations at La Dispensa, I asked Peppe, the foreman of Planeta's vineyards, to drive me up the Belice Valley closer to the epicenter of the '68 earthquake.

A sunny, expressive man of thirty-eight (born two years after the earthquake), he carted me in his small Fiat four-wheel drive to Santa Margherita di Belice. The town was largely destroyed, and much of it was left abandoned as a new town rose up slowly next to the old one. Santa Margherita is also the location of the ancestral summer palace of Giuseppe di Lampedusa, the place that inspired Donnafugata in *The Leopard*.

Now the Lampedusa palace—decimated except for the façade in 1968—has been remade into Villa Gattopardo, a small museum exalting *The Leopard* and Lampedusa's life. Peppe, who speaks no English, had—I soon noticed—the habit of triumphantly announcing in Italian what you are experiencing. And as we stood in front of the sign welcoming us to Villa Gattopardo, Peppe proclaimed, *"Villa Gattopardo!"*

The museum's overseer accompanied us, the only people in the place, up a set of stairs and flipped on the lights. Looking through the period items and photographs arranged in glass cases, we came upon Lampedusa's original handwritten manuscript for the only book he would ever write.

"Il Gattopardo!" Peppe said.

The neat blue script began with a description of vespers in the house of Don Fabrizio Prince of Salina as Garibaldi's troops landed to storm the island and unify Italy under a Republican monarchy:

> *May, 1860*
> *Nunc et in hora mortis nostrae. Amen.*

As is so often true of these places, the ghosts have been evicted by kitsch touches like the waxed figures in the next room portraying a family scene from *The Leopard*—fashioned after the cast of Luchino Visconti's epic 1963 film version starring Burt Lancaster as the Prince of Salina, Claudia Cardinale as the young muse Angelica, and Alain

Delon as the prince's nephew, Tancredi, who delivered the line of the book most often quoted in Sicily: "If we want things to stay as they are, things will have to change."

Leaving the villa, we crossed a plaza being laid with fresh stones and walked up into the ruins of the old town destroyed in 1968. Buildings that were sheared open by the tremors had long ago been picked clean of anything valuable or reusable.

The sun was setting. We walked up through the ruins, grass and dirt underfoot, and as we got to a crest in the hill, I noticed a flock of sheep in the evening light. There were hundreds of them herded by a dog, and off to the left I saw a couple—a man and woman of no more than thirty funneling the sheep down an alley hurriedly away from us. I took out my camera to shoot some pictures, and the man called out something to Peppe. Peppe dramatically waved his hand in the air and called out to the man not to worry—"*Il giornalismo*" ("journalism") is how he explained my camera.

I asked Peppe in Italian why the concern.

"*I Rom*," Peppe said to me. Gypsies.

Why were they scurrying away with the sheep, I wondered; were the animals not legal?

"The sheep, yes, they are legal," Peppe answered. "It is the people who are not legal."

We walked back to Peppe's tiny four-wheel drive, and he took it through more ruins, arriving at a corner of town where it appears that new roads were being laid—where the city was preparing to demolish the ruins and reconstruct new houses.

"A lot of work," I said.

"Yes, there is a lot of work," Peppe answered. "*Ma quarant'anni!*" ("But forty years!")

"Why so long?" I asked.

"Have you read *Il Gattopardo*?" he asked.

"Yes."

"Read it again," Peppe said.

As he pulled back onto the main road, he spoke with his hands, letting the small truck seemingly steer itself. The fragments I picked up went something like this.

"This is Sicily. It is a beautiful place but the Sicilians are particular . . . forty years . . . politics . . . *piano piano* . . . Sicily is sleeping . . . money . . . subsidies . . . government changes . . . confusion . . . sleeping . . ."

In the evening twilight Peppe was whipping the car through some turns up a hillside and then down, talking and shifting gears with his right hand as his left hand gripped the top of the wheel.

"The Mafia?" I said.

"Bravo!" Peppe said. *"Quarant'anni sono quarant'anni."*

Indeed, forty years are forty years, and the Belice Valley provides a surreal setting to contemplate Sicily's past and its future—each seeming to negate the other here. There was the Sicily of the Planetas where revolutions could happen over a few seasons, and there was the Sicily of Santa Margherita where change could take generations.

Night was falling, and to return to La Dispensa, Peppe cut through a vineyard on a dirt road.

"Okay," he said. He wanted to show me something. With the last hint of light now evaporating from the sky, he brought the truck to a standstill and cut the engine.

It was quiet. Not an ordinary quiet but a quiet as silent as the floor of the sea, as still as night holding its breath. I imagined I could hear a bird making a nest at 40 yards. That I could hear a twig snap at 100.

"Silenzio," Peppe whispered, breaking the spell.

He started the engine and released the clutch, leaving the vines to slumber.

5

What Drives Marco

CANTINA MARCO DE BARTOLI SITS like an unfinished poem on the flat, calcareous plain outside Marsala at the western edge of Sicily. You enter De Bartoli's world through an iron gate that opens onto a courtyard scattered with palm and olive trees, an outdoor summer kitchen, and a collection of weathering disparate objects: rusting machine parts, sun-grayed barrels, a faded antique painted Sicilian chariot. A red vintage Lancia racing coupe with De Bartoli's name hand-painted on the driver's door rests in the shade of the winery, which is attached to the ancestral home of De Bartoli's great-grandmother.

I was greeted by Sebastiano, the younger of De Bartoli's two sons, whom I'd met at cos. We walked out behind the winery down a dusty private road through a vineyard of budding Grillo vines, the heat-resistant varietal that's the backbone of Marsala winemaking. Alongside the road next to the vine rows were about a dozen carcasses of Fiats, rusting radiators, and other disembodied car parts strewn in the weeds and yellow dirt. I stopped to look at one of the most beautiful automotive front ends ever made—the hollowed face of a late '50s Alfa Romeo Giulietta Spider staring blankly at us. This was De Bartoli's junkyard; vintage cars were one of three loves of his youth, the others being women and Marsala wine.

Sebastiano took a deep breath and looked at me with apologetic eyes. "This is one of my father's passions," he said, his Italian accent clipping the plural *s* off the end of the word. "He just buys these. To do what, I do not know."

Sebastiano wore a gray cotton sweater and black jeans, and he looked more forlorn than I had remembered him. He shook his head, waved a hand at the metal: "I hope to throw all this away."

Off to one side of the road at the back of the winery was a rectangular pit carved out of the limestone earth—as big as a city block and deep enough to swallow a two-story building. In its belly were more automobile husks.

"Our new *cantina*," he said, ironically.

The story of why Marco De Bartoli's new winery is a hole in the ground that has sat there for more than a dozen years is but one chapter in the long and tragic story of Marsala. Woodhouse's "discovery" of Marsala set the stage for decades during which great English Marsala houses dominated the local trade and Marsala achieved a reputation alongside Port, Sherry, and Madeira. The English merchants brought in the traditional Spanish solera system—a fractional blending method using a stack of barrels at least three high in which every year a small percentage of wine is drawn out of the bottom row of barrels and refilled from the barrels above to create an average aging of five, ten, twenty years or more. In the early part of the nineteenth century, that trade was joined by other major players, including Calabria-born Vincenzo Florio, and in the later part of the century by Sicilian Paolo Pellegrino.

The good times lasted up to the Second World War. While the merchants and big Marsala houses clung to the coast, the vinification and production of Marsala often took place in the countryside in family-owned Marsala cellars known as *bagli*. After the war, as tastes in Europe turned away from Marsala in favor of aperitifs such as Coca-Cola and whiskey, Sicilian winemaking industrialized. Many a *baglio* closed as wine production moved to large cooperatives. Large producers engaged in a price war for cheap Marsala, and more and more of the production went into a cooking wine often doused with flavorings such as egg, almond, and chocolate.

De Bartoli grew up as a scion of the Pellegrino family—and Marsala. As a young man in the 1960s and 1970s, he piloted Alfas and Lancias on the dangerous open-road race circuit in Sicily and southern Italy. During that same period, after earning a degree in agronomy at Palermo, he worked five years for Pellegrino, followed by three as a sales director at Mirabella, another industrial Marsala producer in which his family was involved. Yet, De Bartoli was not content to follow the path that his birthright had placed before him. In the 1970s he began experimenting with traditional methods of making Marsala that had all but disappeared, and in 1980 he broke away to start his own winery. De Bartoli took on the quixotic mission of becoming the sole boutique producer—from grape growing through bottling—of a wine that time had forgotten. As part of that quest, he became an ambassador for what the world then saw as an oxymoron—fine Marsala—at a time when industrial Marsala labeled *fine* was sold on grocery shelves next to vinegar.

De Bartoli also became a vocal proponent of organic agriculture and natural winemaking. Today, the De Bartolis have nearly fifty acres of vineyards, more than half of which produce Grillo and Inzolia grapes destined for Marsala (most of the rest being used for a selection of other dry and sweet, white and red wines). They produce natural traditional Marsala with minimal fortification, requiring low yields of hand-picked super-ripe grapes.

De Bartoli's traditional Marsala used the solera system. To fortify and sweeten the Marsala, the De Bartolis added *mistella* made from Inzolia grape must and alcohol. In modern times the process has become nearly extinct, as major wine houses have either scrapped the solera-and-*mistella* method altogether or use a more expedient cooked *mistella* that adds color and aromas but imparts a heavier, blunter taste. In 1993 De Bartoli, by then a revered figure in Sicily's quality movement, succeeded Diego Planeta as president of the Istituto Regionale delle Vite e del Vino, a post De Bartoli used as a pulpit to condemn the state of Sicilian wine—railing against the anonymous industrial wines that were hurting Sicily's reputation along with the winemakers who sold their wine for distillation.

"My father is not a diplomatic man," Sebastiano said. "He was telling the producers all the time, 'You are doing things the wrong way.' He was telling them, 'You are stupid.' And he made a lot of enemies. There was a lot of . . . you can say . . . jealousy."

As the De Bartolis prepared for the harvest at the end of summer in 1995, a pair of *carabinieri* (officers of the Italian national police) arrived with orders from the local public prosecutor to seize boxes of documents from the winery in an investigation of suspected wine "adulteration." The following day more *carabinieri* came and shut the winery down. The authorities zeroed in on De Bartoli's most prized wine, Vecchio Samperi, named for the *contrada* of Samperi where De Bartoli's vineyards and winery are located. Vecchio Samperi is a traditional solera-aged wine but without fortification. In a sense it is the purest of the pure Marsalas: explosively aromatic, long and dry in the mouth, a revelation in a world of shortsighted shortcuts.

De Bartoli's problem, it turned out, was in the labeling. Vecchio Samperi could not be called Marsala because there was no alcohol added, even though it was naturally high in alcohol at 17 percent. Under Italian law, based on its alcohol and residual sugar level, it should have been branded a *vino liquoroso*—a tag De Bartoli shunned because it implied a fortified wine or sweet dessert wine. So De Bartoli had labeled it *vino da tavola* (table wine). The label certified the wine at what would have been its legal alcohol limit as a table wine—15 percent, two percentage points under the actual alcohol content. And it was in those two percentage points of difference that De Bartoli's world came tumbling down.

The idea in winegrowing Europe that a winemaker would be punished for delivering *more* alcohol in his wine would generally be considered scandalous—a victory of semantics over artistry, or the dark side of sunny Italy. "They accused my father of being a crook," Sebastiano spits out. "But it was shit; it was exactly the opposite of something you would do to make your wine interesting. You would not say it has *less* alcohol to sell the wine. They were looking for something to attach to him and they found this."

In 1997 De Bartoli earned the right to a portion of his production, but his legal problems didn't end until nearly three years later. Only after his term ended as president of the wine institute did a Marsala court find him not guilty of wrongdoing and return him rights to his full wine production.

"My father continued to work hard," Sebastiano said, kicking at some dust as we walked back to the winery. "We still are working to get over the damage."

"IN SICILY WE OFTEN don't know what is good and what is bad," De Bartoli mused over lunch—a reference to his surreal five years of legal purgatory when he was viewed as a trafficker. "Everything is good, everything is bad."

Sebastiano had prepared a meal of grilled artichokes and fresh fava beans tossed with tube pasta in the winery's small modern steel kitchen. We ate at a long wood table in the simple adjacent dining room with De Bartoli's twenty-five-year-old daughter "Gipi" (short for Josephine), who worked in the cantina's office with De Bartoli's longtime business collaborator, Maddalena Susino.

De Bartoli wore a dark sweater and baggy jeans. His eyes were as playful as I remembered them, only more tired looking. De Bartoli picked at his food distractedly and recounted his history in Marsala, alternating between French and Italian.

"There was a lot of work done for Marsala before the war. After the war it was *merrrr-daaaa*," De Bartoli said. "My godfather ran Pellegrino. What he made was *merrrr-daaaa*. The others were even worse. You see, it's easier to make Marsala of *merda* than good Marsala, which takes an enormous investment in aging.

"My grandfather was a great man who made a lot of money with pasta production and Marsala at Mirabella. But after the war, my father's generation wanted to change everything and rejected all the traditions. They did the worst things to Marsala and to everything. Even the old houses were no good anymore, so they tore them down—they wanted to do everything American style.

"It was," De Bartoli said, putting his fork down on his plate, "the time of the devil!"

Agricultural subsidies, in De Bartoli's view, also tended to the diabolical: "For the aging of Marsala, there was no money. But for the industrialization of Marsala there was money. For the quality of grapes—nothing. For the quantity of grapes—money."

"The devil," he repeated. "The love of quality was replaced by the love of business."

"Of course it would have been easier to live like a baron." De Bartoli straightened his back and tightened an imaginary necktie while he peered at me down his nose. "But to me that was not living."

The crimes against Marsala that De Bartoli witnessed included the doping of wine with sugar and water and using other additives to enhance colors and aromas. Yet as a young man De Bartoli had glimpsed another world of Marsala, when he and a Marsala-loving friend would explore the remaining *bagli* in the countryside, tasting from the old barrels of *riserva*. Those old Marsalas left an indelible impression in De Bartoli's sensorial memory and changed the arc of his life. "The aroma of a real Marsala," De Bartoli said, brightening for an instant as if recalling a girl from his youth, "it was for me the perfect perfume."

After lunch, the women, who had said nothing during the meal, cleared the dishes. I noticed the way De Bartoli's daughter with heavy-lidded dark eyes carried herself in the same resigned way as Sebastiano. A telephone sounded from another part of the house, and De Bartoli asked his son whether he had installed a telephone where he had asked. Sebastiano said no, and De Bartoli began shouting, mocking his son in Italian. Sebastiano yelled back, stormed out of the room, and then returned with a screwdriver, which he used to open a wall plate in the dining room. He remained silent as he rearranged wires.

The women stayed in the kitchen, leaving me to sit in the middle of an embarrassing moment between father and son that I wished I had not witnessed.

"We have a problem with a telephone," De Bartoli said. "I go away for fifteen days and I come back and the problem is still there. This is the problem with Sicily: Everything is 'later, later.'"

De Bartoli went to a cabinet and withdrew a series of bottles of Marsala and set them on the table. He lit a small cigar, took a few mouthfuls of smoke, and let it extinguish.

The De Bartoli winery is actually two wineries. There is a modern winery with tile floors and steel climate-controlled tanks. Most of De Bartoli's dry red and white wines are fermented here, along with his modern, easy-drinking Marsala Superiore known as Vigna la Miccia, which at the end of a slow, cold fermentation is fortified with alcohol, then set to age in relatively small 225-liter French oak *barriques* for five years. Then there is De Bartoli's old-fashioned brick-floored *baglio* with large conical barrels or *tini* for fermenting De Bartoli's traditional Vecchio Samperi. This wine is conditioned in a pair of facing soleras—large old wooden casks layered in three rows that nearly touch the roof timbers of a barn ceiling. The small percentage of wine that is removed every year from the top of the soleras is either bottled straight as Vecchio Samperi or fortified with *mistella* to make it Marsala.

Marsala labels can be about the most cluttered in the wine world—so confusing as to induce drinking. Traditionally, vintages are not noted on bottles because the solera system blends wines from different years. Marsala is not considered Marsala until the year it is fortified. So, for example, the 1986 Marsala Superiore I enjoyed at cos was fortified in that year (after many years of blending in the solera). The basic categories of Marsala refer mostly to the amount of wood aging. *Fine* Marsala is the lowest category of Marsala—aged at least one year and typically used for cooking. *Superiore* Marsala is aged a minimum of two years; *Superiore Riserva* Marsala, four years; *Vergine e/o Soleras* Marsala, at least five years; and *Vergine e/o Soleras Riserva* Marsala, at least ten. *Vergine* Marsala is typically dry, as it must be fortified with alcohol only—and no sweetening *mistella*.

De Bartoli and I began our tasting with the young Vigna La Miccia Marsala and ended with a pair of his solera Marsalas. Each was deeper in color, aromas, complexity, and length than the last. De Bartoli described these last two traditional Marsalas as *"vino di meditazione"* ("mediation wine"), an elegant description in a world with little time to meditate, let alone over a glass of Marsala. Great Marsala was all but dead. But to taste De Bartoli's Marsalas provided the proof that De Bartoli was right about it all.

By the time we were done, Sebastiano had installed the phone on a small table at the edge of the room and joined us. The place was quiet now. De Bartoli slowly raised himself up from his chair. He took the unlit cigar from his mouth and made the last of his grand pronouncements of the afternoon: "Sicily is the most important wine region of the world, but unfortunately there are the Sicilians!" He turned to mount the staircase at the edge of the room. "Now, I must take my little nap."

WHILE DE BARTOLI DOZED, Sebastiano drove us into Marsala, passing along the straight dusty roads that cut through the outskirts of town and stopping at the tidy and impressive Pellegrino Marsala plant, where we were met by his father's cousin Benuccio Renda, the fifty-seven-year-old director of the company.

Renda had a full head of salt-and-pepper hair and a quick but nervous smile that showed straight, white capped teeth. He wore black plants and a woven jacket with a crisp new striped shirt and electric blue silk tie. He carried himself with the satisfied bearing of a successful company man, and after exchanging family news with Sebastiano—whom he eyed with a look I interpreted as pity—he offered to show us around.

The place couldn't have been more different from Cantina Marco De Bartoli. It was an industrial campus organized in a series of immaculate hangars with tiled, wood timbered roofs. Outside, palm trees were placed in beds to break up the expanses of asphalt. Renda seemed to glide in his soft loafers across the shiny floors, proudly talking about production and rattling off statistics.

He stopped to lead us into a hangar that held fifty-two conical *tini* containing—he noted—more than 1.5 million liters of Marsala. Annual production was nearly eight million bottles of wine per year—less than a fifth of it now Marsala, which was mostly destined for cooking. (The volume made the company output more than eighty times the size of Cantina De Bartoli.) Renda affirmed that the Marsala portion of the business had shrunk—as it had for all producers—but Pellegrino had, like the others, diversified. In addition to producing dry red and white wines, and sweet wines from Muscat, Malvasia, and Zibibbo (the Sicilian term for Muscat of Alexandria, used to make Passito di Pantelleria), Pellegrino also has a client in the Roman Catholic Church—making both red and white sacramental wine. (Renda explained that the white version was gaining in popularity, as it does not stain altar cloths or vestments.)

Renda had, I noted, an obsessive tic—pausing every time he passed a mirror or reflective glass to look into it and straighten his tie. I thought of the tie-straightening gesture De Bartoli had made at lunch, and wondered what De Bartoli would be like today had he stayed in the family business.

After we viewed Pellegrino's century-old collection of ornately carved Sicilian donkey carts, Renda led us to a tasting room and boutique, where a woman behind the counter set out a plate of biscotti to accompany the wine. A sweet red *fine* Marsala tasted like cough medicine. Pellegrino's best aged Marsalas (like those of the other industrial producer on the other end of town, Florio) were pleasant, but—in comparison with De Bartoli's—fell flat. While De Bartoli's wines had a refreshing acidity that lingered, these tasted as blunt and baked as apricot jam. De Bartoli made meditation wines, I concluded, and Pellegrino made wine to sip with cookies. De Bartoli, I thought, should have been the one making the Communion wine—though his chances of successfully courting the church hierarchy were probably about as good as a scoop of gelato's chances of surviving a day in the summer sun in Samperi.

Cousin Benuccio took Sebastiano with one arm and me with the other and led us across a courtyard to a pair of white towers burnished with the Pellegrino logo. The towers were 1950s wine silos that once held millions of liters of Marsala. The twin towers recently had been renovated into a sleek four-story conference center. We walked in the tower on the right and looked up at the white spiral staircase that coiled to the roof like the inside of a seashell. We took a steel and glass elevator to the private panoramic restaurant at the top. Renda studied his image in the steel of the elevator panel and pushed the knot of his tie up higher on his neck.

OLD MARSALA'S HISTORIC CENTER is surprisingly orderly, monumental, and tranquil with its white stone streets, limestone Baroque churches and gateways, and ancient Punic ruins. Considering that it is not a major tourist stop, I was astonished to see that the decay of many Sicilian cities seems to have stayed out of Marsala, which at night glows yellow in the beam of spotlights.

That evening started with the De Bartolis in better humor. I met De Bartoli and Sebastiano in front of the smart, newly renovated Ristorante San Carlo, where De Bartoli received a hero's welcome. Owner Massimo Bellitteri greeted De Bartoli with embraces and kisses, as did about half the staff. We ate the local pizza *rianata* (anchovies, onions, tomatoes, oregano, and pecorino cheese) followed by fresh seafood carpaccio and couscous (a staple in this corner of Sicily jutting out toward Tunisia) and finished with perfectly grilled tuna steaks.

Three odd things happened that evening—each stranger than the last. The first was not really so unusual, but was a surprise that pumped up De Bartoli's spirits. A German couple seated next to us had ordered a bottle of De Bartoli's signature barrel-aged red Merlot-Syrah blend called Rosso di Marco, and they had drained most of it. When Bellitteri told them that the winemaker was sitting next to them, they sent their compliments De Bartoli's way, giving him many a jolly thumbs-up.

The second thing was truly peculiar. A group of about ten men—mostly local *carabinieri* in plainclothes—walked into the restaurant and took a large table in a dining alcove in back. Both De Bartolis recognized the men—the oldest among them, tall with thinning gray hair, was the public prosecutor who had ordered De Bartoli's winery shut more than a decade earlier.

Sebastiano craned his head to watch, then looked at his father. De Bartoli smiled blankly. Then, after the appetizer plates were cleared, Bellitteri came to the table and spoke with De Bartoli in a near whisper. De Bartoli nodded, and Bellitteri returned with a fresh-faced young man—a few years younger than Sebastiano—from the *carabinieri* table. He wore a pressed shirt and red sweater and shook hands with all of us while he beamed at De Bartoli. He squatted next to De Bartoli, and he spoke to him reverently as though he were addressing an old school professor who'd had a profound effect on his life. De Bartoli's smile broadened, and after a few minutes he motioned to the empty seat next to him. The young man sat in the chair, and for the next quarter of an hour he poured praise into De Bartoli's ear.

The young man, it turned out, was a Carabinieri captain, just transferred from his home base in Milan, where he had come to know and love De Bartoli's Marsalas, Passito de Pantelleria, and other wines. The conversation concluded when the young man fixed an appointment to visit De Bartoli's *cantina* later in the week, shook our hands with an earnest smile, and rejoined his table. After dinner we lingered outside, De Bartoli smoking a cigar in the night air, and Bellitteri came out to join us. At one point the head of the prosecutor was visible as he stood at the back of the restaurant. Sebastiano glared. I said that the man looked not far from retirement.

"And one day we will spit in his face," Sebastiano sneered.

De Bartoli, visibly moved by the turn of events and the sincerity of the young captain, leaned against the building, sucked on his cigar, and said, "Life is fragile—better not to become like beasts."

THE FOLLOWING DAY AROUND NOON, I returned to the *cantina* to meet De Bartoli's older son, Renato, who at thirty-four was the oldest of the three De Bartoli children and now the *cantina*'s chief winemaker. I also wanted to see De Bartoli's collection of vintage cars, which were packed behind a series of steel garage doors into a low warehouse building a few steps from the winery. So while Renato prepared a lunch of spaghetti and roasted tuna, De Bartoli and I crossed the drive.

On that short walk I asked De Bartoli about the previous evening's experience seeing the young Carabinieri officer and the old prosecutor at the restaurant. De Bartoli stopped in the drive. "I still have a good reputation in the north." He held his hands as if in prayer, looking heavenward into a dirty gray sky. "The way of Sicily is not to change," De Bartoli said, then mouthed the two words that most often are used to express this feeling—fifty years after they appeared in print: "*Il Gattopardo*. I am a man of change. I was dangerous."

We entered a series of connected garages and a scene unlike anything I'd imagined—what looked like a small auto factory. Not only were there dozens of vintage cars—1950s and 1960s Alfas, Fiats, Lancias, Porsches, an early 1980s Ferrari, and a collection of minuscule Fiat 500s—but there were many more shells of auto bodies in the rafters prepared and primed for paint. Auto parts were arranged everywhere. The black prewar Lancia from De Bartoli's student days at the University of Perugia seemed fully restored; the shell of his mother's Fiat Topolino (literally, "little mouse") was collecting dust in the rafters.

"In here I am the king," De Bartoli said, walking over to one of his prizes, a red 1964 Alfa Giulia Spider Veloce 1600. It was pared down for racing with a Spartan interior and no top. De Bartoli stroked the paint, which looked original. "To hear the motor is a melody."

"Cars and women—two great stories," De Bartoli said, then grinned. "The difference is that cars don't talk," he held his finger to his lips. "Women talk. A lot." I realized that De Bartoli hadn't said a word about his wife. I had not met her or even seen a photograph. I imagined that Signora De Bartoli stayed far from the winery at the place she was queen—the family home in Marsala.

At lunchtime Maddalena and Gipi quietly joined us as they had the day before. With three De Bartoli men at the table, the tension was as palpable as lamplight. Renato sat to his father's right, his blue eyes seeming to simmer at low boil. We ate in silence. After the meal De Bartoli left the room and returned with a small bottle labeled Riserva Storica 1860.

If you could find a standard seventy-five-centiliter bottle of this ancient Marsala at the time, it would cost nearly $1,000. The story of this historic reserve is this: Over the years, when De Bartoli scouted the countryside around Samperi, old-time country producers giving up production sold De Bartoli barrels of their older prewar solera Marsalas, including some from the nineteenth century. The contents were like syrup, which De Bartoli brought back to life by diluting with his Vecchio Samperi. This particular Marsala was from a friend and noted Baglio producer who, before he died, entrusted De Bartoli with his finest *riserva* made from a solera established in 1830.

"The liquid museum," De Bartoli said. Indeed, the backbone of this wine was older than Italy (unified in 1861), coming from a time when this land was part of the Bourbon Kingdom of Two Sicilies ruled from Naples.

The women cleared the table and De Bartoli poured for the men. The color resembled dark Baltic amber, and it smelled like nuts and fruit that had long ago fossilized. In the mouth it started sweet and finished dry—resting on the tongue for what seemed like minutes.

I was enjoying my meditation, lost somewhere in a now defunct *baglio*, pondering the flavors of the Two Sicilies and the way the flat land met the big sky around Marsala. This reverie was interrupted by the increasing volume of the voices of the De Bartoli men. Renato, suddenly, yelled at his brother and seemed to be berating his father over something I couldn't understand. De Bartoli yelled at Sebastiano, who protested. Renato stood and yelled some more. Another meal at the De Bartolis and I felt embarrassed. The women vanished, Sebastiano slinked off, and De Bartoli stood and excused himself for his nap.

Renato and I went down to the cellar. Here, he explained the changes he was making at Cantina Marco De Bartoli. We passed a chamber of new oak French *barriques*, which contained Renato's new series of white wines called Integer—handcrafted single-varietal white wines in small quantities made from Grecanico Dorato, Grillo, and Zibibbo. The wines, slow-fermented and finished in *barriques*, would fill only 250 cases of each varietal.

As we went through the cellars and the subject turned to Marsala,

Renato revealed that in the past three years he had not made traditional solera Marsala. While he continued to make Vecchio Samperi,
and the De Bartolis were sitting on plenty of barrels of their unsold
old stock, Renato's Marsala production was focused on his modern
Vigna La Miccia. The wine was lighter, less expensive, and easier to
drink as an aperitif. It was as good as any other Marsala being produced in the twenty-first century, but it wasn't a Marco De Bartoli
vino di meditazione, a category that was facing extinction.

"There is no market for quality Marsala—*anywhere*," Renato seemed
to plead. "Look, I don't want to make white wine and red wine, but
I must eat every day. We are famous for making Marsala wine, but
it is the Marsala wine we sell the least!"

"Making Marsala you will go hungry." Renato used the last air
in his lungs to spit out as he hammered his chest: "I am fed up. I
am empty."

At this moment I flashed on a black-and-white picture in a book
on De Bartoli's life by Attilio L. Vinci, a journalist from Marsala.
In the photo, taken more than twenty years earlier, the three De
Bartoli men are—pant legs rolled up—stomping grapes in a wooden
tub in the Samperi vineyards. De Bartoli, lean and tanned, a head of
dark hair, is in his prime, smiling. At his side are his two tow-headed
boys—Renato a head shorter than his father, and Sebastiano barely
up to the level of his chest. It was a snapshot of such youthful, idyllic
peace that it now seemed haunting.

Renato and I walked back upstairs. I was in the process of leaving
when De Bartoli appeared, sleepy-eyed, in a doorway. "Come," De
Bartoli said, and waved me out to the drive where he'd set the Alfa
Giulia Spider Veloce 1600 that he'd so affectionately stroked before
lunch. "Get in," he said, nodding to the passenger door.

De Bartoli beamed like a child on his birthday as he turned the
ignition key and awoke the rumble of steel under the hood. "*La
musica*," De Bartoli cooed, throwing the car into gear.

We set out for nowhere in particular, De Bartoli dodging the pot-
holes as we rolled through the flat stretches of vines and the roadside
ferula. The engine growled—the inimitable and immediate sound

of carbureted gas. Meditation. Like the perfect perfume. De Bartoli spoke of his competitions, how he'd been in shape—to breathe. In racing, he said, breathing is important.

"I was like this," he said, holding up his pinkie to signify how lean he'd been. He pressed his foot into the accelerator, throwing us back against the seats again as the Alfa twisted around a tractor in the road, the driver waving to De Bartoli. "Then with all the *merda* of the Carabinieri, I just blew up."

With every change of gear the car reacted, breathing. It didn't seem so much a machine as an animal, happy to be running and sucking air into its lungs. De Bartoli made the motor roar—a cry from an animal heart still full of life.

6

Palermo Holy Week

THERE IS SOMETHING EERIE ABOUT Palermo on a Sunday afternoon, when—after Mass and the main meal of the day—the city seems to take a collective nap so long and silent you wonder if it's sleep or death. On Palm Sunday afternoon I spent hours walking through old Palermo looking for reassuring signs of life.

Palermo's historic center—the part that wasn't destroyed in the 1960s "Rape of Palermo" by corrupt city officials who replaced much of the city's heart with piles of anonymous Mafia-laid concrete—is full of majestic palaces built by Arabs under Norman rule that began in the eleventh century, and by subsequent generations of nobles up through the blooming of Art Nouveau. It is decorated with Baroque fountains, monumental sculptures, and churches so excessively ornate they appear to have been sculpted in marzipan by hyperactive pastry makers. And six and a half days of the week it is animated by wide avenues of chic boutiques and smart cafés as well as labyrinthine networks of medieval stone streets in neighborhoods that are hives of markets and bars that smell of home cooking and fried street food.

But on Sunday afternoon—with the galvanized roller shutters padlocked in place and the streets emptied—Palermo shows its cold, dark face. What you notice are the cracked windows, the graffiti, the trash, the falling stucco, and the vacuum of quiet.

Early evening at the Piazza Verdi, I found human activity in the groups of men in suits and perfumed women in stoles gathered in front of the Teatro Massimo (setting of the final killing scene in *The Godfather Part III*) for an evening in the gilded and frescoed Belle Epoque world of Italy's largest opera house. I then walked in the general direction of Palermo's historic seat of power—the sprawling Palazzo dei Normanni, started in the ninth century by the Arab emir of Palermo, extended by the Normans, and still the seat of the Sicilian Regional Assembly. I lost my way, however, in the winding backstreets of town. And in a matter of minutes, I'd left the comfortable signs of Palermo society and entered a world closer to the backside of Baghdad: the narrow alleys, where unpaved gray dirt met shanties and ruins.

In these streets there was life—not much different from that captured by the camera of Roberto Rossellini (*Paisan*, 1946) in Sicily and southern Italy more than sixty years earlier. Groups of twelve- and thirteen-year-old boys—the same age as my son at the time—sped around helmetless on scooters that screamed with a sense of urgency. Others sat idly on their motorbikes in jeans and aviator glasses, looking much too street-smart for their own good. In front of a sad apartment block, a group of younger boys—maybe eight or nine, with smeared faces—circled intently around a cement table playing cards. Dogs picked through opened sacks of trash in front of a church dedicated to the Madonna of Lourdes, and farther on I passed piles of uncollected refuse: car tires not worth stealing, worn-out shoes, rotting meat, and mattresses.

I emerged from this squalor to Piazza Bellini and the Dominican convent Church of Santa Caterina. On a high terrace across the piazza, palms were being blessed by a priest at the top of the stairs in front of San Cataldo, a twelfth-century Norman creation topped by three pink Islamic cupolas that give the place the look of another world.

I walked up a flight of steps and behind the sober Renaissance façade of Santa Caterina, entering a world that for most non-Sicilians is an unimaginable explosion of frothy Baroque excess. The walls are decorated with miles of intertwined colored marble inlay, gilded stucco, and hundreds of chubby white stucco *putti*, which climb to the frescoed ceiling and a hovering dome depicting the triumph of Dominican saints. The overall effect is so dizzying that the mind struggles to isolate the details. But any view of any corner of this church (built in the sixteenth century and decorated over the next two centuries) could serve as a pattern for a regal wedding cake. Hanging in front of the altar and its amethyst tabernacle were seven chandeliers; I counted three more on each side of the nave and three closing the back. The oil paintings in the chapels at the side of the church—all of them older than *my country*—were torn, nibbled by insects, giving Santa Caterina a fine patina of neglect that made it even grander. Yet the most amazing thing about Santa Caterina is that for all its gluttonous portions of confectionary art, it is not alone in Palermo.

I thought about dinner and I thought about wine. What do the Palermitani drink with their diet of beauty and decay, divinity and chaos? I wondered. I continued walking. Near Palermo's Norman-era cathedral, I noticed a man lying on his side in some litter-strewn shrubs, a brown mutt next to him. I stared at these two bodies lying there like flour sacks dropped from a truck. The dog, I noticed, was breathing.

THAT EVENING I FOUND my way to the Antica Focacceria San Francesco —one of Palermo's oldest and most storied restaurants and one of the few open on Sunday evening. Established by the Alaimo family in 1834, the focacceria sits at the opposite end of the piazza from the Church of San Francesco d'Assisi, a restrained medieval edifice, the stones of which glow golden at night under soft spotlights.

As you enter the old focacceria, you walk directly into the old focaccia kitchen dominated by the huge original iron woodstove that has long since been converted to gas. Behind the stove, warming a large pot of meat and holding bowls of cheese, is a man working his post in a black apron. Palermo focaccia bears no resemblance to the rosemary-seasoned pizza-like flatbread exported from the Italian mainland to the United States nor to the rolled strudel-like stuffed appetizer of Ragusa in southeast Sicily. The Palermo version—a whole other animal sold by street vendors throughout town—starts with yellow, sweet focaccia bread resembling a sandwich roll. Into the opened roll are placed pieces of dry ricotta. Then a few slices of beef spleen simmered in lard are spooned inside—the focaccia maker cradling the bun in one hand as he squeezes out the excess juices from the stewed offal with the aid of a slotted spoon. The filling is next sprinkled with pungent grated *caciocavallo* cheese. The meatless version is focaccia *schietta* (single) and the full carnivorous version is focaccia *maritata* (married). Slow Food meets Fast Food. The focacceria's recipe uses local products from the countryside near Palermo: flour from Corleone, sheep ricotta from Roccamena, *caciocavallo* from Godrano, beef spleen from Caccamo.

On this night, local families filled the iron chairs and marble-top tables of the ground floor. They ate focaccia and other street foods: *panelle* (chickpea fritters) and *sfincioni* (thick crusted pizza of tomatoes, onions, and anchovies) along with pizzas such as the "Lucky Luciano"—named for the Sicilian American crime boss who frequented the focacceria during his postwar exile from the United States. They drank glasses of wine or soda. The scene felt entirely natural and appetizing—except for the Carabinieri car parked out front of the restaurant in the piazza flanked by a pair of officers wearing bulletproof vests and cradling very businesslike black Beretta machine guns.

The mind does a little calculation when it encounters such a demonstration of arms—determining whether it should tune out or take notice. Big Security is a mundane fact of life in the twenty-first century. But a city as notorious as Palermo makes you ponder the possibilities: for what—or whom—was the firepower stationed here in front of a place that sells food made from ancestral recipes?

I climbed the stairs at the back of the focacceria to the table service restaurant, where there were a few tables of Palermitani as well as tourists from other parts of Italy and from Germany. The walls were colored a deep red and displayed framed black-and-white photos of Italian race car drivers and of Luchino Visconti, the director who put *The Leopard* on film. The floors were marble, the lighting muted, and from the ceilings were draped the same unbleached linens that covered the tables. A pair of doors opened onto the terrace, allowing a light breeze to enter the room along with the friendly chatter of passersby with the machine-gun-toting officers.

A focaccia *maritata* arrived as an unexpected appetizer (as if one could eat the entire thing and still be hungry), smelling and tasting like a Sicilian farm. I ordered *bucatini con le sarde*—a plate of thick spaghetti-like pasta tossed with tomatoes, wild fennel, crushed pine nuts, and raisins and seasoned with saffron. This mainstay Palermo dish is from the first bite a lesson in Sicilian history and *terroir*—east meets west, sweet meets salty, the sea meets the farm. To accompany the typical Palermo meal, I wanted a typical wine and asked the waiter to bring me a glass of the house Nero d'Avola.

Palermo is not a town that fusses over its food and wine. Sicily's handful of Michelin stars (a recent phenomenon) and exhaustive Sicilian wine lists tend to gather around chic Taormina on the east coast below Etna and the island's genteel southeastern Baroque belt around Ragusa. When it comes to bounty from land and sea, modern Sicilians are the most spoiled people on the planet. But Palermitani—conservative and as provincial as the outer provinces —are neither foodies nor gastronomic innovators. They just expect year-round perfection—food that is picked, hunted, or caught not before yesterday, to be prepared as it always has been. And in this context wine plays an important role, but not a very exalted one.

The Nero d'Avola was black, rich, and stout and served in an ample balloon glass. It was a wine (I later learned made by Fatascià, a young winery started in an old *baglio* just outside Palermo) perfect for overstimulated Palermitani—direct and upfront with its fruit and tannins. It didn't invite contemplation, but then who in Palermo had time for contemplation other than the nuns at Santa Caterina? The all-purpose red did its job; the first glass stood up to the rustic focaccia and the second didn't overpower the delicate flavors in my pasta.

After dinner I walked downstairs. The *carabinieri* hadn't budged. I approached the cash register operated by a smiling thirtyish woman with dark, round features who had two small girls pulling on the tail of her sweater as they played. I asked the woman about the *carabinieri*. She smiled and explained that the owner of the focacceria had refused to pay the Mafia *pizzo* (protection money)—she rubbed her fingers together for emphasis. That was not all, she went on cheerily—he had also denounced the Mafia in court. Now he and his business were under constant guard.

With my stomach sated by *Palermitana* pasta and my head lightened by Nero d'Avola, I walked back through empty streets to my hotel, reading the graffiti that demanded *"Basta Pizzo!"* A flier stuck to a lampost elaborated: *Un intero popolo che paga il pizzo è un popolo senza dignità.* ("A whole people who pay *pizzo* are a people without dignity.") It was a moral statement that on its surface seemed to dwarf the world of wine and food. But then, I thought, wasn't it all related? Land, agriculture, exploitation, urbanization, the Mafia, were all part of Sicily's sad and confounding history on view at the focacceria under the watchful beaks of automatic weapons.

I was determined to meet the focacceria owners, the Conticello family—but such a meeting would require a contact. Luckily, the Planetas were family friends, and Alessio helped arrange a meeting for the following weekend on Holy Saturday.

ON GOOD FRIDAY I RETURNED to Palermo and met Francesco Pensovecchio, a fellow writer and a Sicilian reviewer for Slow Food publications who agreed to guide me through some of Palermo's culinary sights. The first thing in the morning, we headed to Palermo's oldest daily street market—the Ballarò Market, sprawling hundreds of yards behind the grand villas of the Via Maqueda.

The Ballarò, dating back more than a millennium to Palermo's rule by Arabs, resembles a raucous bazaar more than a Western conception of a farmers' market. Supermarkets in old Palermo are nonexistent—a fact that has something to do with their inability to compete with Ballarò and the town's other great street markets, which serve as greengrocers, butchers, bakers, fishmongers, public forums, daily operas, and cashiers of the underground (tax-free) economy played out on the streets from every morning before dawn.

The Ballarò is a patchwork with permanent stalls and temporary stands protected from the early sun by a quilted sea of multicolored awnings and umbrellas. On this warm, bright Friday morning it seemed that all of Palermo had turned out, packed as tightly as commuters on a city bus as they brushed against each other: the packs of teenagers, the sprawling families, the new wave of Italian-speaking Africans, the old men in *coppola* caps, and the perfumed women in their oversized Sophia Loren sunglasses.

The landscape was covered with hills of fresh artichokes and fava beans and mountains of blood oranges. There were mounds of fat, pendulous olives—their black and green skins slippery with brine—garlands of dates, and tables filled with disks of baked-brown ricotta. From above, whole small pigs and skinned goats dangled on meat hooks. The smell of fresh fennel and frying oil from the street food vendors selling focaccia, *panelle, arancini* (fried stuffed rice balls), and *crocchè* (fried potato croquettes with parsley and cheese) mingled with Vespa exhaust and the scents of cologne, chewing gum, tobacco, and the press of human flesh.

"*Bello pre!*" ("Nice price!" in Sicilian dialect, which seems to be the primary language of the market) a gruff voice called out, making it sound like an insult.

"*Chiu buone! Chiu mercat!*" answered a nearby fruit seller. ("Better! cheaper!")

"*Amuni!*" ("Let's go!") It sounded like a call to fight.

Beds of ice were covered with whole swordfish—the saber-like snouts intact—human-size blue fin tuna ready to be sliced into bloody steaks, and eel tangled together like giant black spaghetti.

"*Pulpo! . . . sgombro! . . . calamari!*" ("Octopus! . . . mackerel! . . . squid!") With each word, a fishmonger flicked a handful of ice water from a bucket over his sprawling marine still life.

We walked the better part of an hour, arriving at a tiny square, where I noticed a man selling potatoes and artichokes in front of a small corner ruin the size of a one-car Sicilian garage. It looked as though it had been hit by the Allied bombing of 1943 and had yet to be repaired.

My second stop with Francesco required a drive in his car to the edge of town to find one of Sicily's most celebrated pastry chefs. As this was Easter weekend, production was fully ramped up for one of Sicily's most emblematic foods. Cassata was, in my memories of Italian American family gatherings, an overly sweet cake filled with ricotta whipped into cream, coated in white frosting, and topped with candied fruit in unnatural vulgar colors. Various pumped-up Americanized versions use liqueur flavorings, chocolate chips, whipped cream, or just about anything else that showed off our supermarket superiority. In springtime in Sicily, cassata is ubiquitous, filling pastry cases in every town and airport. I once watched a French television special in which cassata was described philosophically as an expression of Sicilian Baroque—a dairy-and-sugar equivalent of churches like Santa Caterina.

Our destination was Cappello, the three-generation bakery run by Salvatore Cappello—a member of Italy's elite academy of master pastry chefs—who employs eighteen other pastry chefs to labor under him. We waited for the maestro in the bakery crammed with Easter weekend customers and breathed in the aromas of butter, sugar, chocolate, lemons, orange water, and dozens of other scents that seemed to swirl in different combinations with every turn of the head. The cakes, tarts, mousses, chocolates, cookies, and cannoli that Cappello produced were placed in chic and sexy packages more emblematic of a Milan fashion house than a Palermo *pasticceria*. The bakery's standard bag featured the photo in profile of a pair of voluptuous female lips set to devour a dangling ripe strawberry. Surely if anyone knew his cassata and its significance, it would be Cappello.

A compact balding man of fifty-one dressed in baker's whites, Cappello appeared, his eyes ringed by dark circles that I suspected had something to do with the onset of Easter. Soft-spoken and projecting humility, Cappello explained that cassata's history was more ancient than Baroque. As old as the Ballarò, in fact. Cassata, he explained, is often attributed to the Arab *quasat* for the form of the round inward-sloping cake mold used to produce its core.

"Cassata," Cappello said, "is a simple cake."

It sounded like one of those ridiculous statements grand chefs always make: the ones in which soufflés are "simple" but boiling an egg becomes an art. But as I listened, Cappello pulled me over to his point of view. What makes cassata are the ingredients, he went on. Starting with the filling, he explained that it should be made from fresh sheep's milk ricotta—neither too humid nor dry—and sugar. "*Ricotta, zucchero. Basta!*" ("Ricotta, sugar. That's it!") he said.

The sloping outer ring of the cassata is covered with alternating bands of sponge cake and a paste of Sicily's emerald-colored pistachios from Bronte on Mount Etna. The cake is then glazed in a white veil of sugar frosting (the Cappello version includes a light second decorative white-on-white sugar filigree) and finally decorated with caramelized fruit. Not just any caramelized fruit—the examples in Cappello's shop looked nothing like my memories of cassata or the plastic-like fruit that topped the versions at the Palermo airport. The slices of mandarins, figs, oranges, and pears, as well as whole cherries, had a pale translucency of vintage Venetian glass—the result of a caramelizing process that uses no coloring and involves keeping the fruit in hot syrup baths for a full week.

A woman behind the counter provided me with a single-portion miniature cassata on a plate. I pushed the fork in and it yielded easily. The sweetened cheese tasted like something that came from an animal, not a can; the fruit tasted like something that came from trees. And the pistachio paste—I don't remember having pistachios in a cassata before—added another dimension. Cassata was not Baroque after all—it was *terroir* that in less capable hands had suffered the same fate as Marsala. Cappello was, in a more restrained and diplomatic way, the Marco De Bartoli of cassata.

"To make a good cassata you need to know good products," Cappello said. "It is really an agricultural product."

FRANCESCO AND I DROVE BACK to the center of town and took the last lunch table in a small osteria in the fishermen's quarter, where we began a lunch with a small whole octopus staring out at us from a plate and a bottle of crisp white Catarratto. That afternoon I walked alone through Palermo's streets, watching as crowds formed from neighborhood to neighborhood for the Good Friday processions. I stopped and waited with a large crowd in the street at the base of the old stone steps that led to Chiesa delle Croci, a sixteenth-century church now obscured by scaffolding for renovation work.

From the church I heard the sound of a traditional funeral march—sad and at the same time carnivalesque. The mood in the street more closely resembled a sporting event than a sacred ritual. As at the Ballarò that morning, there was a cross-section of Palermo, young and old, laughing, exchanging news, ciao-ciao-ing into their telofinini. First out of the church were dozens of boys—not quite at the age where they had begun to shave—aligned in columns and dressed as Roman centurions with bronze-colored breastplates, plumed helmets, shields, and lances.

Then there emerged a priest in white habit and sash, who momentarily hushed the crowd in a recitation of Padre Nostro (the Lord's Prayer). The procession continued noisily from the church and inched down the stairs. More centurions were followed by girls in gold-trimmed, hooded black capes and a small band of musicians, accompanied by the sound of a wood clacker that echoed across the piazza. Then, at a pace of a penitent on his knees, there emerged from the church a gilded litter topped by four golden-winged cherubs and ringed with large thick candles and white orchids. Inside the litter—glassed on three sides—lay a plaster representation of a crucified Jesus with no shortage of blood depicted flowing from his wounds. The appearance was greeted with applause and whistles.

This litter, which easily weighed as much as a mid-sized Fiat, was attached to two wooden rails shouldered by about forty men—as young as sixteen and as old as sixty—wearing black suits and gloves. The men were paired off facing and bracing each other—arms around their partner's torso—rocking back and forth in a deliberate slow dance. As the litter tilted down the stairs, you could feel the weight shift onto the shoulders of the men below, each step requiring physical calculation. Negotiating those few dozen stairs took about a quarter of an hour, accompanied by the drone of funerary music and the flashes of cameras. As the litter reached street level, it was set down on the sidewalk to another eruption of applause. And so it went—the pallbearers carrying the litter another twenty yards and then stopping to pause in the crowd.

When the litter stopped near me, I watched as outstretched hands offered handkerchiefs to a pair of black-suited men who took the cloths and ran them along the arm and fingers of the Christ figure before handing them back to their owners. A woman of about forty standing next to me anxiously reached her arm out to one of the men. In her hand was a photograph. It was a wallet-sized photo, the kind taken at school. The picture was of a smiling boy no more than fifteen years old. As the man took the photo, I could feel her breath stop. Businesslike, the man wiped the face of the photo along the flesh-and-blood-painted plaster, then extended his hand back in the direction it had come from. The woman clutched the photo, squeezing it with two hands against her breast. I could feel her shudder and looked over to see tears streaming down her face. I couldn't help but wonder what had befallen this woman. What sort of violence had pierced her life? I thought of the streetwise kids I'd seen last Sunday. Of the *carabinieri* at the focacceria. I looked back at the litter and the crowd, and when I turned again in the woman's direction, she was gone.

Another statue appeared at the church entrance: Mary—draped with rosaries, head bowed, and tears lacquered to her face—standing upright atop another litter shouldered by another group of black-suited men. There was more applause, another deliberate descent down the steps, and more cheers. After about an hour the procession had made its way into the nearby piazza, melding with the rush hour traffic that had come to a stop.

On that night in Palermo, dozens of such processions wound their way through parish after parish in urban pilgrimages that lasted until the next Holy Mass sometime in the first hours of Saturday morning. Scores of other processions were carried out across the Sicilian countryside—barefoot penitents in hoods carrying crosses in scenes from centuries ago. It was a drama that would play all weekend until the Easter Mass and the family feasts that followed with the Sicilian spring table, the first finished wines of last season's harvest, and cassata.

MY TENTATIVE APPOINTMENT WITH Palermo's most guarded man was confirmed only at the last minute on Saturday morning when I received a call from the focacceria that it was okay to come by.

As I walked up to the piazza on this mild spring morning, I noticed two cars parked in front of the focacceria: one a standard Carabinieri blue Alfa Romeo, the other a shiny black unmarked Mercedes sedan with a blue flasher attached to the side of its roof. Outside were two Carabinieri officers with their machine guns, and standing in the restaurant were four muscular men in jeans and bomber jackets. They were as unsmiling as secret service agents; a couple of them wore a day or two of unshaved stubble and were standing eating focaccia, flashing black steel from inside their jackets.

I introduced myself to the most imposing of these plainclothes cops—tall, with dark clothes and a pair of black aviator glasses, and wearing an earpiece. He stepped aside, and behind him appeared Vincenzo Conticello, a man of medium build who looked impish surrounded by all that muscle. He wore a blue blazer, a light shirt, and baggy jeans. His face was round, his smile haggard. His dark eyes were framed by thin metal-rimmed glasses and his curly jet-black hair was slicked into place.

We sat at a marble table in the corner—Conticello took the bench with his back to the wall. Espressos arrived. The tall security guy called out orders to the others. Another cop brought him a focaccia *maritata* wrapped in paper, which he stood eating a few feet from us, watching the door and the occasional customer who ventured inside.

Conticello spoke little English. The first thing he said in Italian was this: "At this very table where I am sitting, Lucky Luciano used to sit fifty years ago . . . and I am happy to say that thirty years after that, Falcone and Borsellino took this as their favorite table."

Charles (born Salvatore) "Lucky" Luciano's story is not so much a Sicilian one as it is a perverse chapter of the American dream. The Sicilian immigrant rose through the ranks of the Cosa Nostra during Prohibition and then reshaped American criminal rackets with a corporate structure that became known as "organized crime." His return to Italy was forced: he was freed from a New York prison and deported for his help with U.S. port security during World War II. On the other hand, Giovanni Falcone and Paolo Borsellino were the most famous and revered men of modern Sicily and a reason Conticello and I were able to sit here in an interview. The pair of Palermo-born anti-Mafia prosecutors brought about hundreds of convictions before they were assassinated in separate bombings in 1992 and had their names attached to Palermo's airport. Their deaths brought about the public anti-Mafia revolt that changed society.

Conticello recounted the history of the focacceria from 1834 when his ancestors served only focaccia *schietta* on the same old wood-stove. In 1851 the Conticello family added *milza* (beef spleen) to the recipe along with other typical Palermo dishes such as *bucatini con le sarde*.

"Between 1834 and 2005 the Mafia had no interest in the focacceria," Conticello said. He drained the last of his espresso. "In fact, the Mafia came here to eat. They contracted with us for catering events. We did their weddings."

Conticello was now forty-eight years old, married, and the father of a grown daughter. As a younger man he had studied political science in Palermo and left the city for seventeen years, during which time he worked in ecotourism in both the public and the private sectors in South and Central America. He helped design programs that brought humans in touch with whales in Argentina and turtles in the Galapagos. But when it was time for Conticello's parents to retire in 2001, he and his brother, Fabio, took over the focacceria. The new generation of Conticellos expanded the business. They opened a restaurant next door called Hanami, serving sushi and world cuisine. They publicized visits to the focacceria by figures such as Hillary Clinton and Lance Armstrong, and they helped organize events promoting Sicilian food and wine in New York, Tokyo, Beijing, and Miami.

The Conticellos and the focacceria were suddenly known everywhere, and this higher profile, Vincenzo Conticello believes, is what attracted the interest of Palermo's Mafia. The summer of 2005, Conticello remembered, was marked by a series of daily acts of vandalism—too regular and varied to be dismissed.

"One day a window would be broken. The next day a customer's car was broken into on the street, then an employee's car, then my car. One morning we came in and gasoline was thrown on the doors. There was nothing strong, but there was *something* every day. And every day I called the police to report the problem of that day. They came, they made reports and took pictures.

"Then one day in November a man came and asked to talk to me," Conticello continued, motioning beyond the focaccia stove. "We sat at the second table over there. He had a bad face. He said, 'Me and my friend want to help you because we know you have many problems in your business.'"

Conticello paused to deliberately tug the flesh at the corner of his right eye in a Mediterranean gesture of warning.

"He asked me for 50,000 euros for the long time I didn't pay, and for 500 a month. He said, 'If you pay me this, my friend and I will give you maximum protection.'"

I imagined the body chemistry involved with hearing such words: the pounding of blood vessels, the tingling of muscles and nerves, the sick stomach feeling, and the film of sweat.

Conticello touched the back of his head. "I said to myself, 'This is the Mafia. Wow!' This was the kind of thing I read in the newspaper or saw on television or in the movies. I never thought I would see this.

"I said to him, 'You're asking me for *pizzo*?'

"He said, 'Call it what you want, I want to help you.'"

Conticello's face turned red as he described a scene that I found difficult to imagine: this friendly-faced man who'd spent his adult life in the tourism and hospitality industry telling off a street thug.

"I told him I wouldn't pay. I told him, 'I won't pay anything to you or the Cosa Nostra because if I pay once I will have to pay forever!'

"And he said, 'Are you sure, because if I tell my friend you won't pay, it's very dangerous.'

"I said that I was sure. I said, 'I am a free man, and I want to stay a free man!'"

After the man left, Conticello said, he went to the door in hopes of writing down the number on his motorcycle license plate.

"Then three men and a woman from another table came up and surrounded me"—Conticello pressed his arms to his side, dramatizing the closeness of these people in his face—"and they showed me a badge—Carabinieri."

The undercover officers were surveying the focacceria and had recognized the local thug as Giovanni Di Salvo. They asked Conticello to recount what Di Salvo had said. Then they asked if he would write a statement. Conticello shocked them by agreeing. "It was the first time the owner of a company talked about the Mafia."

Di Salvo was arrested along with three others. And during the next two years another dozen business owners came forward, resulting in more than twenty arrests. Palermo's anti-*pizzo* movement flourished and Conticello became its poster boy, testifying in a 2007 trial that resulted in prison sentences of ten years or more for Di Salvo and his accomplices.

The name Libero Grassi is one that weighs heavily on Conticello, who speaks the name in a whisper. A decade before Conticello returned to Palermo, Grassi—a sexagenarian who ran a Palermo pajama and underwear shop—had also refused to pay a *pizzo*. Grassi, who cooperated with authorities and became an anti-Mafia spokesman, was gunned down in the street in August 1991. It is a scenario the Italian state seemed determined to not have repeated. Since the day he agreed to testify, Conticello entered a surreal world of surveillance cameras and round-the-clock teams that live with him and his family and guard his property.

"I don't sleep in the same place from one night to the next. I am always moving around," he said. He pointed to a small video camera perched behind the focaccia stove. "There are cameras everywhere, connected to the Carabinieri. Between me, my brother, and my father there are one hundred cameras!"

Conticello shook his head with a meaningful look: "It's Big Brother."

As the first lunch customers began arriving under the watchful eyes of the security team, I asked Conticello if I might take his picture in front of his business. Conticello agreed and conferred with the head of his security detail. He stood up. Orders were called out. And as he stepped toward the doorway, I felt the dizzying swirl of weapons, adrenaline, and focused attention engulf us—the cage in which Conticello lived. One of the machine-gun-toting officers had stopped a car from entering the small piazza as the men fanned out. I stood facing Conticello and the storefront, and as I lifted my camera to shoot, I could feel someone behind me. I could feel the head cop just out of the frame of the picture, standing between me and the subject: a man who looked as if he were facing a firing squad.

1. Giusto Occhipinti of COS

2. Titta Cilia among cos's amphorae

3. The old *palmento* where cos began

4. Frank Cornelissen

5. Pressing wine at Frank Cornelissen's winery

6. Pippo the mechanic and Sandro
at Bar Sandro Dibella

7. Alessio Planeta at Ulmo

8. Diego Planeta

9. Santa Margherita di Belice, forty
years after the earthquake

10. Marco De Bartoli

11. Vincenzo Conticello in front
of his family *focacceria*

12. Lucio Tasca d'Almerita (*right*) with
his sons Giuseppe (*left*) and Alberto

13. Libera Terra co-op members on
seized Mafia land near Corleone

14. Arianna Occhipinti

15. Francesca Curto looking over the harvest

Summer

7

Where Have the Leopards Gone?

"*GATTOPARDO* DOESN'T EXIST ANYMORE. He is dead." Count Lucio Tasca d'Almerita surprised me with these words. Because if anyone would preserve and protect the ideas of *The Leopard*, I assumed it would be him. After all, everyone from Sicilian laborers to politicians quoted Giuseppe di Lampedusa (whose mother was a Tasca) more frequently than the Bible. I therefore expected the noble overseer of one of Sicily's largest historic estates to embody *The Leopard* and its view of Sicily as immutable.

"My father could have been *Il Gattopardo*. This is a stupid thing," he continued. "In fact, Sicily is changing."

At sixty-eight, Count Lucio—who dismisses the use of a title before his name with the wave of a hand and a "just Lucio"—looks the part of a count with his head of healthy silver hair, the pale eyes peering over a significant nose, and his hint of world weariness. A blue blazer and an open white shirt with gold pants covered the long and agile frame that served him in his days riding steeplechase on the Italian national team. Though he has retired from running the Tasca d'Almerita estates—turning the job of chief executive over to his younger son, the thirty-six-year-old Alberto—Lucio is a businessman with little patience for philosophy or reflecting on the past. A flat computer screen rests on his desk, which is an arc of polished wood. His English is near perfect—his manners impeccable. He asked if I minded if he took off his jacket, and then after doing so rested it on the back of his chair. He pushed a button on his desk phone and asked for coffee, and a secretary soon arrived with espressos in un-*Leopard*-like disposable plastic cups. He settled back in his steel-framed desk chair, opened a window to the bright early summer morning, and after a do-you-mind-if-I-smoke courtesy, ignited a Marlboro Light—the modern affliction, it seems, of all Tasca men.

Despite the "just Lucio," three generations of Tascas live an anachronistic life with cooks and staff in town and country. Town is Villa Tasca, the sixteenth-century palazzo from which Count Lucio and I drove a few hundred yards to this office. The villa is one of Palermo's grandest, with lush gardens at the edge of town insulating it from the blight of apartment blocks and industrial parks just outside. The family's country life is based at Regaleali, the 1,200-acre estate in the remote wheat-covered center of Sicily with about 900 acres of Sicily's most important ecologically run vineyards.

Yet, the Tascas are one of the only aristocratic families to have kept a vast wine estate intact in the twenty-first century—even after more than half of it was taken from them under southern Italy's postwar land reform program in the 1950s. The Tascas, it seemed, have thrived with the right blend of instincts—adapting to the times when others bemoaned them.

"We always worked," Count Lucio said, explaining his family's success as other Sicilian dynasties have gone broke. "They never worked."

The Tascas came to their title and their Palermo villa in the early nineteenth century. An earlier Lucio Tasca, a wealthy cattle rancher from Mistretta in the Nebrodi Mountains of northeastern Sicily, arrived in Palermo with good looks and money and married the daughter of a Sicilian prince, who included the villa—then known as Camastra—in his daughter's dowry. At the time, feudalism and

Bourbon rule were on the wane, baronial lands were being sold, and Sicily was in a state of turmoil as many Spanish families associated with the Bourbons left. In 1830 a pair of Tasca brothers bought the old fortified farm at Regaleali.

The family's main interests were in grain and other agricultural products. Wine—grown in the lands around Camastra now paved with concrete and sprouting high-rise apartments—was cultivated for the family and for estate workers. When he was a young boy at Regaleali after the war, Lucio remembered, the daily ration given to laborers was one kilo of bread and one liter of wine. "Wine was food for them," he said. "They drank it all day long."

"I remember this worker cutting up one olive in such a way to last for one kilo of bread—the whole day," Lucio said, using his hands to illustrate a surgical slicing motion with an imaginary knife.

Around 1920 all of the Camastra production including wine moved to Regaleali. After Lucio's birth at the outbreak of the war in 1940, about eighty people, including relatives, friends, and workers' families, moved there as well. After the war Lucio's grandfather and father "made revolution," instigating the Sicilian separatist movement and its doomed pair of secessionist plans: first to be annexed by the United States and later to have the deposed Italian king Umberto II installed as king of an independent Sicily.

Some historical accounts have linked members of the aristocracy, including the Tascas, with the bandit Salvatore Giuliano. (Lucio's father, Count Giuseppe, served as a consultant to Michael Cimino for his screen adaptation of *The Sicilian*.) But Lucio says he never saw Giuliano at Regaleali, and he said that if a relationship did exist, it was a matter of practical convenience. "When you make revolution, you need to have some people who know how to kill," Lucio said matter-of-factly.

The Tascas were not great political revolutionaries. They were, however, revolutionary in the stewardship of their lands—bringing one of the first tractors to central Sicily before the war, and building one of the first high country lakes in the years after. In those postwar years, while the government created cooperatives and handed out subsidies for producing *more* wine, the Tascas instead worked to produce *better* wines. They shunned herbicides and pesticides, introduced vineyard techniques such as short pruning of vines that improved quality and limited quantity of fruit, and were among the first to use temperature-controlled fermentation tanks.

Count Giuseppe was the wine lover who transformed Tascas' wines—and in so doing left a lasting mark on Sicily. In the early 1960s—enlisting the help of Ezio Rivella, one of Italy's top oenologists —he began bottling white wines from Inzolia, Catarratto, and a grape variety on the estate they called Sauvignon Tasca (believed to be a cross of Sauvignon Blanc with Grecanico). Among Giuseppe's favorite wines were reds from Châteauneuf-du-Pape in France's Rhone Valley, and in 1970 he began bottling a red wine (the first bottled from 100 percent Nero d'Avola) called Rosso del Conte.

"We don't work for money," his son, Lucio, was now telling me with another wave of the hand. "We have never worked for money."

"We work," Lucio said, "for what we Italians call *la bellezza di lavare*" ("the beauty of work").

Unlike his father, Lucio is not a true wine lover. He studied economics, not agronomy or oenology. Wine, he freely admits, is something he enjoys a few minutes of the day with meals. His loves are the land, his business, and *la bellezza* that is evident throughout the Tascas' growing world.

As a younger man he had worked briefly for his father but then launched other small businesses—wholesaling nursery plants and textiles from Villa Tasca. "I was married and had two children, but I couldn't talk with my father about money, so I did other things," he said. "Also, there was always competition between my father and me."

Finally, approaching forty years old in 1979, Lucio joined his father at Regaleali. "Back in 1980," he remembered, "if you went around the world with a bottle of Nero d'Avola, people weren't interested. People—the Americans—were just starting to learn about the French *cepages* (varietals) . . . nobody could imagine that in Sicily you could make a good wine. They thought you could only do it in France."

Thinking that if the world wanted French varietals, Regaleali could produce them. Lucio asked his father to experiment with other grape varieties.

"He gave me half a hectare at Regaleali—one acre." A smile creased Lucio's face. His long fingers toyed with the Marlboro pack on his desk. "The Chardonnay and Cabernet were wonderful."

Next, Lucio wanted to experiment with raising wine in small French oak *barriques*. "My father said, 'If you bring *barriques* to Regaleali, I will leave,'" Lucio remembered. The wines at Regaleali were traditionally aged in large chestnut or Slovenian oak *botti*. Lucio had to trick his father by hiding French *barriques* he'd bought with his own money. He later had his father blind taste his experiment: the *barriques* and the count stayed.

VAST ENOUGH TO BE MARKED on roadmaps of Sicily, Regaleali is planted in the immensity of the Sicilian interior, in which twisting roads lead through mountains and rolling hills covered with wheat and no buildings to be seen for miles. As summer arrives, the oceans of wheat dry to the palest shades of gold—ready for harvest. In the middle of this sea of grain, Regaleali is an island of deep green and meticulously plotted vineyards in brown clay soils along with vegetable gardens, olive groves, and irrigation lakes fed by small rivers.

The entry to the main house is an arched tunnel of peeling blue paint and mortar that leads to a courtyard of worn cobblestones and a series of old farm buildings from which the Tascas have built the seat of their country dominion—adding onto, but never erasing, their past. Inside, in a large reception room, two hundred years of family patriarchs stare down from dark oil paintings. Propped on an easel in the same room is a sunny painting with bright bold strokes of Count Giuseppe and a glass of his prized red wine.

Behind the old farm complex, a large state-of-the-art winery sprawls through a pair of modern buildings. But amid all the steel and computer-controlled vats and new barrel rooms, the Tascas have kept some old cement fermenting tanks and cellars of large casks that go back generations—a conscious effort which never allows modernity to entirely erase history. Outside the winery, exposed to the elements, is a stand of shiny refrigerated tanks—tall as a three-story building and topped by a stainless steel representation of Mary of Lourdes, specially commissioned by Count Giuseppe.

After arriving at Regaleali, I hid from the midday sun by napping in a ground-floor room in which a small, dark oil painting of the Crucifixion rested above the bed made up with fresh white linens. In the evening I found Giuseppe's namesake—Lucio's eldest son—in a small modern house down the road, where he and his family stay when at Regaleali. At forty-five, Giuseppe was the earthiest of the Tasca men. With a head of untamed gray curls, matching beard, and epicure's paunch, Giuseppe actually looks like a winegrower. Bicycles were scattered in front of his house. Inside, he and his fifteen-year-old son, Lucio, and his son's friend from Palermo were jamming—jazz—on acoustic guitars. After an espresso, Giuseppe and I set out for the vineyards.

"There is always music in my house," he said, adding that his favorite instrument was drums—rock drums.

As we walked down the road to a station wagon parked in front of the farm compound, the hills were bathed in a golden evening light that electrified the contrast between the deep green vineyards and everything else. Swallows circled overhead, and on a hill to our left a herd of Regaleali goats ate wild grasses and nibbled at the lower branches of olive trees.

"My passion," Giuseppe said as we paused to look down the valley, "is the countryside. I love winemaking, vineyards, olives, wheat—everything." He pulled on the handle of his car door and clarified: "Drums and the countryside."

This countryside has been known for centuries as Regaleali, a name that derives from the Arabic *Rahal Ali* (Ali's place). "But who was Ali—we don't know," Giuseppe said.

As he drove through the vineyards, along washed-out irregular roads, stopping every so often in a different vineyard plot or a field of wheat, Giuseppe—who worked as manager of the estate for eight years—reflected on the principles that guide Regaleali.

"My grandfather understood that you make wine in the vineyard," he said, "not in the winery."

Unlike his father, Giuseppe loves talking wine. He professed his love for the whites of Burgundy. But when it comes to Regaleali Chardonnay, the grape of Burgundy whites, he said that after years of experimentation he'd learned that the Sicilian climate was incapable of producing a white wine acidic enough to finish like a Burgundy.

"We want to make a Sicily high-in-the-hills Chardonnay," he said. Over time I have come to appreciate what this means. Regaleali Chardonnay—a full shade lighter than Planeta's and fresher in the mouth—tastes of mint and wild herbs that I've never tasted in another Chardonnay.

Nestling at a relatively high altitude, between 400 and 750 meters, Regaleali has the kind of hot days and cool nights that winemakers covet for making complex wines. There also seems to be a constant mountain wind, good for warding off mold and mildew. Though Tasca d'Almerita's wine production is larger than Planeta's wine production by about one-fifth, in most years Regaleali's vineyards are cultivated organically. About once every decade the farm uses some nonorganic treatment to combat vineyard outbreaks, as in 2007 when the spread of downy mildew claimed much of the crop in western Sicily and the Tascas treated their vineyards with antibiotics.

In winter, sheep graze the vineyards, leaving their droppings as fertilizer. Soil-enriching fava beans are planted between rows, and once every five years vineyards are fertilized with a barnyard blanket of manure and hay. More than a decade ago the Tascas commissioned a geological mapping of their vineyards to better understand their soils. Through this research they determined that 30 percent of their vineyards needed to be equipped with drip irrigation, and the rest—softer soils with less evaporation—are dry-farmed.

Beyond science, what distinguishes the Tascas among large Italian wine producers is the intuitive farming practiced at every level. Giuseppe stopped the car, and we stomped through the brown soil of clay laced with sand between a stand of Inzolia vines. The vines—short-pruned and tied to galvanized wire between wood posts—dangled nascent bunches of tiny green pendulous grapes. The earth was light, spongy.

"If you walk in the soil, you can tell how it is. So in summer, if we go and walk in the soils and it is good, we leave more clusters. Where it is not so good—where it is hard—we leave less clusters," Giuseppe said. Then he caressed a bunch of vine leaves. "We teach our people to touch the leaves. They should be velvety. If they are sharp there is a problem."

"All the people who work in the vineyard—they are at the lowest level of society," Giuseppe said. "They are like what in New York would be . . . Puerto Ricans. We try to give them value because they are the real value of the company. So we give them freedom to make decisions. We tell them, 'Push on the soil—touch the leaves.'"

Tasca d'Almerita employs about 50 people, plus 150 seasonal workers, many of whom have their own nearby farms and sell grapes to Regaleali. "We pay them three times what the market pays them because we know where the grapes come from and know they work in a good way."

Back in the car, which he steered through more vineyards, Giuseppe stopped next to a field where we listened to the wind whistle through wheat, and then continued down a hillside to Regaleali's oldest vineyard, San Lucio—about twenty acres of fifty-year-old vines alternating Nero d'Avola and Perricone rows. This southern-exposed vineyard at about 450 meters was planted by the late Count Giuseppe—his Sicilian answer to Châteauneuf-du-Pape. The soil was light in color and laced with sand, and the vines looked like small trees in the traditional *alberello* form without any supports or wires.

On the drive back, I looked over the miles of hills that made the Tasca heritage. Giuseppe spoke of how he was shaped by his father, grandfather, and other Tasca men.

"They taught us that if you cry, to cry in public; if you laugh, to do it in public," he said. "They taught us to be real."

I asked Giuseppe what it meant to him—a rock 'n' roller, *vignaiolo*, and future Count Giuseppe—to be Sicilian.

"In this crazy world where everybody is selling their souls for money, the people here in Sicily are very attached to their soil," he said. "The Sicilian people have always had too many people invading. French . . . Bourbons . . . Arabs . . . so the Sicilian people needed to find a way to show that they were not really dominated inside . . . this is the Sicilian character—a mixture of being open and being closed."

THAT EVENING, DINNER WAS IN the family dining room upstairs in the main house. I joined Giuseppe and his wife, Luisa, along with Count Lucio's older sister, Anna Tasca Lanza—the Sicilian cookbook author who runs a cooking school from Case Vecchie, another farm on the estate—and her husband, the Marchese Venceslao Lanza di Mazzarino (known simply as "Vences" around Regaleali).

Anna, at seventy-one, and Venceslao, approaching eighty, were more reserved than the younger Tascas I'd met and seemed to have been schooled in the very un-Italian—and disconcerting—practice of keeping their hands at their sides when they spoke. They dressed smartly for dinner. Over the course of a couple of days and several encounters with Venceslao, I never saw him not wearing a coat and tie (the latter fastened in place with a gold tie clip), even in the heat of a Sicilian summer day.

After a half century of marriage, the slender, white-haired couple seem not only to finish each other's sentences in perfect English but to complete their thoughts. "Venceslao is like a machine," warned Anna, a handsome woman with long features, her green eyes shining. "If you let him talk he will go on and on, so you have to push the button when you want him to stop."

As we sat in the small drawing room before dinner, I asked Anna how a woman who grew up with cooks and servants and attended a girls' finishing school in Switzerland had become an authority on Sicilian peasant cooking. Anna answered that after she married, she didn't know how to cook, yet she and Venceslao wanted to eat as well as they had growing up. More and more they wanted to eat simpler.

"When I was a child, we ate Sicilian cuisine, Arab cuisine, French cuisine, and we didn't know what we were eating, but it all came completely from the land," Anna said. "Every aristocratic family had what we called a *monseu*—the Sicilian way of saying the French *monsieur*." A *monseu*, Anna and Venceslao went on while alternating phrases, was a chef who had trained to work in glamorous hotels in Paris or northern Italy or on large ocean liners—a tradition that was interrupted by World War II but resumed soon thereafter.

"We grew up with a cuisine of lots of butter and foie gras of the *monseu*, who served it with caponata and pasta." The more Venceslao spoke, the more reflective aristocrat—the more *Leopard*—I saw in him. In fact, Venceslao's brother, Gioacchino Lanza Tomasi, a renowned musicologist who has been artistic director of operas from Palermo to Bologna, is the adopted son of Giuseppe di Lampedusa—chosen to manage the writer's intellectual property after his death.

Venceslao was born in Rome, but when he was seventeen his family moved to Sicily, closer to their landholdings that included almond plantations, vineyards, and a sulfur mine near Enna. Venceslao recounted how the two generations that preceded him had traveled the world and accumulated debts of about $1.6 million by the end of World War II—an almost unthinkable sum by Italian postwar standards. "My parents and grandparents lived in a very grand style and spent the fortune," he said. "I spent my life paying off their debts. I just finished paying five years ago."

Dinner—served by the house cook, a younger woman who addressed Anna as "Marchesa"—began with two pastas: *ditalini con cucuzza* (small tube pasta with young local squash) followed by *bucatini con finocchietti* (thick tube pasta with wild fennel), which we ate with the 2006 vintage of Regaleali's signature white Nozze d'Oro, a wine created by Count Giuseppe for his fiftieth wedding anniversary. Made from Sauvignon Tasca and Inzolia, it is a dry but robust wine—thoroughly odd by modern standards.

This *Leopard*-like wine got Venceslao going. A passionate history buff, he recounted—with my encouragement—how up until 1812 Sicily remained a feudal state run by one hundred families and the Bourbon Spanish king.

"Vences, maybe this is bit of a tangent," Anna politely suggested, "and everybody may not want to hear this."

With no other protests, Venceslao continued, explaining the turmoil of Sicily in the nineteenth century: changes in land ownership out of feudal estates, the end of the Kingdom of Sicily, which was attached to Naples (as the Bourbon Kingdom of Two Sicilies), the short-lived revolution for independence in 1848, and the unification of Italy in 1860 with its compulsory military service. In fact, Italy was so divided, Venceslao said, that an official Italian language (based on Florentine Italian) had to be invented so that army soldiers could communicate with each other. He remembered his grandfather telling how, in order to make himself understood on a trip north to Turin, he spoke in Latin.

The unrest and lack of stability in Sicily produced a climate, Venceslao offered, that germinated what came to be known as the Mafia. "The Italians were divided in two and are still that way to some extent," Venceslao said, hands on his lap and sitting upright as the plates were cleared. "There are the Italians who feel that they are citizens, and there are the Italians who feel they are subjects. If you feel you are a subject, your enemy is the state."

As the main course of *involtini di carne* (stuffed beef rolls) was set out, Giuseppe poured from a bottle of Rosso del Conte 2006—spicy, velvety, and surprisingly clean. Absent were the barnyard and mystery aromas of Giuseppe's grandfather's beloved Châteauneuf-du-Pape.

Venceslao dabbed at the corners of his mouth with a napkin, then sipped and savored the wine. Setting his glass back down, he continued: "There are two mafias, in fact. There is the mafia that is not criminal but a mentality. For years I remember there were two entrances to the post office. There was the front door, and then if you didn't want to wait in line, you went to see the postman at the back door where you got a special service. And then one day when you went to the back door the postman would ask you do something . . . it was not *necessarily* illegal."

About the future, Venceslao was less certain. The families that once ruled Sicily were all but gone, as was the professional ruling class that followed. For the first time Sicily was being run by an entrepreneurial middle class—Venceslao called them "traders." Did he mean it derisively? I wasn't sure. No one at the table seemed to have any idea what this new spirit of enterprise would mean for Sicily.

WHILE VENCESLAO IS A WINDOW into Sicily's long and complicated past, Alberto Tasca is a direct line to its future. Young, dynamic, barely able to restrain cockiness, and constantly in motion, Alberto is emblematic of a generation of young Sicilians who came of age around the time of the Falcone and Borsellino assassinations and vowed not to leave.

Alberto arrived at mid-morning the following day by helicopter from Palermo, with the idea that the two of us would take the chopper to visit some of the family's other vineyard projects on the north face of Etna as well as on the Aeolian island of Salina. He introduced himself as the CEO, though he added in perfect English that the structure of the company is "very horizontal." He confers constantly with a team of young managers and his brother, Giuseppe, with whom there is no discernible rivalry.

"My brother is like this," Giuseppe had told me, drawing a straight line in front of his face with his open hand. Both brothers manage the estate by finding smart, motivated people and, as Alberto put it, "letting them do what they are passionate about." He pals around with his staff, and they with him—exchanging backslaps with the guys and fraternal kisses when arriving or leaving, or watching a soccer match together under the gaze of his ancestors on canvas.

Handsome with a lean frame, wavy dark hair, a Roman nose, and an easy smile, Alberto seemed as though he could just as easily head a technology startup company. He wore khakis and a plain white cotton shirt, and while he often fiddled with a cell phone, he wore no watch. Alberto took me on a tour of the winery, repeating the mantra he uses to describe his family legacy—and at the same time putting *The Leopard* in its grave.

"Experimentation," he said, "is in our DNA."

Alberto is sharp—a quick-witted whirl of statistics, perfect catchphrases, and business acumen. He spoke of the geology of Regaleali—"so many variables, so many *terroirs*, 360 degrees of exposition"—and of the move for Regaleali to isolate and select its own yeasts starting in the 2008 vintage. In the barrel room, surrounded by thousands of *barriques* in steel frameworks, he spoke of the problem of buying new wood *barriques*, which have become a permanent part of winemaking here.

"No two *barriques* are the same: 20 percent are great, 60 percent are good, and 20 percent are bad—they destroy the wine," he said, explaining that the goal of the winery is to oxidize the wine slightly and soften it—and not to add flavors and tannins from the oak barrels.

"This is Sicily, so we don't need to add anything to the wine; we need to take it away," he said—a reference to the cool climate-controlled steel tanks that limit the baked effect of fermenting ripe grapes at high temperatures.

Alberto took over in 2003, propelled into that position by his handling of a potential distribution crisis faced by the company. Shortly after the death of Count Giuseppe, Lucio sought to break with the Tascas' longtime distributor—a hostile move that was set for January 2002. Alberto took charge of the task of setting up a distribution unit within Tasca in 2001—recruiting a group of business school friends and building a computer database and distribution procedures from nothing.

"Before that, we didn't know anything about distribution," Alberto said. "We sent out two and a half million bottles of wine a year and we didn't know the name of one customer!"

The Tascas' biggest problems, he remembered, were in the domestic Italian market, which is responsible for more than half the consumption of Tasca wines. (Within Italy about half their wine is consumed in Sicily.) The previous distributor had accumulated the equivalent of millions of dollars in unpaid invoices.

"In Italy it's one thing to sell—another thing to get paid," Alberto said. "In the United States the system of payments is controlled. In Italy there is no regulation—everybody does what they want!"

For lunch that day Count Lucio joined Alberto, Giuseppe, and an old school friend of Alberto's from Palermo who had flown out with him. Just as interesting as the lunch—eggplant and tomato-based *Pasta alla Norma* served with fresh ricotta and grilled lamb from the Regaleali flock—was watching the two brothers eat. Giuseppe heartily savored each course and paused to carefully taste the first sip of wine—a fresh, citrusy Regaleali Bianco 2007 (a blend of Inzolia, Catarratto, and Grecanico). Alberto skipped the meat course in favor of a salad, took water instead of wine, and was also the only one to not touch the cannoli that followed.

A wind had kicked up—a hot dry Scirocco from North Africa. Through a door that led to a terrace in the dining room, I saw the landscape turn almost white under a hazy sun as the wind rattled the windows and whistled through Regaleali. Because of the wind we were grounded for the day, unable to take the helicopter until the next morning.

That evening, Alberto and I sat on a stone wall in front of the farm entry, and he talked about his life—the two years after high school he spent racing on the Alfa Boxer automotive circuit, followed by the six months he spent finding his life's direction by working in the fields at Regaleali. That was followed by two years at Palermo's elite business management school, which he'd tested into without the usual university degree. He spoke of his family—his wife, Francesca, and their two toddler sons—who spend about half the year in Rome, where Alberto travels on weekends during that period.

Alberto told of his program to reset Regaleali's business strategy every five years, and of his plan to create three rotating commissions—one of wine lovers, another of business people, and a third of "opinion leaders" to critique the company and its products.

"I don't want to hear how what we are doing is great," he said. "I want to know what we are doing wrong. And in that there is an opportunity."

His restlessness and his faith in modern business management were astounding by the standards of southern Europe. In Sicily they seemed unimaginable.

It appeared that the *Leopard* had been bred out of the Tasca men in two generations. Alberto had spent his life in Sicily, but it was hard to tell. His generation seemed to be the first to see opportunity where others had been resigned to fate.

"My generation is over the idea where you have to be rich. We are completely free but we decided to stay here in Sicily. We could go elsewhere. I mean, if you make an analysis of this as a business—wine is not the best business. Sicily has problems. It doesn't have the best economy. We are a poor country. There was not a culture of entrepreneurs. Sicilian wines are not so well known. But the guys of my generation have decided that in the problem is an opportunity.

"We have a beautiful place," Alberto said in a voice that seemed almost pleading. "We say we have all the potential to do something here. My generation is making this a mission, saying, 'Why go to Milan?'"

The Scirocco continued to shake the trees in a nearby olive grove and kick up dust. I imagined that if it continued to blow, such a wind could make people listless or mad. And I thought that for all Alberto's smart business school concepts and ways, Regaleali and Sicily managed to touch him intimately.

"Look at this place. We don't try to make it a perfect château, because there were hundreds of people who worked here who made it what it is today." He stood and pointed to the deep rounded out corners in the wall—there were four or five that looked as though the rock had been spooned away.

"These places were where the men would stand and talk and sharpen their knives waiting for a piece of bread." He'd lowered his voice and solemnly moved his hand back and forth—miming the rhythmic sharpening of two sides of a blade.

THE FOLLOWING DAY, UNDER A blue sky and gentle wind, we flew over the heart of Sicily in a four-seat California-made helicopter. As we approached Etna the landscape turned green with chestnut and oak trees—divided by the long dribblings of black lava flows. We landed on the north face near Randazzo in one of the last great flows, from 1986. It was mid-morning and already 90°F.

We walked up a narrow leafy road through vines—the soils that were black in winter had dried and turned to a brown dust. In 2007 the Tascas had bought several parcels, including an early-nineteenth-century *palmento,* and twelve acres of terraced land here in the *contrada* Bocca d'Orzo. The *palmento* still had its great lever press intact, but the roof was broken, and as we walked inside the high building, pigeons fluttered out—everything inside was painted with droppings. We walked through a small iron gate through some brush and entered into what was a large amphitheater of terraces—long abandoned—facing the Peloritani Mountains. Once a vineyard, the terraces were now covered in neglected olive trees and chestnut trees that had sprung from bird-dropped nuts.

To cross through the terraces, you walk along walls accessible by stone steps—created as level, raised paths that could support mules for bringing the harvest to the *palmento.*

"When the agronomist came from Regaleali, he said, 'Please don't buy this—it will be too difficult to restore everything,'" Alberto laughed. Then he enthused about Etna as having the "highest potential" in Sicily—not just for the climate, soils, and grapes.

"Randazzo to Solicchiata is about 2,500 acres with sixty producers," Alberto said, back in CEO mode. "When you have sixty producers all competing, it is much better for quality. With sixty all working for quality, you can do much more experimentation than if you are on your own."

Yet I wondered if the influx was all for good. It is always exhilarating to see a place just as it is "discovered," and crushing to find that same place after it's tamed by accountants and the winery gift shops arrive. I mentioned California's wine country and Tuscany.

"California?" Alberto objected. "California is about doing whatever you want. Here the mountain—the nature—is greater than all of us. Tuscany was California style. It became chic. *Chiantishire.* Here it is nature that will tell us what to do!

"Look, what can you do with this nature?" he asked, flinging his hand toward the plume of smoke that rose from a crater high up the mountain. "All you can say is, 'Do what you want, I will do my best.' Look at it—it can destroy everything in minutes!"

Having literally dropped onto the mountain from the sky, I felt the brooding nature of Etna more pointedly than at any time before or since. Etna was black, magnetic, with a mountainous energy as heavy as iron ore that seemed to weigh on everything around it. You could see it in the gray film of dust that left its patina on houses and buildings and in the hunched gaits of toughened old *contadini*. We climbed back into the helicopter and headed north, over the Tyrannian Sea toward the Aeolian Islands, and a world that was Etna's inverse.

After about forty minutes in the air, we touched down on a cliff at a lighthouse point on the island of Salina. Here in 2001 the Tascas bought more than fifteen acres covered with vineyards, which were renovated and replanted for making the archipelago's sweet appellation white wine, Malvasia delle Lipari, from overripe Malvasia grapes that are either left to dry in the sun or—as is the case with the Tascas—placed in special drying rooms. While recent harvests had been ferried back to the main island in refrigerated trucks and driven to Regaleali for vinification, the Tascas were constructing a nearby winery.

Salina, with a population of about 2,500, feels like a Greek island. Light and breezy, it is swept by salt air that blows off a brilliant blue sea and is punctuated with bougainvillea and umbrella pines. Here, right in the middle of the working vineyards that fall to the sea, Alberto Tasca has created Capofaro Malvasia and Resort, with twenty luxury hotel rooms, a swimming pool, and an open-to-the-elements restaurant and bar. Everything at Capofaro, inside and out, is white. Buildings and the intimate bungalows in the vines are completely repainted every spring so as to remain pristine. Even the young staff wears white linens, accessorized by the calm contented look of yoga instructors.

While Alberto talked business with the resort manager, I walked with the vineyard manager, Corrado, a young man with red hair and a pointed goatee. Corrado happily told me how most of the year he worked with hand tools so as not to disturb the guests, how he placed memos in the rooms telling them what he would be doing in the vineyards, and how they could participate in the late summer harvest. (Corrado said most last for only about twenty minutes before they find it too hot and head off for some shade or the pool.) Then, with the blissed look of a man who has stared in the face of an Eternal Truth, Corrado told me about the joy he experienced in March when he was working alone in the vineyards and dolphins who come to feed here splashed in the waters below the cliff.

Lunch was made of beautiful servings—a tiny Zen presentation of zucchini soufflé and smoked local shrimp decorated with a sprig of lavender, followed by a prawn salad. Dessert was the Tascas' Malvasia mixed with fine crushed ice in a granita served in martini glasses. Poolside, a few well-manicured guests—mostly British couples shiny with sunscreen—lounged in the quiet, ensured by a policy excluding children under fourteen.

Capofaro—judged in the context of an international luxury compound—seemed perfect. But it was a creation in Sicilian waters completely disconnected from Sicily. Like Chardonnay.

Alberto said that when he came to Salina he was welcomed by the locals. But experimentation, he learned, is not in the local DNA. The more he encouraged his neighbors with opportunities for developing the island's tourist potential, the more they resisted.

"I was telling them, 'Wouldn't it be great? You could do this, you could do that,' and they said, 'Why? Why would we want to do that?' Finally, I said, 'I know, I am stupid.'"

Alberto shook his head. It was a lesson in humility for a young man in a hurry. We spooned and sucked on the granitas, and I asked Alberto the same question about being Sicilian I'd asked his older brother.

"To be Sicilian is not to be a son of consumerism. It is to be direct and human—a son of real life," he answered. "Sicily tells us: You can be rich from a noble family—or poor. We are all the same."

I have no doubt Alberto meant what he said. It was an ideal as good as the granita was cold—and just as fragile. I drank it down before it could melt.

8

Return to Corleone

BEFORE ACTUALLY SETTING FOOT in Corleone, the only impression I'd had was formed by Francis Ford Coppola's film version of *The Godfather*. The fictional ancestral home where Michael Corleone (Al Pacino) spends his exile from New York mob wars was a remote pastoral hamlet filmed in several rural locations near Taormina in northeastern Sicily. The real Corleone—on the other side of the island, in Palermo province in the northern Belice Valley—is a modernized country town of about 11,000, surrounded by vineyards, expanses of wheat, and a winery once owned by some of Sicily's most brutal Mafia dons.

The story of Corleone in the latter part of the twentieth century is many times more violent and less honorable than the imaginary one. There have been no empathetic portrayals or smart television series about the real *Corleonesi* clan that seized control of the Sicilian Mafia in Palermo in the 1980s (a life-imitates-art twist: this happened after *The Godfather* film) under the direction of Salvatore "Totò" Riina, also known as "the beast."

Legend has it that Riina—who committed his first murder as a teenager—once told his hesitant future in-laws that he would have to shed some blood were he not allowed to marry their daughter. In another sentimental moment he was reported to have cried at the funeral of an associate whose killing he ordered. In all, Riina was responsible for hundreds of assassinations—of rivals, politicians, and their families—culminating in the spring 1992 bombings that killed the popular anti-Mafia prosecutors Giovanni Falcone and Paolo Borsellino along with their bodyguards and Falcone's wife. In January 1993—following public outrage over the assassinations—Riina was arrested in Palermo traffic: Italy's Most Wanted criminal had in fact spent decades as a "fugitive" living comfortably in his house in downtown Palermo. In 2006 Riina's successor, Bernardo "The Tractor" Provenzano—under whose reign the Sicilian Mafia is believed to have abandoned drugs and killing for the more discreet and lucrative business of infiltrating and embezzling public finance systems—was arrested in the Corleone countryside after more than four decades in hiding.

Riina's two sons joined him behind bars, but in March 2008 Riina's youngest son, Giuseppe—serving a fourteen-year-sentence for money laundering, extortion, and Mafia membership—was set free on a technicality. (His trial took too long, according to Italian justice.) When Giuseppe returned home to his mother's house in Corleone, carrying a box of pastry for Mamma, Corleone's reformist mayor and a group of protesters futilely asked him to leave.

What drew me to Corleone—just a few months after the twenty-eight-year-old Riina's release—was not the usual *Godfather* tourism, on which a few local businesses feed. I was drawn by the surprising anti-Mafia movement known as Libera Terra that had taken root here and spread north to the Italian peninsula. Now, Mafia wine and landholdings seized by Italian courts were being turned over to nonprofit cooperatives that produced "liberated" Nero d'Avola and Catarratto wines, along with organic pasta, tomato sauce, and olive oil. It was a new dimension of *terroir* that I hadn't yet considered.

My first impression of Corleone was of a friendly, open place that seemed untouched by decades of notoriety—a confirmation of the idea that while mafioso did their dirty work in the cities, they liked to keep their hometowns quiet and free of the crime and drugs that might disturb Mamma. Nestled in the belly of a mountainous cirque topped by the remains of a Saracen lookout tower, Corleone is neither prosperous nor poor. The center of town is a collection of intimate public squares and narrow stone streets with a hundred churches, chapels, and shrines in varying states of upkeep and decay. Beaded doorways lead to bakeries, pasta makers, barbershops and hairdressers, butchers, tobacconists, and bars. There are a few fashion boutiques and jewelry stores and almost no graffiti or other signs of vandalism or lawlessness. A local cooperative sells its wines in bulk for less than one euro a liter.

All day long, groups of old men line up like crows on telephone wires in front of bars and cafés—staring in unison at the occasional tourists who pass in shorts and sandals. Evenings, more old men show up in the town's central sprawling garden, with its gurgling fountains and umbrella pines, to stroll in their uniformly crisp ironed plaid or striped shirts. Teenagers sporting droopy jeans, bared flesh, and enough hair gel to withstand a Scirocco cavort at the far end of the park.

Almost every bar in town pours a Sicilian after-dinner herbal *digestivo* called Amaro Don Corleone. The café that faces city hall—the Central Bar—is decorated inside and out with movie stills of Don Corleone as played by Marlon Brando and Al Pacino (whose grandparents came from Corleone). Across the street from the bar, in the plaza of palms where the Central Bar has a few plastic tables, is a bronze bust of a young mustachioed Placido Rizzotto, the labor organizer abducted from Corleone in 1948 and murdered by the local Mafia boss.

For those who care to look, the eighteenth-century Palazzo Pretorio, on a shady side street, houses not only the Corleone public library but also the city's anti-Mafia museum, known as the Centro Internazionale di Documentazione sulle Mafie e del Movimento Antimafia. The low-key museum is a series of rooms containing trial documents and the stunning black-and-white photographs of Mafia hit victims by the Palermo self-taught photojournalist-turnedcouncilwoman and anti-Mafia symbol, Letizia Battaglia. In guided tours of the museum, visitors are told some of the more sensational aspects of modern Italian history now taught in public schools. On my visit I was alone in the place. The guide, a young woman in a red skirt and matching clacking high heels, coolly announced that the 1982 assassination (ordered by Riina) of the newly appointed Mafia-fighting prefect in Palermo, General Carlo Alberto Dalla Chiesa, along with his wife and driver, "was allowed to happen by the corrupt Italian state at the time."

In Corleone I'd expected to find a climate of, if not fear, at least deep suspicion. But I found instead locals who were not shy to talk about their notorious residents. Locals eagerly directed me to the large villa that Riina was in the process of constructing at the edge of town while still a fugitive.

"It had gold toilets!" I was told of Villa Riina. After the removal of the supposed gilded latrines that Riina never had a chance to piss in, the house was first converted to a public school and now serves as a customs office.

Over morning espresso at the Central Bar with Brando's jowly Don Corleone looking down at me, I waited for other patrons to leave before leaning over to the barman and asking in a hushed tone where I might find the sanctuary of Riina the younger—his mother's family house.

The barman, with neither a blink nor showing a need to whisper, directed me to Via Scorsone, a tiny street up the hill. Finding Via Scorsone was not easy. When I did finally find it—directed there by a postman—I understood why: it seemed to be the only street not marked by a cement wall plaque. Via Scorsone also seemed to be Corleone's quietest street; the facing rows of old houses were shuttered, drapes drawn. Though I found the block, I wasn't sure which one of the similar-looking doorways belonged to Riina's wife. Just around the corner I asked a bent, white-haired woman who was sweeping her doorstep where I might find Signora Riina. Before I could even finish the name, she silently turned and disappeared inside her doorway with her eyes trained on the ground.

LIBERA TERRA WAS BORN in the mid-1990s in Corleone when Don Luigi Ciotti, a leftist Mafia-fighting Catholic priest from Turin, began collecting petition signatures for a change in Italian law allowing confiscated Mafia properties to be turned over to social cooperatives. The law was approved in 1996 and the first Libera Terra nonprofit cooperative—named for Placido Rizzotto—was established in 2001 near Corleone. By 2008 it controlled hundreds of acres of wheat as well as nearly seventy acres of vineyards—most of which had been replanted after years of abandonment.

The grain was turned into Libera Terra pasta, and the vineyard harvest, beginning in 2006, was turned to wine marketed under the name Centopassi—a label derived from the film *I Cento Passi* (*The Hundred Steps*, 2000), which tells the story of Giuseppe "Peppino" Impastato, a Mafia-fighting labor organizer and radio broadcaster from Cinisi who was killed in 1978 during his campaign for the local town council. (Impastato's body was tied to railroad tracks and exploded with TNT. The man ultimately convicted in the murder by an Italian court was Gaetano Badalamenti, the Mafia heroin trafficker of the famed "Pizza Connection," who died in a U.S. federal prison in 2004.)

Centopassi produces about 200,000 bottles of wine a year, including a white made from a blend of Catarratto, Grillo, and Chardonnay, a pure Catarratto white, and a red blend of Nero d'Avola and Syrah. To arrive at the heart of Libera Terra, I drove about a half hour northwest of Corleone to San Giuseppe Jato, a town fractionally smaller than Corleone and surrounded by the leafy green vineyards of the Jato Valley.

I found the Placido Rizzotto cooperative headquarters above a gas station at the edge of San Giuseppe. The strip of functional offices felt more like a student newspaper than an agricultural cooperative: most everyone was under thirty, wore T-shirts and sandals, and shared desks in rooms papered with anti-Mafia wall posters and slogans.

At twenty-six years old, Francesco Galiante, the son of a Palermo physician, had worked for Sicily's anti-Mafia movement since his graduation from the University of Palermo—first as a volunteer for a group called Addiopizzo and now for Libera Terra's Placido Rizzotto cooperative, where, owing to his degree in journalism, he served as a communications officer.

Francesco's mission over the next couple of days was to show me the ex-Mafia lands around Corleone. From the moment we shook hands I noticed he had the earnest, pragmatic air of a man at least twice his age—not so much as idealistic as he was determined. We met at lunchtime and the two of us walked to a local panini shop. There would be no hedonistic meals or even home-cooked pasta here in the belly of Sicily's most significant social movement. The *panineria* catered to bare-armed construction and field workers who were sweaty from a morning's labor in the sun. We ordered at a long deli-style counter, pointing to the ingredients we wanted stuffed into our sandwiches before they were grilled. The thought of some of the combinations made me queasy: pork and vegetable salads, mushrooms, ham, beef, cheeses, squid, shrimp, and a selection of mashed and camouflaged meat products I couldn't begin to identify. Then we sat at a plastic table on the terrace overlooking a street crammed with parked trucks and small cars. Francesco—a pair of dark sunglasses propped in close-cropped light hair—ate slowly, chewing deliberately.

"The idea of the project here is to create opportunities. The more opportunities you create, the more you create lawful work," Francesco began. "It's defeating the Mafia through real work."

"It is important to show," he said, "that legal work can work even in these lands."

I wasn't sure if it was a poetic flourish or the result of his translating literally from Italian, but whenever Francesco spoke of the Sicilian countryside he ended his sentence with the same two words: "these lands."

"The first year it was difficult to get people to work in these lands," Francesco continued. Three local Libera Terra cooperatives now employed forty full-time staff and also used volunteers and seasonal workers. Their success had led to a reverse problem—too many applications (more than one hundred for every job opening).

"When you work illegally in agriculture, you get 40 euros (about $62 at the time) a day," he said. "Here, you get 60 euros a day, plus health and pension benefits."

Certainly that was a social victory. But I was interested in something more personal. Sicilians can have a profound attachment to their land—but what about the Mafia? How did people like Riina and his murderous associates view "these lands"? Why would someone trafficking infinitely more profitable heroin bother with wine? Could a megalomaniac mafioso appreciate *terroir*?

"The Mafia has a completely different vision of the land," Francesco said. "They like to possess land to show power. They of course don't want to *work* the land . . . the Mafia economy is not in the fields, not in the villages. Not in Corleone. By the 1970s it was in the cities. So what is left is prestige—to *own these lands*."

Surely, showing off real estate is not a vanity limited to the criminal class. In the United States there are hundreds of municipalities that exist solely for this purpose. Yet to me there is no more important distinction in the wine world than between those who view land as a possession or a factory and those who care for it intimately.

We finished lunch, and I went up to the bar to get a pair of espressos as thick as motor oil. I asked Francesco if he thought the attachment that many Sicilians have for their land had evolved into anti-Mafia passion among his generation.

"First of all, it is not a passion," he corrected, stirring a sugar cube into the muddy liquid with a small spoon. "No. A need. I can't say it's a passion because so much of what we do is not exciting. A need because we have five thousand mafiosi in Sicily who cause problems for five million people. But the five million let it happen!"

WE DROVE SOUTH TOWARD San Cipriello and turned up a washed-out road, arriving at a construction site surrounded by vineyards: the winery being built by Libera Terra–Placido Rizzotto for the 2008 vintage that would be picked at the end of summer. (The first two vintages were produced at a local wine cooperative.) The unfinished shell resembled an airplane hangar—with modern steel exposed beams and an earth-colored steel roof, rounded like a barrel to match the flow of the rolling hills. A few workers, arms shining with sweat in the afternoon sun, were finishing the exterior masonry. They looked suspiciously at us two strangers coming toward them, until Francesco called out and introduced himself.

We walked up a slope of brown clay soil filled with rows of young vines exploding with head-high foliage and trained to wires between wooden chestnut posts.

"Cabernet Sauvignon," Francesco announced blankly. When I showed my surprise that a French-International grape was being showcased at a new consciousness-raising winery in northwestern Sicily, Francesco shrugged. He said he knew that the selection of Cabernet (the recommendation of one of Libera Terra's consulting oenologists in the first days of the cooperative) was a poor symbolic choice in "these lands" so charged with symbolism. What did Cabernet have to do with Sicily? Perhaps the leaders of the cooperative had been too busy focusing on other things to worry about the meanings and provenance of the grapes they were planting.

The symbolism on which the group had focused was choosing to put its new winery on land seized from the Brusca clan, for whom Dante surely would have created a new inner ring of hell.

Bernardo Brusca, once the capo of San Giuseppe, died in prison in 2000. The most telling achievement of his life was raising his son Giovanni, a Mafia soldier who once said he didn't know how many murders—between one hundred and two hundred—he had committed. It was he who detonated the explosives under the highway that killed Falcone and his wife and bodyguards. One of his more monstrously notorious acts had been to kidnap the eleven-year-old son of an informer and send his father pictures of the boy's torture over more than two years before he finally ordered his young victim strangled and his body dissolved in acid. After his arrest in 1996, Giovanni Brusca became a *pentito* or state's witness, living in a secret place—though it is inconceivable to think of a man having his record actually being repentant.

At the top of the hill, the vines ended and we came upon a plateau of golden-white fields from which wheat had recently been harvested by combines. Here Francesco explained one of the timing problems of Libera Terra cooperatives. After several incidents in which fields were burned by arsonists, Libera Terra is now sure to schedule all its harvests before its neighbors do—the idea being that arson is unlikely to happen when the crops of other locals would be put at risk from a fire's spread. In the heart of Sicily, even Mafia sympathizers have become sensitive to public relations.

I dropped Francesco off in San Giuseppe and took the circuitous country road back to Corleone, stopping at an abandoned winery that was fenced and padlocked. The Cantina Kaggio—once the local wine-producing cooperative owned by the elder Riina and Bernardo Brusca—sits on the Jato Valley floor, an eyesore in an otherwise idyllic Sicilian interior setting.

The Mafia has never been known for its architectural aesthetic. Even here in their own backyard, the characterless concrete gray winery buildings seemed as if they were designed to erase hope. The place had few windows and the aura of a Soviet-era munitions plant.

The asphalt on the grounds was now sprouting weeds, and the paint had almost entirely peeled off the steel outdoor vats that once held wine. A dog sat outside the gate as if waiting for someone to come home and feed him; when I approached, he meekly hobbled up to me and hung his head. From the entry I turned and took in the views of the countryside that were nothing short of dramatic. Across the small road shaded by eucalyptus trees, a flock of sheep grazed in a pasture that climbed up a hill topped by a great phallic boulder pointing the way back to Corleone.

The Placido Rizzotto cooperative had petitioned the government to use this confiscated property for storing vehicles and grain, and a decision was imminent. Still, for more than fifteen years, it had sat in decay—not only a scar on the land but also what Mafia fighters believed was perhaps the region's most potently malevolent symbol.

"People see this big winery and it is abandoned," Francesco had complained to me earlier that day. "And the people say, 'At least when the Mafia had it people worked there. Now the state has it and . . . nothing.'"

THE NEXT MORNING, AFTER BREAKFAST of a *cornetto* and espresso at the Central Bar, I met with Corleone's young mayor, Antonino Iannazzo. A center-right politician elected in 2007, Iannazzo was the latest in a string of local anti-Mafia mayors. Tall, balding, and with a sky blue Lacoste shirt that matched the color of his eyes, Iannazzo looked at least a decade older than his thirty-three years. In his office at city hall with its palatial ceilings and oil paintings was a modern table that held his computer and was piled high with documents.

Iannazzo had the quiet, serious bearing of a family doctor. Yet beneath the calm, patient exterior I sensed there was a man in a hurry. It was understandable: For more than fifteen years, the battle against the Sicilian Mafia appeared to have borne fruit, and a business class was restless for real success, giving the island the feel of an emerging nation. His was a generation of Sicilians at war with inertia and fearful of the return of Sicily's dark days.

"Being mayor of Corleone is more difficult than in any other town," Iannazzo said in Italian. "The presence of Riina and Provenzano still influences the behavior of people here." He was talking about the casual sympathizers and the way in which former Mafia associates were still treated with respect by a population that was hedging its bets—watching and waiting to see what happened.

The mayor himself had been made uneasy by the release of Giuseppe Riina (the younger) from Italian justice into the loving arms of his mother in Corleone a couple of weeks before Easter Sunday.

"He could be the first step for the rehabilitation of the Mafia," Iannazzo said calmly. "He's watched 24/7. He doesn't show off. He's smart. He only goes out with his mother and his sister. And . . . his presence here makes me nervous."

In his battle against unseen forces, Iannazzo had cut through red tape to assign all criminal confiscated properties in Corleone to cooperative associations. His administration had reduced the time for confiscated property to be assigned from an average of seven years in all of Italy to four weeks in Corleone. "The message is to show that twenty-eight days are enough," he said.

What's more, Iannazzo's administration, like others in a handful of traditional mob bastions around Palermo, required all prospective public contractors to sign a no-*pizzo* pledge authorizing an investigation by the Carabinieri in their business dealings. Palermo, the city that had narrowly escaped total destruction by the Mafia, had yet to enact such a policy.

"Ordinary people have to be free to change. That means that when they get a job they don't get it as a favor," the mayor said.

For Corleone to progress, he said, it needed economic development, which meant expanding, modernizing, and diversifying Corleone's biggest sector of activity—agriculture. The mayor—a Nero d'Avola man—was working on creating a town appellation for Corleone with production standards and a common label for Corleone wines, flour, pasta, and other products. At the same time, the mayor was eager to market Corleone's charms to visitors.

"About seven to eight thousand tourists come to visit Corleone every year—about six thousand of them come from the USA. But they stay for a day and no more," the mayor said. "They take a tour around town and look for the Godfather of Corleone, but they don't stay to appreciate our architecture or our hospitality."

Marketing Corleone, of course, would not be easy, the mayor acknowledged. It would require a delicate balancing of imagery. Most anywhere in the world the name Corleone evokes a romantic image of lawlessness, tradition, family values, *omerta*, and the codes of loyalty explored in the *Godfather* films. Restaurants from Morris, Illinois, to Mumbai, India, to Marseille, France, to the Metropolitan Hotel in Dubai cheekily bear the town's name.

"Corleone is a brand," the mayor said reflectively. "But it has to be done carefully. We have to control what kind of brand we want."

As the minutes passed that Friday morning, Iannazzo's electronic devices—his computer, his desk phone, and his cell phone—all seemed to be making noises calling his attention to the mortal enemy that never rested: the inexorable passage of time.

I MET FRANCESCO AT CITY hall and followed him as he drove back toward San Giuseppe, turning up a dirt track to a vineyard of more than twelve acres of Catarratto vines. Planted in light, sandy soil on a well-exposed slope at an elevation of about 1,300 feet, the vines were being tied up on shoulder-high guiding wires by a half-dozen cooperative members, day workers, and volunteers.

What made this Catarratto vineyard different from Placido Rizzotto's others was its age; it was planted more than twenty years earlier. Catarratto is Sicily's most common wine grape; it thrives in the Sicilian heat and, on the best high-altitude *terroirs,* produces some of the island's finest floral-scented white wines. The vineyard once belonged to Salvatore Genovese, who succeeded Bernardo Brusca as San Giuseppe's crime boss. Genovese was arrested in 2000, but because the vineyard was quickly turned over to the cooperative, it survived whole, without falling into abandon and having to be replanted.

Francesco and I and a worker named Angelo—dark, lean, and wearing a pair of what I assumed were counterfeit Ray-Ban aviator glasses—walked to the top of the rise on the hill. A wind blew from the south, and Angelo pointed out another slope of a facing vineyard, still owned by the Genovese family and looking neglected: there were spaces in the rows where vines had died off, and tall grasses were crowding the soil. This branch of the local Mafia did indeed seem on its heels.

I again followed Francesco as he drove along twisting country roads that every once in a while seemed to run out of asphalt and turn to dirt, as though chunks of the route had been embezzled. We drove along cliff sides past rock outcroppings stained the color of rust, through parched hills dotted with the purple thistle flowers that seemed to thrive in the roadside dust.

We stopped in a rugged mountainous area known as Portella Ginestra a few miles east of San Giuseppe. Here the co-op runs a small, quaint bed-and-breakfast and organic restaurant in what had been the dilapidated eighteenth-century farmhouse belonging to Bernardo Brusca. On the hillside above the *agriturismo,* the cooperative created a small horse farm named for Giuseppe Di Matteo, the young boy who had been kidnapped, tortured, and killed by Brusca the younger.

It was a hot day at the beginning of summer, and I saw no signs of guests at the inn or takers in the restaurant. No one was selling postcards or T-shirts of Marlon Brando up front. There were no signs beckoning motorists to sleep in the bed of a real Godfather. There was just a big sky and a landscape as vast and empty as the backdrop of a spaghetti western.

Up at the horse farm I spoke with agronomist Antonio Castro, whose family came from Corleone and who was one of the founders of the Placido Rizzotto cooperative. At thirty-five, with flowing dark hair, deep brown eyes, and a beard covering hollow cheeks, Castor looked like a Mediterranean cliché of Jesus.

"The Mafia isn't finished—it's just changed," Castro stated somberly. What he had to say was something I'd heard universally from the anti-Mafia movement and others including Mayor Iannazzo. The twenty-first-century Mafia was globalized, embedded in government and finance far beyond Sicily's shores in northern Europe and America. "*Pizzo* is just a way to help the families of the people in jail," Castro shrugged. "Before, the Mafia controlled the politicians, the state . . . now they are politicians."

Castro spoke in a way that convinced you he was more prophetic than crazy. Of course, it was difficult to name names and point fingers, because this new Mafia was invisible. At the beginning of summer 2008, the suggestion of a scenario in which the Mafia was manipulating world finance and institutions sounded far-fetched—a potential Hollywood thriller plot. By the end of the year, as global markets collapsed amid audacious financial scams that probably made the remaining *Corleonesi* jealous, it all seemed plausible.

What concerned me, however, was that for a group so clear about its social mission, Libera Terra seemed a bit lost when it came to a vision for wine. I mentioned this to Castro, who shrugged when I brought up the Cabernet planted in the flagship. When I asked him about the future of the local liberated wine, Castro didn't hesitate.

"Catarratto," he answered. "I hope we'll be planting more of it . . . in high places it is like Chardonnay."

Centopassi does not make fine boutique wines. The wines are made

for popular consumption at popular prices and distributed throughout Italy by the Coop supermarket chain. Later that evening—my
last in Corleone—I bought a couple of bottles of Centopassi, and at
dinner at my hotel I shared them with the couple who ran the place.
We agreed that the Catarratto—a light, floral wine with a dab of
butteriness—was the most drinkable wine of the 2007 vintage. The
Nero d'Avola–based red, in contrast, was flat and flabby—a wine that
didn't yet match the high-minded ideals of this movement.

BEFORE I HAD RETURNED to Corleone, Francesco and I drove through
San Giuseppe, where we met a bright-eyed young man in his twenties
named Gabriele who had come from *Addiopizzo* in Palermo. We ate
lunch at the same panini place as the day before and opened a bottle
of chilled Centopassi white, which we drank on the terrace with a
view of the neighbor's drying laundry. Given the context—drinking
from plastic cups with our sandwiches—it was not bad.

I listened as these two sons of Palermo who grew up amid the
anti-Mafia fervor of the 1990s talked about the "new Mafia." *Pizzo*,
Francesco said, amounted to only 5 percent of Mafia income, but
he said it remained just one more important symbol. "It's through
extortion that the Mafia qualifies itself as a state," he said.

We spoke of Vincenzo Conticello at the focacceria as well as Conticello's *Carabinieri* guards. Was Conticello's life in danger, the two
wondered aloud, or were the *Carabinieri* also some sort of dramatic
symbol? To hear these two young men talk, modern-day Mafia wars
weren't being fought with bullets, but images. Like political parties. I
tried to ponder it all but my American mind didn't like the nagging,
murky uncertainties. Was Italy fighting the Mafia as it exists today?
Or was it fighting the shadow of a former enemy?

"It's not the old Mafia anymore," said Gabriele, the picture of
youth that is honest and wide-eyed, and that in Sicily also has a
tremendous capacity for processing ambiguity. "There's no blood
in the new Mafia . . . it's *Godfather Part III*."

9

Due Donne

THE GLOBAL POSITIONING SYSTEM, OR GPS, was one of the U.S. Defense Department's more creative inventions of the latter twentieth century. In its practical application as portable satellite navigation system, GPS has become a modern-day miracle, delivering automotive travelers from Point A to Point B without having to decipher roadmaps or ask for directions.

GPS works almost anywhere in the world—except, it seems, on the surreal roads of southeastern Sicily where there are few fixed points. Roads that appear in global mapping systems—that may have been paid for with state funds—sometimes dead-end in a field of trash in the middle of nowhere. Or they simply do not exist.

In Ragusa Ibla, the historic Baroque town rebuilt on its medieval grid after the earthquake leveled the towns of the Val di Noto, GPS tried to lead me through walls and down staircases at the end of streets exactly the width of a Fiat Panda (with its side-view mirrors tucked in) plus one inch. It was as if GPS mapping were looking for some pre-earthquake street configuration—understandable except for the fact that the earthquake occurred in 1693!

I'd driven to Ragusa from Catania in early September. The

landscape, which in early spring had looked as green as the Scottish highlands, was now parched—the grayish brown of cardboard left out in the summer sun. Everywhere, I noticed patches of land burned by fire. The tall thistle flowers that had painted the June countryside with explosive strokes of pale purple were now corpses along the roadside littered with a season's worth of trash.

After spending the night in Ragusa Ibla, I continued on the road to Vittoria. On my first trip to this area (back in January when I visited cos), I got helplessly lost in the maze of provincial roads and traffic roundabouts with signs that seemed to lead everywhere and nowhere. I did not fare much better with the help of precision satellite guidance. What should have been a forty-minute drive stretched more than two hours on roads that seemed to lead me in circles. It was as if the forces of nature in the countryside around Vittoria had conspired to confuse outsiders and keep their secrets hidden.

If those forces took human form, I imagined they would approximately recreate Arianna Occhipinti, whose family farm sits on a gently sloping hillside in a *contrada* called Fossa del Lupo ("wolf's ditch"). At twenty-six, Arianna, the cousin of Giusto Occhipinti of cos, was a reed of a woman with dark hair that flowed to the middle of her back, black Byzantine eyes, and the intense, concentrated look of a girl who has been up at night experimenting with alchemy.

As I pulled up to the farm, Arianna appeared, wearing a striped golf shirt, khakis, and black flip-flops. A pair of thick-rimmed eyeglasses sat on top of her head, and at her side was a large, friendly white Labrador retriever, Paco. I was struck by how small she seemed—easier to picture her running around in her silver convertible Miata parked in the dirt drive than aboard a tractor or working her biceps in the winery. But Arianna does everything on about seventeen acres of vineyards with the help of two full-time employees and several seasonal workers.

That day a scirocco blew from the south, packing the heat of North Africa with the humidity picked up on its voyage across the Mediterranean. By late morning the temperature climbed to 100°F and the air felt molten. Arianna led me below the farm to a sloping vineyard where she cultivates Frappato and Nero d'Avola. Up to this point, Arianna has refused to mix the two varietals. She made a wine of 100 percent Frappato, of which she said, "I wanted to make a Frappato that was elegant and *grande* because it is the most feminine grape in Sicily." She also made a pure Nero d'Avola, arguably the most masculine. She had only recently experimented with the idea of combining the two into a classic Cerasuolo di Vittoria.

The Frappato was growing along steel cordon wires—small violet bunches of no more than a half dozen per plant and no bigger than a toddler's fist. The Nero d'Avola stood upright in *alberello* goblets supported by wood posts. As we walked through a stand of Frappato, the vine leaves looked droopy and burned around the edges, and they were brittle to the touch.

In just about every way—aside from their shared Sicilian-ness—Arianna is a foil to the old sage of modern Sicilian winemaking, Diego Planeta, and just as firm in her convictions. "In Sicily it is stupid *not to* do *biologico* [organic]," Arianna said. Unlike the Planetas and a few other large-scale producers, she doesn't ever irrigate her vines. On this day a soaker hose was dripping water at the edge of the vineyard, not for the vines, Arianna insisted, but for the grasses and wildflowers she encourages for biodiversity and to attract insects.

Arianna's methods were not unique in the wine world. If anything, they were part of a trend practiced by increasing numbers of winemakers from Italy to France to California. Arianna was on the verge of becoming something of a winemaking star among the alternative wine set in New York and San Francisco. What was unusual about her was what she represented in Sicily—a young woman who had chosen to stay on the land of her ancestors and challenge the thinking of the *contadini* of her grandparents' generation.

As we walked through the vines, I looked down and noticed that my shoes had dug holes in the earth and were covered with fine sand. Arianna's narrow feet, which seemed to glide across the soil in her flip-flops, somehow remained unsoiled.

Growing up around Vittoria, Arianna became taken with wine in her teens, working the harvests and hanging around at cos. After high school she studied oenology in Milan, earning her degree in 2004. As a graduation present her father gave her a couple of acres of vines to test her skills.

The Italian oenology curriculum—like most modern oenology —deals mostly with the chemistry and technology of correcting wine defects in the winery. Yet from the start of her winemaking, Arianna was bent on throwing the oenology books out the window. "This is my idea of wine: a natural wine where you squeeze the fruit, let it ferment, and *basta*," Arianna told me confidently.

While her first vintage of about 1,500 liters was still in barrels, Arianna met a representative from Velier, the Genoa-based wine importer and distribution company that in 2003 had committed itself to representing natural wines. Struck by her sincerity and focus, the company launched her career.

We walked back up the hill to the small, barnlike building where Arianna makes her wines—now almost 30,000 heavy Burgundy-style bottles per year with their corks sealed with wax. In her simple laboratory—air-conditioned against the heat—Arianna ferments her wines in steel or plastic vats. She uses no other extraction technique than gently pushing down on the cap of skins and seeds that forms during fermentation and leaving those solids to macerate with wine for extra-long periods of forty days to some months.

After pressing in a 1970s wood pneumatic press, her wines are left to be raised in traditional large *botti* or smaller Bordeaux *barriques* for twelve months. Her experiments have included making a blend using half of her Frappato and half of Frank Cornelissen's Nero Mascalese from Etna, and putting the mixture in 300 magnums called 1708 (she and Frank share an August 17 birthday) that they gave away to friends.

Light streamed in through a window as Arianna withdrew one of many samples from the barrels and stainless tanks, pouring them into tall, oversized glasses. Her Frappato wines were a light ruby color and their "femininity" was not the dainty kind. These weren't simple wines or wallflowers. Their feminine qualities demanded attention with a complex mix of scents like tea tree oil and sandal leather and Neolithic rock.

"I don't know if I can say, 'My wine is the best wine,' but I can say it's the wine of here—this territory," Arianna said. "The old people here they tell me, 'Ari, this is like the wine of forty years ago.'"

Critiques like that satisfy her. Across a patch of soft, deep, green and well-watered grass was the Occhipintis' sprawling farmhouse made from an old *palmento* that was abandoned nearly half a century earlier and renovated by Arianna's father, Bruno, an architect like his younger brother, Giusto, at cos. The farm serves as the family's summer house outside Vittoria. Arianna, who lives here fulltime, noted that there are advantages in having the family around. Typical of her generation of Italian women, she seems to appreciate traditional roles when it's her parents in them.

"Mamma does the cooking," Arianna grinned. As we entered the main room of the *palmento* through an open door, I smelled herbs and game and edible combinations that made me glad that, for that moment in Italy, some women still chose to be Mamma.

One open room served as living room and dining room, with its tall beamed ceilings resting on limestone rock walls, polished terrazzo floors, and a pair of red fabric couches around a fireplace. But the back half of the room, where Arianna's cat lounged in a wine box, was left primitive—the heart of the old *palmento* with a pressing area and four large, rectangular openings in the floor that drop a good eight feet. These old vats that once held thousands of gallons of red wine were now unprotected—a hazard, I imagined, for an errant guest who backed away from the table, after too much Frappato.

We sat at the family dining table and Arianna poured some of her bottled vintages. The Nero d'Avolas were surprisingly red in color, muted compared with other supercharged deep black versions.

"I don't have to do anything to make elegant wines. Most of the wines in Sicily are pumped up," Arianna said, listing the sins of modern oenology: selected yeasts, oxygenations, added chemicals, added tannins, acidification. To illustrate the doctoring of wine, as undoubtedly practiced by many of her classmates, she turned her thumbs toward her glass and pumped her hands up and down as if making a cocktail.

"I didn't start to make wine to make it for the *mercato*. I wanted to make a wine that was *buono*." She rolled her hair up into a bun and clipped it in place with a black plastic hairclip that had been dangling from a belt loop. "The problem with modern oenology is it makes wine to please people right away. It makes wines that have a big perfume that please people in a restaurant and then ten minutes or an hour later or even the next day . . . it's over."

"If I was a producer who had to produce a million bottles, I would have to force nature, but for small producers it is stupid," she said, turning petulant. "For me I don't like that wine is the product of industrial processes. I hate this!"

There was something so entirely childlike and unselfconscious about Arianna as she talked that it was captivating: her hands flew in the air or tugged at her hair, her feet hooked around the legs of the chair or tucked beneath her on the wood seat. Every once in a while she would saunter off and show affection to a family pet. When I asked Arianna about being a woman winemaker in Sicily, she was curled up, hugging her knees in a fetal position.

"Working in the vines was a man's work," she said as she rocked back and forth. "In Sicily, the work of women was to crush the grapes with their feet."

As we spoke, Arianna noted, an Italian association of women wine and restaurant professionals known as Le Donne del Vino was marking its twentieth anniversary in Milan. Arianna defiantly mocked the idea, saying she had received many requests to join. "When they make an association for men in wine, I will join the association for women!"

So far her struggles have not been with the media, the market, or the residents of Milan, London, or other urban centers. Her difficulties have been with farmers in her neighborhood.

"I contract with two *contadini* who help me prune the vineyards in January. The first year after one hour they were at the end of the row and I was still way behind. One of them called out to me, 'Hey what are you doing, taking a picture of every plant?'"

"Then later he said to me in a Sicilian dialect: 'Listen, my son went north to work and he is a man. And you who are female, what do you want to do, stay here and work in the countryside of Sicily?! Go north and you will have some hope!' These men were seventy-five years old, and to them the idea of me making wine was something that was not possible."

Making matters worse was Arianna's fundamental disagreement about nature and how her vines should be worked. Unlike most growers in Vittoria, Arianna lets weeds and grasses grow in her vineyards, and she doesn't till her soil until late spring. In the arid climate of Sicily, where anything other than vines in the vineyards is seen as impermissible competition, Arianna's "green" methods were viewed as heresy. "I think in Sicily, people work the vineyards too much," Arianna said. "For most of them, green things growing in your vines are like monsters!"

Arianna—arguing that the roots of non-irrigated vines descend six yards or more into the earth in search of water—told the *contadini* it was ridiculous to obsess about superficial weed growth. She works the land three times in late spring and summer—not with a plough but with a scarifier that cuts rather than turning the top layer of soil and eliminates evaporation galleries.

"In spring I like the flowers in the vines," she said. "It's good for my eyes and it's good for the vineyards. The insects, the bees help the pollination."

"I think that men are not part of nature at certain moments," Arianna offered, and by men, I took it she meant my gender as opposed to the generic "mankind."

"Sometimes the other growers come here and they tell me what I need to do," she said, amused, flashing a row of white teeth. She removed the clip from her hair and let it fall down her back. Holding the hairclip, she then waved it as if scolding. "They come in February and say, 'You must go out and work—look at all the grasses in your vines . . .'

"Now they know I work in a different way. And the most important thing is the grape, and if the grape is good the grape is good. And they see my grapes are good.

"The nature is happy because you are giving it more expression. In my wine I like that you can find the expression of nature, the spring and the winter, in every vintage." Arianna was again hugging her knees. "I accompany the vineyards, but I don't want to *control* nature."

Controlling nature—the statement bristled with overtones of earth-hugging manifesto. I asked the obvious question for which I already knew the answer.

Did she think *men* try to control nature?

Arianna let out a spontaneous eruption of laughter so hearty that it kicked off one of her flip-flops, which fell and smacked the floor.

"Yes, in agriculture, I do."

Arianna's mother, Rosa Aura, a light-haired, roundish, smiling woman in a linen dress, collected herbs from the garden, spread out a white table cloth and set it with the halfhearted help of Arianna's elder sister, Fausta, who was staying with the family while preparing to go to Paris to work on her master's thesis in landscape architecture. Arianna's father, Bruno, a compact man with a floppy moustache and skin tanned the deep color of espresso, arrived and kissed the women. Arianna selected her wines and sat at the head of the table.

What followed was one of the most convincing arguments I have witnessed for keeping Mamma in the kitchen—at least in Sicily. Rosa Aura's creations were something you can't find in restaurants: simple revelations that made the preparations of Sicily's top Michelin-starred (male) chefs seem clumsy and overwrought.

She first brought out a dish of Pesto Ragusana—thick tube pasta coated in a green pesto with dashes of subtle flavors that sang out one after another in a divine chorus. Aside from the usual base of homegrown basil and olive oil, this Ragusa version uses local almonds, raw fresh onion, and lemon rind.

I ate, sipped Arianna's long, earthy Frappato, and felt a warm breeze through the open terrace doors. It was a transcendent moment broken by what seemed the explosion of a hunter's rifle somewhere off in the distance.

I noticed that Rosa Aura was studying me. There was discussion in

Italian about me—who was I and where was I from? After all, I lived in France, claimed to be American, and had a Sicilian name. I explained, in Italian, that I was born on Sicily's westernmost island.

"Pantelleria?" Bruno asked.

No. Manhattan.

I was savoring Rosa Aura's pasta and looked over at Arianna. She barely weighed a hundred pounds but had already cleaned her plate with the gusto of a field hand.

The main course was coiled rounds of rabbit meat with Bronte pistachios. Rosa served with it strings of raw zucchini seasoned with vinegar and sugar. Again, the soaring transcendence of the first few bites was broken by the sound of gunshot.

In fact, Arianna clarified, the sound was not of a rifle but of gas cannons in neighboring vineyards that regularly fired off their blasts to drive off swarms of birds. The mere mention of this device set off a round of animated discussion around the table, for apparently Arianna was thinking of buying her own cannon to place in the vineyards.

"Every two minutes: boom!" Fausta shook her head.

Rosa Aura laughed at the idea of taking such a measure to scare away birds.

"So what if the birds come and pick a few grapes," she said, adding that because it is so dry, even pecked grapes wouldn't contribute to rotting in the vineyards.

Bruno, the family's sole male, looked grave.

"In the 1940s and 1950s this whole area was planted with vines; now there are fewer vines, but the same number of birds. That is the problem!" he said. "And they like to come to the places that are organic and have no chemicals!"

Rosa Aura laughed and shrugged with a *"va bene"* that I interpreted as a "Leave the birds alone."

Sicily is known among birdwatchers as a crossroads of migration between Europe and Africa. The island has more than four hundred species of birds, some of which evidently like Frappato and Nero d'Avola. Earlier, I hadn't noted any more than a few swallows darting above the vineyards.

"When twenty thousand birds arrive at once, it will be a big problem!" Bruno warned, conjuring a picture of Hitchcockian menace.

Rosa Aura smiled, unconvinced. Arianna listened. Her thick eyebrows furrowed. She pondered aloud about the food chain in the vineyards and the birds that feed on the insects.

With a troubled look, she explained, "Last week I called the store to ask about buying the machine that goes *boom*. It cost 250 euros. I was going to buy it but . . . I don't know."

"I don't want to listen to that noise all the time!" Fausta erupted as she carried dishes to the kitchen.

Arianna sneered at her older sister's outburst. She explained that this year she would lose 10 percent of her crop to birds. And she was obviously caught between her heartfelt desire to let nature express itself and the male impulses she so disliked.

"I should use it," she said, "Really, you only have to use it twenty days a year when the grapes are at their ripest . . ."

"*Venti giorni!*" ("Twenty days!") Fausta cried, mocking as she marched heavily across the room. She went through the open door, sat in a lounge chair, and lit a cigarette in the shade of a parasol. She called back through the open door: "Twenty days—all July, August, and September! Twenty days!"

Arianna glared at her sister as though she could be conjuring a hex. She found the family cat, Patti, in her wine box and spoke to her softly. Then she ran outside and tackled Paco the Labrador. Fausta had disappeared, leaving her sister to contemplate her first unwelcome conflict with nature and her ambivalent desire to—perhaps just once—control its forces.

THAT NIGHT I STAYED IN Noto, with its impressive inventory of Baroque palaces that radiated 90° of heat even hours after dark, as swallows darted overhead. The following morning I set out for nearby Ispica and got caught in another GPS no-man's-land (landing in a mass of sheep and goats on a backroad that dead-ended in a field of weeds) before arriving at Azienda Curto.

This southeastern tip of Sicily—torrid, windy, and dotted with ancient ruins—juts between the Mediterranean and Ionian seas. It is one of the sunniest parts of Europe and the home of Nero d'Avola ("the black of Avola," a reference to the nearby town on the Ionian coast), Sicily's best-known, and most potent, red wine grape.

The Curto family has one thousand years of history as overseers of feudal lands, or *latifundi*. The family now controls some 500 acres, more than seventy of which are planted with vines. The rest are mostly olives, wheat, citrus, carob, and almonds. The Curtos claim winemaking roots that go back to the seventeenth century, but wine wasn't taken very seriously until the last years of the twentieth century, when this family's sole heir, Francesca, came of age.

The Azienda sits atop a limestone-rich dusty hillside covered with drywall terraces, olive and citrus groves, stands of carob trees, and stone burial chambers that date to the fifth century BC. At the top of the hill is a faded, sprawling eighteenth-century Baroque villa—with a family crest and cracked, peeling shutters—that hasn't been lived in for a hundred years.

The Azienda looks over gentle hills and a plain that slopes to the two distant seas, which—this day in the heat of the continuing Scirocco—were smeared by haze. The grounds of the villa are evocative in their barrenness: the occasional bougainvillea, rose, or caper plant sprouting magnificently from earth that looks as white, dry, hard, and barren as old mortar. At the western edge of the villa is a simple modern winery crammed into what were once the carriage stalls and chapel of this farm complex; at the bottom of a set of rough limestone stairs is another outbuilding that holds an air-conditioned barrel room for raising wines.

Francesca Curto appeared at the top of the stairs, in a blaze of confident Italian womanhood. She wore a black rhinestone tank top announcing the Pink Panther fortieth anniversary, with black knee-length shorts, and she balanced atop a pair of high gold-trimmed wedge sandals. Her hair was black and coiffed to straight perfection, a pair of oversized violet sunglasses rested on top of her head, and in her right hand she carried the gadget of the time—an iPhone in a pink case.

Her smile was warm and full. After spending a day with the ethereal nature child Arianna, I couldn't help but notice little details. Francesca wore lipstick. At thirty-six she was now a decade older than Arianna, and she was fleshier—part of the new generation of Italian working mammas you see chatting on their *telefonini* as they wait to pick their kids up from kindergarten.

By midmorning the heat felt like noon. Francesca led the way into the shade of the Curto tasting room, an old grain storage building that had been painted white. There were long tables inside standing on worn stone floors. In this corner of Sicily the harvest was now on, weeks ahead of Vittoria. Francesca's hands were not wine stained. Though she wasn't wearing nail polish, she was certainly one of the most put-together winemakers I had seen at harvest time. Which led me to ask how hands-on she was in Curto's winemaking.

"No, I don't drive the tractor," she smiled—earthy, ironic. "I am not Arianna!"

Francesca, a mother of two infant daughters who is married to a local dentist, runs and oversees the family's wine operations, which consist of the production of about 75,000 bottles per year—nearly two-thirds of which is exported to outside Italy. Her father, a retired judge, and her mother, a retired schoolteacher, run the business of the rest of the farm. Francesca had once gone away to law school but quit to return here to help her parents' business, organizing work crews and assisting with administration.

"I knew my place was here," she said. "At the end of the '90s I said to my father, 'Why don't we try to commercialize the wines?' My father made a good wine, but it was just to drink with friends and the family. I thought with modern techniques we could make a really great wine."

In 1997 Francesca went off to learn about winemaking by visiting a pair of Saint-Émilion châteaux over a period of months and put together her plan for the winery back home. She said she chose Saint-Émilion because the highly calcareous soils of the appellation are similar to southeastern Sicily. The following year, Curto launched its first commercial vintage.

Nero d'Avola was traditionally used to make deep-colored syrupy wines of up to 18 percent alcohol to fortify vintages from northern Italy and France. In recent decades, Sicilian winemakers have cultivated Nero d'Avola—often compared with Syrah—for single-varietal wines that vary wildly in quality and character.

Francesca flexed a muscle with her tanned right arm and said, "There is a lot of *muscoloso* (muscular) Nero d'Avola . . . I don't want to make wine that is *muscoloso*. I want to make wine that is classic and elegant."

The Curtos do not irrigate their vineyards or use herbicides. To make a classic Nero d'Avola—to, as she puts it, "exalt Nero d'Avola" —she uses the two most basic technologies that have transformed Sicilian winemaking. The first and most important is air-conditioning systems that allow for cooler fermentation of potentially "hot" wines. By fermenting at cooler temperatures, wines preserve aromas and finesse without being overwhelmed by the power of the fruit.

The second bit of technology that Francesca insists on is selected Sicilian yeasts. And for this reason: *"Sardine,"* she said. There was no mistaking the meaning; it's the same word in English: sardines. But what sardines was she talking about? "The typical smell of Nero d'Avola from Eloro," she said, "is sardines . . . a little bit."

I was still confused. Wine? Smelling like fish?

"You will see at first in the beginning before you oxygenate the wine, you just put it to your nose and it smells like salty sardines . . . then it goes away," she said. "And the wild yeasts from here are too wild—they really give the smell of sardines, they make the wine too salty, too acidic. And I am a woman, I don't like this, so I use selected yeasts."

She picked up a stray piece of paper and fanned her neck. "We use a little cold, a little yeast, *basta.*"

Throughout the morning, Francesca's iPhone blipped messages at her. Occasionally she would look at the screen and fiddle with the touch pad. Once she showed family photos of her husband and daughters, ages four months and sixteen months. She is of a generation in Italy that sees the *telefonino* as an extension of self. But when it comes to wine, Francesca was dubious about too much technology.

"You know, oenology can do everything now, but to me it's like a woman who redoes everything with plastic surgery. Yes, she is perfect, but she is no more. She is finished."

The Curtos' winery makes four wines with Nero d'Avola—a rosé, a New Worldish Merlot blend called Ikano, and two reds. The most interesting is called Curto Fontanelle, from the Eloro appellation that covers the southeastern tip of Sicily. The wine is made from low-yielding vines (about a pound of grapes for each) planted in the 1960s in a single Contrada of Pachino known as Fontanelle. The wine is fermented in stainless steel, raised in a mixture of new and used French *barriques*, and later aged a year in bottles before release.

After tasting our way through Curto's other wines, Francesca poured glasses of Fontanelle 2004. One of the first things that struck me about the wine was the color. Like Arianna's, it was red—in this case, ruby, rather than the color of the ink that fills this page.

Before I could touch the glass, Curto had me lean my head toward it and smell it, while she did the same with her glass.

"Do you smell the *sardine*?" She looked at me curiously.

I snorted deeply, detecting a vague smell of sea water, and for an instant I could have sworn I was smelling . . . anchovies. Close enough, I suppose. But, frankly, I can't honestly say that I would have detected any sea life if Francesca not been there, smiling and repeating "*sardine . . . sardine . . .*"

(In the months that followed I was dogged by this *sardine* question. Eventually, I phoned another Ispica producer, Massimo Padova, who with his wife, Marianta, runs a small organic winery, Riofavara, which makes my favorite Nero d'Avola wine in all of Sicily called Sciavé. Massimo, who uses ambient or Eloro selected yeasts depending on the vintage, said that off odors in Nero d'Avola typically come from high-production vineyards and not the traditional vines like those in Fontanelle. When I mentioned "*sardine*," he shot back with "*acciuga!*" ["anchovy!"] and insisted that the fish odors came not from wild yeasts but from a reaction of Nero d'Avola with older wood containers.)

I picked up the glass and swirled it, letting the fish odor swim away. I smelled again and tasted a wine that was complex and long in the mouth and seemed to bear marks of the fruit from the carob trees down the road.

I started to offer my opinion to Francesca—to tell her that she should dump all her other more-or-less forgettable wines and make only this wine. But I was interrupted by a dove that flew in through the tall open doors and flapped around in the tall wood rafters.

Francesca watched the bird for awhile, then returned to the subject of Nero d'Avola and its odd position. Like most anywhere in Sicily and much of Italy, any official efforts to organize ended in the Italian specialty known as confusion. And so it is with Italian wine appellations. Here the local Nero d'Avola was labeled DOC Eloro—prized by wine merchants familiar with it, but obscure to most of the rest of the world.

"Most of the Nero d'Avola now is made as IGT—Sicilia [Indicazione Geografica Tipica—designating regional wine]. It can be anything! It can sell for one euro. They put Nero d'Avola IGT Sicilia on bottles in Trieste [in northeastern Italy] and the wine is terrible!"

At one point Francesca's friend Sabina joined us. The two women tried with no luck using animated Italian to direct the dove out the high open window. Minutes later the dove found the window on its own. Not long after that, another dove—or perhaps the same one—flew in and flapped around in the rafters.

I was curious about Francesca's experience as a woman in wine, having come of age a decade earlier than Arianna. In the corner, where she had taped up press articles about the winery, there was a wall poster from Le Donne del Vino, to which Francesca belonged.

As a woman winemaker, Francesca said, "It's easier in the beginning because you are a woman, so people are nice, but then it's harder to show you have value. You have to show that you are not just an image.

"In the beginning, almost ten years ago, I would go to the trade fairs and people thought I was a hostess. I was so angry I was not being recognized!"

Le Donne del Vino "is good for organizing events together but not when they do these promotions that say . . ."—here Francesca mocked an Italian fashion model pose, throwing her head back and letting her black hair fly—"*I am woman. I am beautiful. I make wine.*"

"Sometimes for a promotion they say, 'Okay, everyone wear skirts.' I hate these things!" Francesca rolled her eyes. Not the cynical eye rolling of an American, but a roll of the eyes that used her whole head and body and nearly sent the sunglasses flying off the top of her head. "Yes, I have high-heeled shoes!" she announced. "But I wear them because I want to wear them, not because I must. I hate that!"

Before noon, Francesca's father, Giambattista, arrived. A dapper man, he was then sixty-six, with linen pants, a rolled-up blue cotton shirt, and a straw short-brimmed hat covering his nearly bald crown. He had, I noticed, the same quick and all-consuming smile as his daughter and looked like a man who was not afraid of women but had been well fed and well loved by them.

We were going to lunch, but before we left, Francesca greeted the first of the harvest loads that were coming to the winery. The weathered truck parked out in the sun behind the winery. Cases were manually unloaded by one grape-stained worker and placed on a rolling belt of a sorting table where leaves, other debris, and bad bunches were removed by another man. The clusters were fed through a destemming machine and a crusher, and then the mash was sucked by a tube thicker than a fire hose through a hole in the wall inside the winery and into steel fermenting vats. Francesca bounded up onto a platform where the sorting table was balanced—her high sandals no impediment—and she randomly picked a few grapes and tasted from the 2008 vintage that was likely to make wines more *muscoloso* than usual.

On the way to lunch I rode with Giambattista in his sedan, and Francesca and Sabina followed in her smaller two-door. On the way, we stopped in a vineyard where Francesca looked at the morning's work and conferred with her harvest foreman. We ate in the small, evocative Mediterranean fishing port of Marzamemi (from the Arab *Marsà al hamen* or "harbor of the turtle doves," for the large spring dove migration). In Marzamemi, the old small blocks of Arab fishermen's houses (some now restaurants) are gathered around a central piazza that ends a few steps from a limpid harbor. The plaza was lit by a blazing white sun, and the restaurant tables were empty. Inside the Taverna La Cialoma we found locals packed in like sardines trying to take advantage of the small air conditioner, which was struggling to keep up with a kitchen turning out Pesto Ragusana and fresh grilled fish drizzled in olive oil.

After lunch we drove through Pachino and the vineyards of Fontanelle, where we walked among low, twisted, untrained vines shaped by the wind into forms that Francesca called "chicken feet." We tasted the blue-black, nearly ripe-for-picking grapes and crunched on the seeds.

"They are still a couple of weeks away," Francesca announced.

There were starlings and crows above, and I asked Francesca about the birds. She shrugged. Birds were not a problem. I thought of Vittoria and Arianna's father's dire warnings. They were perhaps thirty miles away as a crow or any number of species might fly, but for some reason birds preferred to swarm in Vittoria to feed.

Was it some migration habit? Some particularity of the land? A preference for Frappato or the Nero d'Avola of Vittoria? Or perhaps an aversion to "sardine"? Giambattista, reaching for science, said something about the tomato growing in Vittoria attracting birds.

The soil was deep-brown soft clay; Francesca marched through it with little concern in those high gold stomping sandals of hers. We walked through a vineyard to an old *palmento*—its roof sunken in and the structure invaded by a giant prickly pear cactus ready to give its fruit.

Every hundred yards, on a slope that rolled down to the sea, there seemed to be another tiny *palmento*—once the presses of sharecroppers—now abandoned. I watched Francesca march so naturally through the dirt; you could tell she had grown up running through these fields. It was land that once had been abandoned by so many sons of Sicily, and was now being cultivated again by its granddaughters.

10

The Jet Set

I FOLLOWED THE WINDS NORTH to Etna where the vineyards were greener, the air more breathable, and the heat less insistent. The white wine harvest had begun, but the Nerello varietals were still a month or more away from being picked. At the southeastern tip of Sicily, summer showed no sign of relenting. Here on Etna, you could smell that *something* new was coming.

My first night back on the mountain, I had dinner in the deep woods near Bronte with three winemakers who were part of Etna's new wave: Frank Cornelissen, Alberto Aiello Graci, and Giuseppe Russo, a young classical musician who'd abandoned his career as a professional pianist to take over the family winery known as Girolamo Russo.

Alberto is the scion of a Catania construction fortune, who after working a few years as a financial analyst in Milan in the '90s ("Every day in front of a computer inside a room—impossible!") returned home to Sicily. In 2004, at twenty-nine years old, Alberto sold his family's vineyards in the Sicilian interior and bought a massive, abandoned three-story *palmento* and vineyards below the village of Passopisciaro for his new winery, called Graci.

With the help of one of Italy's most renowned oenologists, Donato Lanati, Alberto produces some of my favorite Sicilian reds: soft, velvety, ruby-colored, and easily mistaken for Pinot Noir from Burgundy's Côtes de Beaune. But there is another astounding quality I find in Alberto's wines that becomes more pronounced when drunk alongside other wines. His wines have this—I don't know a better way to put it—this purity. It's like a long, perfect sustained note with little to analyze and dissect. It's just there and it doesn't give up. It can make other more complex and expensive bottles seem overdone and suddenly undesirable.

Alberto is slight, soft-spoken, and serious, with dark features and heavy rimmed glasses—sort of a grown up Sicilian Harry Potter. He is the kind of impeccably mannered and discreet young man that older generations complain doesn't exist anymore. The kind that mothers wish for their daughters to bring home. He carried not one but two cell phones: one to which only his fiancée, Carla (also the architect for his winery), had the number and the other for everybody else. He speaks careful English, pausing to analyze the meaning of the particular words and their translations. In ways that seem prophetic in the Sicilian countryside, he can carefully cite both Sicilian grandmothers' recipes and Bob Dylan ("You don't need a weatherman to know which way the wind blows").

Frank and Alberto had become close friends and collaborators who shared some vineyards, and both produced what would broadly be considered natural wines. Yet their approaches and manners are completely different. Frank combines the vocabulary of a sailor with a pilgrim's quest. Alberto, whom I've never heard use profanity, is a lover of beauty—happy to make smaller quantities of wine (at the time he produced about 10,000 bottles annually) "because I can make the wines I like—not what the market likes at the moment."

Driving to dinner that night Alberto turned up the volume on the car stereo, which sang out Maria Callas in *Cavalliera Rusticana* ("Rustic Chivalry"), the nineteenth-century opera set in Sicily. As the car wound down the black roads toward Bronte, Callas belted out the aria "Voi lo sapete," and we breathed in the warm night from the open windows. Alberto drove with his left hand and delicately waved his right hand, giving form to the music. This is the image —with soundtrack—that is permanently etched in my memory and unearthed whenever I now drink Graci wines.

We ate at the Hosteria della Stazione, a family restaurant (the young chef Giovanni Leonardi has since opened a new restaurant in the center of Bronte, called Omnibus) in what was once the waiting room of the tiny train station for the Circumetnea railroad—a dwarf-sized single-car train service that still connects the towns below the volcano. We drank the three men's wines—Cornelissen's apricot-colored and honey-scented "white" MunJebel Bianco 2007, followed by Russo's delicious fruity 2006 Etna red, and Alberto's guileless 2006 "Quota 600," named for the metric elevation of the vineyards from which the wine was made.

It was a long and enjoyable evening with multiple courses—from rabbit to pasta—that appeared before us seasoned with Bronte's famous pistachios—greener and more floral than other pistachios. Frank seemed to have aged years since I'd seen him last. His skin looked weathered, his face gaunt—the result, I figured, of his working months under the summer sun. His girlfriend, Aki—he now referred to her as "my wife to be"—had flown back to Japan but, he said, was set to return in October.

"I am so sick of the wine business. I just don't want to have anything to do with it," Frank blurted at one point. "I mean, I want to do something in wine that is almost . . . religious."

"I mean, wine should be the blood of Christ," he continued, with the fervor of an early Jesuit. "But most of what is made is the urine of Christ!"

After wine, food, and more wine, the conversation took a turn into the definition of "elegance." Here, clearly, we had turned into Alberto's territory. He said—waving the hand as if conducting "Voi lo sapete"—that he wanted to make wine with the softness—and yes, elegance—of Monica Bellucci. The wine he eventually planned to make at 1,000 meters (Quota 1000) would be leaner, longer, cooler. Like, he said, Nicole Kidman.

I BEGAN THE FOLLOWING morning at Passopisciaro, Andrea Franchetti's winery above the village with the same name. Perched at 850 meters and looking over the Alcantara Valley, Franchetti's lair is one of the largest, sitting at a higher altitude than the rest on the north face.

From town you take a climbing road up the mountain until it runs out of asphalt a few yards in front of Franchetti's tall rustic iron gates and the imposing set of old stone buildings—*palmenti* now turned into a modern winery. Continuing up a rutted black dirt road that climbs behind the winery, I parked next to the ruin of a stone outbuilding.

I crossed the dirt to an open painted door. On entering I heard a voice call out in English—a low, nasal growl with an accent that seemed to come from another place and time—beckoning me up a flight of stairs tiled in worn terra-cotta. I climbed them and came into a large loftlike room that seemed to serve as office, dining room, living room, and wine-testing lab. The place was simple, except for the pair of colorfully ornate Murano glass chandeliers that hung dramatically from the whitewashed wood roof beams. For windows there were a couple of sets of rustic double doors that opened onto small terraces and views over Franchetti's vineyards, now bathed in a white sunlight.

Franchetti stood behind a table positioned in front of the pair of doors that looked up the face of Etna. Over six feet tall with an upright posture, golden hair, and thick horn-rimmed glasses, Franchetti resembled an Italian Michael Caine. His white button-collared shirt, dark pants, and brown wingtip shoes completed the image of a patrician in the wilds.

Franchetti wasted no time in leading me outside and into a shiny black, new-smelling four-wheel-drive Indian Mahindra truck. He exchanged his glasses for a pair of sunglasses. He started the engine, shifted, and headed up a short, steep incline of black sand and lava stones. The truck rocked and heaved itself halfway up the rise and then stalled.

Franchetti restarted the engine and fiddled with a dial on the console between the seats. He accelerated and the truck leaned and shimmied without moving forward. He moved the dial and put his foot to the gas again. We went nowhere. He cursed his new truck, shifted into reverse, and bounced us down the hill backward.

"It's obviously not working so well," Franchetti grumbled. "We'll have to go up another way."

That other way was an ascent about fifty yards to the west that put up less resistance. As we climbed the hill I looked east, over the acres of densely packed vineyards that Franchetti had replanted on the mountainside—the tightly spaced short-pruned vines trained on steel wire between chestnut posts.

"It's tough to be here—humanly," Franchetti said suddenly, giving me a grave look. I thought I knew that voice, that accent from somewhere. But where?

I didn't know what to make of his statement, until I followed his gaze over my shoulder as we topped the hill. I looked to the west and saw that the land—mostly scrubland of low shrubs and trees—had been burned to a black crisp, not by lava flows but by fire.

"It's primitive," Franchetti said, "it's no joke."

I had traveled through enough Sicilian countryside to know that brush fires happened more often here than in most places—usually explained as accidental occurrences such as a lit cigarette stupidly tossed from a car window. But Franchetti was indicating something more sinister.

"Shepherds," he said.

As in sheep? Those shepherds?

"They come and they light fires to clear the land so that these small plants grow back for grazing." Franchetti said, "It's not their land, but they don't care."

Weeks earlier, Franchetti had lost thousands of vines in a fire that had spread to his vineyard. Now he snorted: "They don't care if they kill you!"

"The law here is a joke anyway. There is no law . . ." He stopped the truck and cut the motor. "And these shepherds, they challenge you. This is the way they deal with things here and you . . . you are supposed to take a stance like they would.

"And how the hell can you do that when you come from . . ." Franchetti's head was turned toward me, sunglasses staring at me as he alliterated ". . . these soft cities."

He spoke the last three words as though he were reciting a poem—made even more striking by that accent. What was it? A cross of Roman and New England (birthplace of his mother)? A hearing impediment? Then I realized where I might have heard it before: Franchetti seemed to speak the sort of theatrical English used by Hollywood actors in the films of his youth.

EVERYTHING ABOUT FRANCHETTI'S BEARING indicated that he was a product of cities. The son of an American mother who was heiress to a South Carolina textile fortune and a Roman father, Franchetti was born in Manhattan in 1949 by the contrivance of his parents, who wanted their son born in America. The family moved back to Italy soon after, and Franchetti grew up in the postwar Rome of *La Dolce Vita*.

The Franchettis lived in a world of art and culture. His Roman uncle was an influential collector and promoter of contemporary art. Another uncle was the American abstract painter Cy Twombly, who joined the Franchettis in Rome. Franchetti dropped out of high school in the eleventh grade and, as he puts it, "played" in the eternal city.

Franchetti once described his young adult years to the wine writer Jancis Robinson as "a beautiful tunnel of dope." In the 1970s, he told me, "I didn't do anything . . . I hitchhiked through Afghanistan and Morocco and wrote some articles about it for *L'Espresso*." In the '80s he moved to New York for awhile and started a wine import and distribution company that dealt in edgy, innovative wineries in the Italian Piedmont and Tuscany. He took enough time out to play a supporting role in an independent Italian film noir called *Fuori dal Giorno* (1983), which Franchetti characterized as "an adventure of another life; they didn't even pay me and the movie was pretty bad."

After New York, he opened a pair of restaurants in Italy, sold them after two years, and left Rome to move out to the country—to a ruin of a house he'd bought in the 1970s and forgotten in the vast (coincidentally) shepherding country of Tuscany's Val d'Orcia.

"I stayed for years alone there—it was completely empty and abandoned. Vines hadn't been planted in the locale for more than a century." But Franchetti—looking for something to do—began planting. "I made wine simply as a way of staying in the country," he said. "You know you're out there in the middle of nowhere—what do you do? It was something I started doing not even knowing what I was doing."

What he planted at Tenuta di Trinoro was not the native Sangiovese that dominates Chianti and Brunello di Montalcino, but Bordeaux varietals such as Cabernet Franc and Cabernet Sauvignon and spicy Petit Verdot. He aimed for the same sort of extreme wine being made by the Bordeaux vanguard of the early '90s—among them his good friend Jean-Luc Thunevin, who launched the *garagiste* movement in Saint-Émilion by producing highly concentrated explosive wines that were championed by the American critic Robert Parker.

The keys to the formula (which created a backlash among some consumers) included severely cutting back vines in summer to produce a much smaller, concentrated crop, waiting to pick overripe fruit, extracting the maximum amount of matter from grape skins in the winery, and raising wine in new oak *barriques*. Tenuta di Trinoro rode the new wave, and with ninety-plus scores from Parker and other wine critics, collectors happily paid up to $200 a bottle.

Franchetti's arrival on Etna—in the same year as Frank Cornelissen's—was a turning point for north face reds. The presence of an eccentric Roman with a successful Tuscan estate gave the first idea that a wine scene was developing.

Unlike Cornelissen or de Grazia, Franchetti didn't come to Sicily for Etna. He came to Sicily in 2000 for a vacation near Siracusa. "I loved it here and I said, 'Where can I find a cool enough place to make wine?' . . . and I went up into the mountains all over eastern Sicily until I found this place."

FRANCHETTI OPENED THE TRUCK DOOR and climbed out, walking to the edge of the vineyard above his winery. The young vines were pruned, orderly, and carrying the minimum of dark fruit that Franchetti would harvest as late as November. There was no Nerello planted here. In fact, Franchetti saw no need to plant local varieties when he could buy or lease Nerello vineyards already established. This vineyard was planted mostly with Franchetti's Bordeaux favorite of Petit Verdot along with another lesser-known varietal, Cesanese di Affile from outside of Rome.

Franchetti's selection of varietals is, of course, telling. Most winemakers were coming to Etna to make their interpretations of Nerello, but Franchetti was here, it seemed, to interpret Franchetti. The others were like landscape painters who had come to paint the volcano; Franchetti was an abstractionist who had come to paint on the volcano. His top wine at Passopisciaro, called simply "Franchetti," is dominated by Petit Verdot (a grape used sparingly in Bordeaux to add spice) with a bit of Cesanese. It sold at more than $100 a bottle—about three times the price of his Nerello-based red called Passopisciaro.

For other winemakers, Nerello Mascalese, with its delicate Pinot Noir color and structure, was part of the attraction. Franchetti, on the other hand, was here on Etna *in spite of* Nerello.

"I hated the stuff—I thought it was coarse," Franchetti said. "I didn't want to use Nerello to make wine. I looked at it as a bad ingredient I had to use."

In the years since, Franchetti claimed to have undergone a slow "conversion" to the charms of Nerello. It might also be viewed as a truce after a long battle. For his first Nerello vintages on Etna, Franchetti rolled out the Bordeaux new wave formula that had worked so well for him at Tenuta di Trinoro. The results were disappointing. The extraction techniques, including long macerations and aging in *barriques,* produced a wine that was as rude as it was rustic. And Franchetti tried to cut the result with wine made from his French grapes. "I was doing everything to make it the least Nerello possible," Franchetti said.

But soon, he said, he realized that the problem was not with Nerello but with his own intensive winemaking techniques. The errors he made were akin to trying to serenade a new lover with the favorite music of one's ex. The Bordeaux grapes danced to '90s pop winemaking. Nerello demanded something more traditional. In 2004 Franchetti changed his tune: he cut out maceration on skins, lowered the temperature of grapes during fermentation, and ditched *barriques* for large oval Italian *botti* more than twenty times the size of the Bordeaux barrels.

"You see, I learned that the best part of the Nerello grape is not in the skins, like with Bordeaux grapes," Franchetti said. "It's all in the juice."

Before he climbed back into the truck, Franchetti bent down and touched the soil, letting it sift through his fingers. It was dry, deep brown, with a texture of dust.

"I've never seen soil so light," Franchetti mused.

"Look," he said, and he offered an analogy that could not have been any more incongruous with our surroundings. "It's like face powder."

He brushed off his right hand with his left, then slid it with a sort of gentlemanly reflex into his pocket. I thought, Franchetti was right: How could he confront local shepherds who had probably never even touched face powder?

Franchetti drove up the ridge; off to the west were more acres of burned landscape, and he murmured something about the "violence of it all." He pulled onto the paved road that circles Etna at 1,000 meters, drove less than 100 yards, then stopped. We walked along the ridge. To the north, down the mountain slope, was the high vineyard in the *contrada* known as Guardiola, where Franchetti grew Chardonnay.

"If I can make a great white here, I want to try it with a great white grape," Franchetti said, as if dismissing any idea that a great white could be made with Sicilian grapes.

One thousand meters was an important number. Franchetti and other winemakers like Cornelissen and Graci were reclaiming vineyards at higher and higher elevations, believing that Etna's greatest wines would come from the highest possible growing areas with the latest maturation cycles.

Franchetti's Chardonnay below us was bordered by a couple of strands of barbed wire—to keep grazing herds out of his vines. I looked up the mountain on the other side of the road into the wild brush and stands of oak and pine. This public land was also sealed off with barbed wire.

"Shepherds," Franchetti spat again, waving the back of his hand at the wire barricade.

The wire had been placed there, logically, to keep animals out of the road, but it seemed there was a secondary purpose of keeping out the *stranieri*, like Franchetti, and their encroaching vineyards.

"They put this shit up and it doesn't even belong to them," Franchetti protested. "It's ridiculous—people are scared shitless to go in there and go up higher to make better wines."

We drove back down to his winery, turning onto the dirt and bouncing down the hill that Franchetti's truck had failed to mount earlier. On the way down, Franchetti talked about the chemistry of his winemaking. He added yeast for consistent fermentation in his wines, and if his ripe fruit resulted in a wine lacking acid, he added it at the end. Lots of it, he said.

Adding yeast to make red wine is an unnecessary and unfortunate shortcut that circumvents the natural yeasts that grew naturally on the grapes that season. Adding tartaric acid powder to wine is common practice in hot climates like California and among big producers in the Sicilian lowlands. In Bordeaux it is normally forbidden except in years of extreme drought. I was shocked that a maker of fine wine like Franchetti would need or want to acidify Etna wines. In fact, I loathed the practice; if Franchetti wanted more acidity, he should have just picked his fruit earlier. Yet at the same time I was charmed—how many winemakers were so forthright about their winery tricks?

"Frank would never do it [acidify] because he has this thing that the juice comes from the ground," he said. "But that's his trip—not mine."

We walked back up to the second floor of the winery and tasted Franchetti's wines together, sitting at a long table with a red-and-white checked tablecloth under the Murano glass chandeliers. Franchetti was dismissive about his 2007 Guardiola—the Chardonnay from the high vineyards we had just visited. "For a moment it seemed like it would be a good idea here," Franchetti said ambiguously. "The sun bakes out all the minerality. Still you have to wait—it will take a few years before this plant shows what it has."

Franchetti's Australian oenologist, Anna Martens, came and huddled with her boss, as did Vincenzo, the chief of his vineyards. Then we tasted his 2006 reds, starting with the Passopisciaro made from Nerello. It was the color—pink around the edges—of Pinot Noir, only a fraction of a shade darker than Graci's wine. But where Graci's wine was seamless and silky, Franchetti's smelled and tasted more of licorice and spice. It was more primped, more Franchetti, but it was still Nerello.

"Thunevin can't stand it," Franchetti said. "Something like this is anathema. It's hard for the people of Bordeaux to like it."

Later, after we had gone through the cellars tasting from Franchetti's barrels, we came back to this spot and tasted from a freshly opened bottle of 2006 Franchetti made with Petit Verdot. The color was deep purple, the wine lush and substantial and velvet—a concentrated package of fruit and violets and tannins that surely Thunevin would approve of.

"You can see the structure in this like—it's like Lego," Franchetti said. "This wine is me."

"And this," he said, offhandedly gesturing to the glass of Nerello, "is what I've learned to do."

ON THE ROAD THAT CUTS from Linguaglossa across the eastern face of Etna the terrain changes: the slope of mountain levels and the lava fields give way to a landscape that is softer and lusher, with dark stands of oak and chestnut trees mixed in with olive groves and small vineyards that look out onto an endless panorama of Ionian sea.

Sant'Alfio is a typical country hill town of less than 2,000 people —famous for its Castagno dei Cento Cavalli (the One Hundred Horse's chestnut tree)—a miraculous sprawling tree believed to be more than three thousand years old that has inspired writers and painters for centuries. The town looks directly over the Riposto, the port that was expanded in the nineteenth century for exports of Etna wine.

With its face exposed to the sea and shielded from the afternoon sun, this side of the mountain is more humid and less sunny than the north face—making for conditions that generally favor white wine grapes over sun-craving reds.

I went to Sant'Alfio to meet Salvo Foti, a man who had been an engine for the revival of Etna wines long before the arrival of Franchetti and the other *stranieri*. As a freshly degreed oenologist in the 1980s, Foti, who is from Catania, had the idea of restoring Etna's wine glory by cultivating local grapes in traditional ways that respected the environment, and making wine from them with minimal technological interference. Foti's dream took flight when he found a client with money and passion for local wines in Dr. Giuseppe Benanti, a successful pharmaceuticals entrepreneur. Benanti's grandfather had planted vineyards on the southeast side of Etna near Viagrande, and in the 1990s the Benanti (Foti) mineral-rich white wine called Pietramarina Etna Bianco Superiore—made from local Carricante vines planted in the early twentieth century at 950 meters on Etna's eastern slope—was hailed among Italy's finest. Pietramarina is a wine that ages—sometimes taking years to show off its nuanced flavors. It inspired a generation of Sicilian winemakers, including Alessio Planeta, who was now working to make a great Carricante wine on the north slope.

The success had propelled Foti's consultancy. He worked on all corners of the mountain and had also formed a consortium of growers known as I Vigneri (from the Catania winegrowers' guild established in the early fifteenth century as the Maestranza dei Vigneri). Foti's own wines, which he labeled I Vigneri di Salvo Foti, were barely commercial—after he distributed about half his production to friends, he sold what remained (only about 1,000 bottles) to the world.

I found Foti in a vineyard with a restored *palmento* on the property named Il Cantante ("The Singer"). I had seen dozens of *palmenti* in all states of abandon with old wood presses gnawed by generations of insects, and I'd seen others recycled into wineries and homes. But this was the first *palmento* I'd seen turned into something resembling a museum. Outside it had a fresh coating of pink stucco that contrasted with the black lava doorways and windows. Inside, the floors and old vats were worn lava stone. The massive wood beam that was once used to press grape pomace—at least twenty feet long with the girth of a man—was preserved, lacquered, and illuminated by spotlights. Suspended above was a transparent Plexiglas floor and steel handrails.

Foti, at forty-six, was a lean man with flowing silver hair and a gray stubble of beard. A pair of clunky Blues Brothers–style shades covered his blue eyes, yet there was nothing hip about him. For the most part he carried himself and spoke with the focused brow-furrowed look of a university professor.

Foti also seemed more than a little distracted, and I soon learned the reason. The owner of Il Cantante—one of Foti's main clients—would soon be arriving. Il Cantante's owner was a singer—Mick Hucknall, of the British pop/soul band Simply Red. This morning Hucknall was coming to film a segment for an Italian television program, followed by lunch for about forty people.

Foti, the ideological wine consultant, who had overseen everything at Il Cantante—from the renovation of the old *palmento* to the planting of vineyards and bottling the wines—would today have to play unruffled co-host and stage manager of a modest piece of wine theater.

Foti and I took a short walk up through the vineyards, where Nerello grapes were grown in tight and upright *alberello* goblets planted a meter apart and supported by traditional chestnut tutors.

"This was the system of the Romans from two thousand years ago," Foti said, with a pleading edge in his voice. "Why change the system that has worked for two thousand years. Why?"

I couldn't help but think of Franchetti, on the other side of the mountain—a modern-day Roman who would surely ask *Why not?* It was clear that Foti looked at wine as something greater than himself. It was liquid testimony, history, archaeology—a record of the footprints and sweat of generations—and the *alberello* form was an icon so sacred that he refused to tamper with it. "If you told me that you wanted to work in the *spalliera* [the short prune trellis or *"guyot"* system], I could not be a consultant for you," he said.

Foti and I walked back to the *palmento*, which he looked at forlornly. He denounced the European health regulations that made winemaking in old stone *palmenti* illegal, partly because the uneven and porous stone surfaces used to crush grapes were judged as harbingers for bacteria.

"It's not possible to make the wine in the old system anymore," Foti said, shaking his head in disgust. "For two thousand years the system worked. Now . . . *basta* . . . it's no good."

Foti's discourse was interrupted by the arrival of a series of panel vans that pulled up into Il Cantante's drive. Doors flung open and a small army of caterers poured out—unloading tables, dishes, and glassware and ice to be set up under shade umbrellas on Il Cantante's terra-cotta brick terraces with the sea views.

The caterers had questions for maestro Foti about the buffet, the cocktail tables, and dozens of other details that yanked him back from antiquity to the here and now of this afternoon's lunch.

A television producer from the Italian station Rai Uno appeared: a woman in her mid-thirties wearing a tight black tank top. Her black hair was pulled into a taut ponytail and her face was the mask of perpetual anxiety worn by TV people everywhere. She was trailed by the reporter/ interviewer for Rai Uno's agricultural program: a young man with light hair and the sculpted features of a Roman deity wearing the clingy white button shirt and the self-assured cockiness of a guy who could be dining that evening with Miss Italia.

Suddenly, everybody wanted Foti. It was showtime Italian-style—with all the requisite drama and confusion. The only people who seemed to be relaxed were Foti's vineyard crew in their I Vigneri T-shirts. These were men accustomed to long, hard days working *alberello* vines in stifling heat, but now they just leaned against a shaded wall, quietly watching, waiting for instructions.

More people arrived. At around noon, Hucknall appeared—the

aging, soft-around-the-middle rocker who'd sold fifty million albums—with his trademark red floppy curls and the faded tattoos that made him look older than his forty-eight years. At his side was his young wife, Gabriella—a tall, sturdy beauty of Greek and German stock with black hair and high cheekbones. Now, everybody wanted Mick.

The television producer directed Foti, who directed a group of five vineyard workers to move a ceramic-topped iron table from the terrace down into the vineyard. The men obliged. There was discussion. A guy in shorts and an engineer's cap directed the men to move the table to the left, then to the right—trying to get the perfect placement for the prop in the vine rows.

The table was filled with bottles and wine glasses. Boom microphones appeared and the TV interviewer chatted calmly with Foti and Hucknall, who nodded and answered in fluent Italian. When the television cameras finally began taping, the interviewer instantly changed languages, from Italian to TV Italian. The difference is that television Italian is spoken at about five times the speed and is delivered with the animated urgency of an automatic weapon.

The interviewer mowed down Hucknall, who looked wounded but smiled anyway. Hucknall said some nice things and raised his glass. Hucknall told the story of how the vineyards of Il Cantante had belonged to a friend—an officer in the Italian motorcycle police—who had bought this place for his retirement but died of a heart attack three days after moving there in 2001. Hucknall bought the property to continue his friend's dream. Il Cantante now had about seventeen acres under cultivation here and on the north face of Etna.

By the time the shooting was over, about twenty minutes later, Hucknall looked a darker shade of red and was coated with a film of perspiration. He fled indoors for shade and water. Hucknall's young interviewer hadn't even broken a sweat.

Over a glass of white wine Hucknall told me—a diamond filling flashing in his front tooth—that while he had numerous offers to buy vineyards, making wine on Etna was an opportunity to do something unique in the wine world with grape varieties that were unheard of outside Sicily.

Dozens of people filled the terrace. The wine flowed from tables stacked with fresh cheeses and marinated olive-sized caper berries. The buffet was spread out on natural hemp-colored fabric: beef and sausage cooked on the barbeque, pastas, and caponata in pastry shells. The vineyard crew sat in their own corner looking amused and taking it all in as part of a day's work.

I had expected none of this when I set out for Sant'Alfio. The Hucknalls seemed like good conscientious people, and Mick was certainly more knowledgeable and engaged in winegrowing than the average "celebrity winemaker." But the perfect garden party setting struck me as odd—as odd as Franchetti in Passopisciaro cursing the local grapes.

I thought what a tragedy it would be if Mount Etna actually became fashionable.

For a moment I wanted the mountain to rise up, to resist, to swallow this whole scene. It was a crazy thought, tempered by two occurrences that afternoon. The first incident was something that Hucknall's wife, Gabriella, said as we sipped the good Il Cantante wine.

She looked around the party at the well-dressed smiling guests and sighed, "You know, it all looks very beautiful now, but I can't tell you how many times we were ready to give up and run away from this place."

She complained of the endless permits, the dishonesty, and the official corruption that had dogged them and their project. It made me admire the Hucknalls more. At the same time it relieved me to think that more singers would not be on the way.

THEN, LATER THAT AFTERNOON, I was cheered at witnessing Ciro Biondi's dick.

I'll explain.

Biondi is an architect (he designed de Grazia's new winery) who at forty-nine had been making wine for nearly a decade on the east slopes of Etna—in a modern garage-type building in a tiny industrial park. Here, in a setting that was neither stylish nor aesthetic, Biondi not only made about 35,000 bottles of his own wine but also allowed his oenologist Foti to use the place to make Hucknall's Il Cantante. Biondi is a stocky man with a shaved head and gray lamb-chop sideburns who can't help but emote like a Sicilian. He humbly calls his wine Outis (Greek for "no one"—a Homeric reference to Odysseus's encounter with the Cyclops in *The Odyssey*) and sees himself as the heir of a craft that had been practiced by his grandfather—one of the rare Sicilians who bottled his wines in the early part of the twentieth century for fairs in mainland Europe.

That afternoon I followed Biondi on his motorcycle to his vineyards planted with smatterings of local red and white grapes that he vinified by mixing together for results that were earthy and unfussy.

In one vineyard I saw the system of hand pulleys and cables that had been used for generations to bring the harvest down the mountain; in another we went inside a small, dusty, but well-preserved *palmento* that the architect described as perfect because "it wasn't designed by an architect!"

The third vineyard belonged to Biondi's grandfather. It sat in a natural amphitheater against a pair of extinct volcanic craters on the side of Etna. To get there I had to hop on the back of Biondi's bike, which bucked up the stone path and delivered us to the old antique stone well that gave its name to the vineyards: Cisterna Fuori.

Around the well, Biondi had built some white columns and long plaster couches and had fashioned a rustic bamboo sun awning to rest above it all. He'd placed a long plywood dining table here—used by day for work breaks in the vineyard, and on long summer evenings for entertaining friends by candlelight. When he'd inherited this five-acre vineyard from his father it was in a state of abandon, and with his nephew and other workers he'd replanted. He had once considered building a home for his family on this spot but couldn't bring himself to do it: "The place is already perfect."

Biondi told me stories—one about how he was up here eating alone one night (his wife, Stephanie, was in her native England) when he felt a womanly presence and scent surround him.

"It was strange, I mean, I felt there was somebody there. I mean

really there! I stopped eating and looked around me and . . . nothing . . ."
In fact, Biondi said, it was a trick of the full moon. "Scientifically
you would say the moonlight caused the wildflowers to open, which
gave off their perfume," he said. "But what would the ancients have
said? They would say, 'I was visited by a goddess last night.' I prefer
to think I was visited by a goddess!"

Just as the image and scent of a night goddess was setting in, I
heard Biondi say: "Look . . . the dick." That was followed by something like, "My dick." I looked over by the wall where Biondi was
standing, and he pointed to a relief carving made in lava stone. The
carving was indeed of a penis more than two feet long, and where
the stem met the head there were holes for some sort of ring.

Biondi explained that he had unearthed this "dick" when replant-
ing the vineyards. He'd researched the dimensions and found them
to correspond to ancient Greece. A fertility symbol—used to tie
down farm animals.

"I may not have a lot of money, but I have this," Biondi said triumphantly of his dick.

In fact, Biondi made no money from wine and seemed not to
care. He was driven by other things: the footprints of his ancestors,
the land that made him not want to build buildings, the black eruption carved into a phallus of a talisman, and the scent of a goddess
of the night.

Fall

II

Child of the Wind

THE 2008 HARVEST TURNED OUT to be an odd time to be traveling to a wild volcanic island in the Mediterranean. By early October the tourists and seasonal residents have abandoned Pantelleria, that speck between the Sicilian mother island and Tunisia, leaving behind a landscape that is primitive and desolate. Compounding the strangeness, in the fall of 2008 the world that most of us inhabit seemed headed for the financial abyss. The planets and stars seemed out of alignment. People in the worlds of cities and finance were binging on antidepressants and huddling about what "we" should do to avoid a Depression. In Palermo banks posted handwritten notices warning clients that cash withdrawals were limited to 500 euros. It was against this backdrop that I left civilization to learn the secrets of the ancient sweet wine Passito di Pantelleria.

I would be spending a few days at Marco De Bartoli's wine outpost on the island as Sebastiano De Bartoli while two workers started the long process of making the amber-colored meditative nectar. I met Sebastiano on the daily turboprop from Trapani—a twenty-minute flight that is often grounded by the winds that gave Pantelleria its Arabic-derived name meaning "daughter of the wind."

Sebastiano was in good spirits that seemed only lifted by the worldwide panic. "I hope the crisis gets much worse," Sebastiano smiled. He seemed to be watching for my reaction—which was suitably outraged. I liked many of the things that the modern world had given us: airline travel, central heating, electricity, refrigerators, my car stereo. I didn't want to have to give it *all* up.

"People are too comfortable and living crazy . . . it is my fantasy that we return to medieval times with everyone on a horse. I think it was better."

He was serious. He had inherited the petulance of his father, with whom—he informed me—he was not speaking this week. Sebastiano was unmarried, without children—a strapping young man in blue jeans and work boots who managed his family's properties around Marsala and Pantelleria and bragged, "I can grow everything I need."

Like most Sicilian men in the countryside, Sebastiano also knew how to construct anything he needed—walls, structures, roofing—and plumb, wire, and paint it. Of course, in a medieval world, Sebastiano would not be able to fly between the Sicilian main island and Pantelleria—a concern, considering that he would be stuck on the smaller island for longer periods in the off-season when there were few young, eligible females.

"That's a problem," he said. "I would just need a helicopter. Medieval times—except for my helicopter!"

From the window of the plane Pantelleria looked like another world. The coastline was far less developed and more expressively sculpted, with volcanic crags and inlets against a turquoise sea. Trapani had seemed an island of concrete public housing projects surrounded by parched brown clay and haze. Pantelleria was as moist and vibrantly green as a Celtic countryside. The interior of the small island rose up to a pair of mountains whose peaks were now shrouded in low clouds, and the landscape was dotted with houses—small lava stone cubes with domed roofs—that looked like they were inhabited by a people who worshipped deities by moonlight.

The main port town of the island, also known as Pantelleria (with about 3,000 inhabitants), appears insignificant from the air. It was largely razed by Allied bombing in 1943 and rebuilt with some unfortunate concrete building blocks. The rest of the island's 30 or so square miles are either cultivated terraced farms, marked by endless lengths of volcanic dry stone walls, or covered with *macchia*, wild Mediterranean brush.

When we landed at the airport—slightly larger than a bus station—it was a little after one. "Let's go," Sebastiano urged. "We are late."

I had reserved a small rental car—a tin box of an old Fiat with sun-faded paint. We drove toward the De Bartolis' place, which shared the old Arab name of its *contrada*—Bukkuram. The air felt hotter and smelled saltier than it had on the main island. I had no idea what we were "late" for, but heeding Sebastiano's sense of urgency, I raced along the more-or-less paved roads from the airport—past the barbed wired fences of a Mussolini-era air base.

Black and brown lava stone was piled into orderly dry walls that lined the road and cut across vineyards and fields. Prickly pear cacti and the occasional agave stood tall above olive trees that spread out horizontally at no more than chest height—cut this way as a defense against the wind. Similarly, in the vineyards I noticed the way the *alberello* vines grew low and horizontal, trailing leaves and shoots along the ground. The lava stone cubes I'd seen from above looked even stranger up close: the design, known as *dammuso*, was developed during the Arab period more than one thousand years ago, with small windows and meter-thick walls. The domed roofs were made to channel and collect rainwater.

The De Bartolis' Bukkuram lies on a plain with vineyards that run southwest toward the sea, a couple of miles away. The winery complex is a centuries-old Spanish-era two-story house—boxy with vaulted ceilings and water channeling domes on the white roof. I parked the car in the entry scattered with the De Bartolis' signature hulks of junked cars and machine parts. Off to the side were the ruins of an old *dammuso* along with an equally strange-looking *giardino arabo*, a high-walled circular enclosed garden designed by Arabs to protect precious citrus trees from the Pantelleria's winds.

We walked past the open metal doors of the small winery, then to an entry around back, where a piece of burlap sack served as a doormat. Inside the typical country kitchen of plaster and tiles and improvised wood shelves, the two field hands who did most of the work in the De Bartoli vineyards greeted us. I then realized the reason for Sebastiano's hurry: lunch.

The two men in their early thirties wore stained clothing and open, smiling faces. Angelo, tall with a receding hairline and thick beard, was setting plates on the table. Francesco, smaller with laughing eyes, was standing over the gas range, stirring sauce in a large skillet as pasta boiled on a back burner.

We sat and ate at a wood table—penne with a sauce of tomatoes, tuna, basil, and almonds on which we grated salted ricotta cheese. We drank a simple white wine and finished the meal with a chilled round of the De Bartolis' basic Passito di Pantelleria. It tasted like the sun—the long relentless summer without shade in Bukkuram that roasted the local white Muscat of Alexandria grapes, known here on Pantelleria by their otherworldly sounding name: Zibibbo.

Sebastiano made espresso in a small conical electric pot and slapped four small cups on the table, filling them halfway. Francesco and Angelo spooned sugar into the muddy brew and downed it. Time to get back to work—they drove off in a van to harvest more Zibibbo in a nearby vineyard. A hot slow wind blew from the south and through the kitchen door, and I had to fight off the sudden, overwhelming urge to nap.

Passito di Pantelleria tastes like what it is, a wine made with a mix of three stages of Muscat: fresh harvested grapes, sun-dried grapes (*uva passa*), and semi-dried grapes (*uva passolata*). "Straw wine" or "raisin wine" is made throughout Europe. But the particular recipe for Passito di Pantelleria is believed to be one of the oldest—about the closest thing to the original *passum* of ancient Carthage.

Sebastiano and I walked west through the vineyards in the direction of the sea. The sprawling vines were now turning gold and red, and towering over them were bouquets of tall flowering weeds. We stopped at the edge of a vineyard by the entrance to a long tunnel-like greenhouse made from a galvanized steel frame covered with taut plastic sheeting. Running the length of the structure, about 50 yards, were rows of long steel drying tables supporting tons of grape clusters in various stages of dehydration—from green to gold to a reddish brown. Sebastiano slid open the metal door and went inside—the temperature about twenty degrees hotter than outside. We did a tour of the grapes, pausing to taste the fruit. Sweet, fragrant, and unmistakable, Muscat is one of the most seductive flavors of the edible plant world. The greenhouse was a laboratory that used the sun to stretch the Muscat into a whole spectrum of sensations from fresh and tart to concentrated and baked.

Making a traditional *passito* is far more laborious than making most wines. The low trailing vines resist the use of tractors and usually require at least some manual tilling. Grapes must be handpicked, and the bunches drying in the greenhouse require turning by hand every couple of days over periods of weeks. After drying, the large, fat raisins must be separated from their stems before they are added to the wine. Because of the fragility of the dried stems, the separation must be done by hand; mechanical de-stemmers don't work.

The demands of labor have led to a drop in production in recent decades, and many old vineyards have been abandoned as new generations sought an easier life elsewhere. Yet Passito di Pantelleria has refused to go away. As it has become rarer, it has also become prized. Artists, poets, and celebrities—from Giorgio Armani to Gabriel García Márquez to Truman Capote to Madonna—have taken refuge in the seclusion of Pantelleria. And the island nectar has developed a following in Milan and the rest of the pleasure-seeking world.

Marco De Bartoli first came to Pantelleria in 1984 and learned the traditional methods of making *passito*. Nine years later he bought Bukkuram with its 10 acres of vineyards, and in 2003 he doubled his lands. While new technologies such as electric drying ovens allow for quicker production, the De Bartolis and other small producers have patiently clung to the old ways. Grapes are picked in two harvests—the earlier-ripening bunches closest to the vine trunk are picked as early as August, and the slower-maturing fruit at the edges of the vines is harvested in October. The first grapes—also the sweetest—are dried to raisins in the greenhouses. The last grapes—more acidic—are pressed along with partly dried grapes into a juice that ferments into a high-alcohol dry white wine. Then, the sweet raisins are mixed in—adding color and sugar to the blend. The rest of the recipe lies in the waiting: usually years, during which small doses of oxygen (the De Bartolis age their *passito* two years in used Bordeaux *barriques*) turn the wine from golden to tawny.

There is a dramatically exposed, capricious quality to Pantelleria that gives you the sense that the earth and sky are likely to revolt at any minute. *Terra firma* it is not. As Sebastiano and I walked back to the winery, low wisps of clouds flew overhead—disconcertingly faster than I'd ever seen clouds move—veiling and unveiling a brilliant white sun. I looked up beyond the winery to Pantelleria's principal mountain—with the obvious name Montagna Grande; its peak was shrouded in an ornery blanket that wasn't budging. As I turned my attention to the ground, I noticed something else I'd never seen: the floor of the vineyards seemed lit with a million specks of light. I examined closer—the volcanic sand was full of microscopic reflecting particles that turned the earth into a glittering carpet.

Sebastiano had to deliver a small tractor and trailer to Francesco and Angelo. Back at the winery he hopped onto the tractor seat and gave me the choice of either balancing on the back while holding onto a steel frame around the seat, or getting in the trailer. I took the latter option and squatted on a plastic harvesting crate. This system worked smoothly for the first few minutes as the tractor rolled at about fifteen miles an hour down the paved road. Then Sebastiano turned onto a dirt path that led into the hills below Montagna Grande. I bounced up and down more times than I care to remember and gripped the sides of the trailer until my hands turned white. After the crate slid out from under me, I knelt—knees banging on the metal floor as my insides struggled to keep down the afternoon's pasta.

Sebastiano turned and turned again through terraced vineyards, mercifully slowing as the grade grew steeper. Here in this *contrada* known as Kufura, the jungle of growth between the vines was greener and the stones looked blacker. Long, trailing caper plants—Pantelleria's other prized agricultural product—sprouted wild from crevices in the dry wall. We passed abandoned *dammusi*—their roofs taken over by grasses—and groves of low, gangly olive trees loaded with fat whitish green fruit.

We arrived at the van and I saw Francesco and Angelo—straw hats shading their faces from the sun—kneeling and picking the last small bunches of Zibibbo. This was grape picking as I'd never seen it before: the vine shoots were so low the men had to lift them to find and pull the last small bunches—locally called *sgangnune*. The whole exercise resembled the milking of sheep.

Sebastiano loaded the crates into the back of the van, and we drove it back to Bukkuram. There we climbed into his jeep and headed southeast to buy food for dinner in a nearby hamlet perched on a cliff above the sea. Pantelleria is sprinkled with end-of-the-earth hamlets like Scauri—each with a few streets lined with low buildings, one general food store with beaded curtains, a church, a public dance hall, locals who scrutinize every car and its passengers as though they were aliens, and dogs that stretch out in the middle of the road.

From Scauri, Sebastiano made a detour up the winding roads that climbed Montagna Grande. Very quickly it seemed we were in another place and climate. Among the black drywall stones were pieces of shiny obsidian. The vineyards and the fragrant Mediterranean *macchia* gave way to ferns and stands of pine and holm oaks, their trunks wrapped in coats of moss. In the minutes it took to climb to the peak (at about 800 meters), the intense evening sun was swallowed by a gray wet mist. We got out of the jeep and walked along a ridge. It was cool and smelled of rain, and from this panoramic spot we saw nothing. Looking west, the sun was merely a faint smudge.

We drove back down the mountain to a low brilliant sun that reflected off the sea. Sebastiano stopped to pick lemons from a tree limb hanging over the roadway. In the hamlet of Siba we were forced to stop and wait for the passage of a religious procession of about fifty singing pilgrims—seemingly the entire population of the town.

A group of men shouldered a statue of the Madonna draped in rosaries, and as they passed Sebastiano dutifully crossed himself. Then he turned to me and said, "To stay here would not be good. The brain does not work so well."

"It is too . . . relax," he said, a common grammatical error among native Italian speakers. "Can you feel it? You are in the middle of the sea. The air is different."

I could feel it. I could also sense it in the faces of the villagers and their animals. We were all "relax."

"The Panteschi," Sebastiano continued with a critique of the island's inhabitants, "are the worst people in the whole world. They are closed, stupid; they don't help you. Very few of them are nice."

After the procession passed, we headed down towards Bukkuram and a sun that was melting orange into the horizon. Just below Siba, Sebastiano stopped again—this time by a small spontaneous roadside dump from which he scavenged an old rusted hand grape crusher and an antique metal gasoline container, both of which he tossed in the rear of the jeep with the groceries.

"We have this passion for old things—me, my brother, my father—we all have it," Sebastiano said. "It is a . . . *malattia* [sickness]."

That evening was the celebration of the end of the De Bartolis' harvest season that had begun six weeks earlier in Marsala. The following morning the men would be pressing the fresh grapes they'd picked that day. Sebastiano sautéed swordfish with capers and tomatoes, which we ate beneath the vaulted ceiling of the informal dining room with some of the De Bartolis' dry white wines.

Sebastiano—like all the De Bartolis I'd met—was as moody as Pantelleria: lighthearted one minute, and short-fused or bitter the next. In contrast, Francesco shone with what seemed a constant inner brightness. To have a conversation with him and try to penetrate the source of the light was, in some small way, a life-changing event. I spoke for a while with him that evening and he relayed his life story. When he was an infant, his parents, too poor to support him, had placed him in an orphanage. From the age of six he was reared by and worked for a shepherd. From sixteen on he had worked in the vineyards, most of that time for the De Bartolis. He loved what he did—communicating with vines and knowing how to cut them and care for them. When he wasn't working for others, he was working for himself—making his own white wine and raising snails to sell at the market. He took a *telefonino* from his pocket and showed me pictures of his three small daughters. The idea of a financial crisis was to Francesco an abstract: he worked with his hands, he made food, and he would provide for his family no matter what. I was thinking of how much more fragile existence was for most of us Westerners—dependent not on the soil and its seasons, but on money and sophisticated systems created to keep it circulating.

Francesco pointed to his shoes. They were fancy new athletic shoes with silver soles. He didn't need such shoes, he told me. "When I was twelve, to go to school I learned how to fix my own shoes—to keep the soles from coming off—with nails," he said, making a delicate hammering motion with his right hand. The most striking thing about his story was the joy with which he told it. He was possibly the happiest man I have ever met.

After dinner we sipped several vintages of the De Bartolis' premium *passito*, Bukkuram—starting with the latest 2005 vintage and ending with a finer, deeper 1991. I was beginning to see that *passito* is, as the name suggests, all about the passage of time: the lateness of the harvest, the weeks the grapes spent baking in the sun, and its years of aging. Unlike most wines that absorbed time haltingly and unevenly, *passito* seemed time's perfect reflection. If you knew it well enough, I figured, you could set your watch to it.

I slept in a vaulted room above the winery—part of an apartment that mixed antiques with makeshift plumbing and Sebastiano's do-it-yourself electric wiring. The housekeeping was on the level of a college dormitory, with clothes and shoes strewn everywhere. I turned out the dangling bulb that hung above the bed and drifted off into the still night of Bukkuram.

The peaceful sleep didn't last long. I was awakened by the splashing of water from a heavy rain that slapped the roof with astonishing force. I'd left the window open and it swung on its hinges and banged against the wall with a wet gust. I jumped up and closed it. Looking out to sea, I noticed the sky painted in shades of black and creased by lightning. How was it possible, I wondered, that lightning on Pantelleria could seem more *electric*?

I pulled the bed covers over my head and awoke after daybreak. The rain had stopped but the sky still looked as if it had more to unleash. The morning was cool—about half the temperature it had been on my arrival. I looked for the others downstairs, taking a cup of lukewarm espresso from the pot in the kitchen, where the previous night's dishes sat in the large stone sink.

Outside, I noticed the men had positioned a large metal de-stemming machine on stone blocks. More than one hundred crates of grapes from yesterday's harvest were stacked a few yards away on the pavement and covered with a plastic sheet. Inside the *cantina*, in a corner between the tall cylindrical stainless steel vats and a bottling machine, Sebastiano, Francesco, and Angelo were wrestling with a horizontal vat, trying to balance it on chunks of uneven wood beam stacked about a yard high.

The way it would work was like this: Grape bunches would go into the top of the de-stemmer and crusher, and the resulting mash would get pumped out the tail of the machine into a fat hose that would bring it around the corner to an automated cylindrical press that rested under an overhang. The grapes would then go into the press, where the internal bladder would squeeze them into grape juice, which would spill into a long rectangular tub at the press's base. Another pump would suck this juice from the tub through an open window and into this horizontal vat recently acquired by the De Bartolis. Fermentation would start spontaneously, semi-dry *passolata* grapes would be added to the fermentation, followed later by the sweet dry *uva passa*. The result would be on its way to becoming *passito*.

This scenario, of course, left out one element: the dose of Sicilian confusion due that morning. For starters, the men were having a difficult time stabilizing the new vat on its improvised perch. Sebastiano raised it with an electric forklift as the others slid lengths of wood underneath. They went into the yard and pulled out more lengths of beam. A chain saw appeared. Sebastiano sliced through the thick pieces of wood, spitting sawdust that turned to mud in the puddles from the previous night's rain.

This went on for some time, but in the end the men's engineering efforts failed. "Forget it," Sebastiano said. "It's too complicated."

The vat was lifted, slabs of wood removed, and the men set up for the juice to be pumped into one of the vertical 5,000-liter tanks at the back of the winery. Large hoses were attached between the machines with thick washers and clamps. Electrical cords were fed inside to a central power panel, and within an hour all the pieces were in place to start the process of making wine.

Sebastiano clapped his hands and looked at his watch. "Wonderful!" Sebastiano exulted. "We are on time!"

On time? I wondered. For what? We were on an island with a total of two gas stations, and we had nothing to do all day except press some grapes. Sebastiano called out *"caffè!"* and the men gathered for their espresso break in the kitchen. Cups were lined up on the table once more with the sugar and spoons, and the men downed the stuff standing in their high rubber work boots. The cups slammed to the wood and it was time to return to work.

Sebastiano switched on the motors of the wineworks assembled that morning, and Bukkuram roared into production. Francesco carried crates of grape bunches to Angelo, who stood on an empty crate and dumped the contents into the maw of the de-stemmer. I could see the grape mash surging through the fat translucent hose at the other end of the machine on its way to the press. I followed that hose around the corner and noticed something very wrong: the other end of the hose had been dangled into the mouth of the press but it had broken free and fallen to the ground—spilling the freshly crushed grapes onto the pavement.

"Shit!" I yelled as loud as I could, instinctively choosing an English word that everyone would understand. Sebastiano ran and cut the power to the machine. The wasted grapes were cleaned up and thrown out in the vineyards; the hose was tied down to the edge of the mouth of the press, and the process restarted. Only now, a light rain began to fall. Sebastiano stood on a stack of wood pallets at the press and watched the grape mash flow inside. Juice soon flowed into the tub below. Surprisingly, it looked nothing like the golden liquid I'd expected: raw and unfiltered, it was as green and murky as swamp water. It didn't look like anything you'd want to put in your mouth, let alone something that would become limpid meditation wine sold for significant sums.

With all seeming in order, Sebastiano returned to the winery and I followed him, watching the juice flow into the upright vat. My gaze wandered around the room and up through a small window that looked out at the press. I noticed movement and looked closer to see the end of the hose that fed the press thrashing wildly in all directions like an angry trapped snake. Another "Shit!" sent Sebastiano scrambling outside in a hail of cries of *"vaffanculo!"* ("fuck it!") as the mouth of the hose vomited grape mash in all directions except into the mouth of the press.

There was more cleaning up to do. Grape skins and juice now stained Sebastiano's jeans and stuck to his arms and hair. After another delay the tube was forced down deep in the throat of the press, and the action started up again. That worked for a while—almost enough time to finish the job. But now the force of the rain was building. Suddenly thunder cracks rattled the building and all of Bukkuram as the men ran about to feed the last crates of grapes into the machine. A bolt of lightning zipped across the sky and produced the sound of a home appliance being fried. Another thunder crack made the lights flicker, and yet another came and the machines ground to a halt.

The electricity in Bukkuram was out. We huddled under the shelter at the entrance of the winery. The rain now was a wall of water, bathing the last grapes. With no electricity there was nothing to do but wait. I thought of the hand-cranked machine that Sebastiano had found by the side of the road and wondered if it had something to do with fate.

"Life is not easy," Francesco sighed and then laughed in Sebastiano's direction. "Who is medieval now? Eh?"

"Sebastiano said he wanted to do things the medieval way,"

Francesco taunted, *"medievale . . . medievale.* Now, God gave to him *medievale."*

Sebastiano shook his head in disgust. "I have been here every year for ten years and it's always like this on Pantelleria . . . nothing works," he sputtered. "The climate . . . it's always complicated . . . always . . . it's in the air."

THAT AFTERNOON, SEBASTIANO AND I crossed the island—he in his jeep and me following in my rented tin cart. Sebastiano had agreed to show me the way to the hamlet of Tracino and Salvatore Ferrandes, a man who I reckoned knew Pantelleria and its *passito* better than anyone.

I found Ferrandes and his Swiss-born wife, Domenica, in the center of the hamlet in their small, meticulously kept *dammuso*. The place exuded a yogic energy opposite that of the frenetic casa De Bartoli. A beaded entryway led from their terrace patrolled by house cats to a small kitchen and an orderly living room with a computer and their fourteen-year-old son's video game console.

Salvatore, at fifty-four, was a slight man with a gray beard who seemed worn from decades of manual labor. Domenica—who had advanced literature degrees—was slightly younger and tall with sharp features and long brown hair. Both of them had quiet, patient blue eyes, and when they spoke they delivered their words with thoughtful care. Salvatore explained that they had been up all the previous night pressing their harvest in order to beat the rain—the same rain that had drenched Sebastiano that morning.

The Ferrandes name has deep roots in Pantelleria. The family, originally from Spain, had been farming on the island for seven hundred years, and there were scores of Ferrandeses around Tracino. In addition to making *passito*, Salvatore and Domenica cured capers and olives and made olive oil.

Despite their differences in education (Salvatore quit studies at a science-based high school in Palermo), the Ferrandeses seemed to be intellectual equals. Salvatore reflected on how the isolation of the island had shaped its society and people. *Panteschi* families had learned to be autonomous—living off of scattered plots of land that were minuscule compared with the vast feudal holdings of the main island.

"Each family had their own animals, grew their own fruit and vegetables," Salvatore said. "They made their own milk, meat, capers, and wine."

Salvatore saw himself as a continuation of that tradition. For a while in the early 1990s he had helped give birth to the Passito di Pantelleria of the large Sicilian producer Donnafugata—working as a consultant and winemaker before they parted ways.

"For me what mattered most were human relations," Salvatore explained. "Other things were second: commercialization, organization, administration. We valued different things."

The four of us drove in a pair of jeeps up to the vineyards in the contrada of Mueggen on the north-facing flanks of Monte Gibele. The sky was now infinite and cloudless, and the sun cast sharp late afternoon shadows on the dark sand.

"The methods of agriculture in Pantelleria are particular in their difficulty," Salvatore announced. With only one field hand to help him, Salvatore cultivated about five hectares of vines planted in the traditional *Pantesco* method. Each of his thick-trunked vines in this vineyard—a minimum of seventy years old—was rooted in a sloping hole as much as two feet deep. This form of planting had two benefits: protecting the vines from high winds and conserving water during dry spells.

All work was done by hand, and though Salvatore had finished the harvest, it seemed there were still plenty of small grape bunches on his vines. Salvatore said he simply couldn't justify the extra effort and expense to pick them. As it was, he produced the equivalent of about 2,600 half bottles of *passito* under his own name. A percentage of those were imported into the United States by Marco de Grazia and were sold for about $40 at a few specialty wineshops. But the bulk of his production—the equivalent of another 4,000 small bottles—was bottled by the Etna winemaker Giuseppe Benanti and sold under the Benanti name.

Salvatore said he had enough grapes to more than double his production but lacked for cellar space and labor.

We got back in the jeeps and climbed higher up the mountain to a ridge where the Ferrandeses' winery was perched in a fastidiously renovated *dammuso*. There were no exposed wires or spilled wine or forgotten objects collecting dust as at the De Bartolis'. The main low arch-ceilinged room contained only a series of nine 500-liter stainless steel vats standing around the perimeter of a spotless, polished tile floor. His cylindrical press and other winery equipment similar to the De Bartolis' was neatly arranged outdoors and covered with tarps.

Ferrandes explained why he wasn't picking those additional grapes: his micro winery was at full capacity. So small was the place, Ferrandes said, that his application for a permit to bottle his own wine had been rejected by provincial authorities in Trapani. The winery that had allowed him to use their bottling equipment had closed earlier that year, and he didn't know where he would bottle his wine the next year.

"As local producers, we are required to bottle on the island," he sighed. But because of a wrinkle in the law, some Sicilian producers (such as De Bartoli and Donnafugata and others) were allowed to bottle on the main island. "It's not normal—Benanti can put our wine in bottles in Catania. But us—no!"

Salvatore spoke like a man with no fight left in him. He might be the last of his line to work the land. His son, a bright and bookish fourteen-year-old, was obsessed with video games and one day would probably leave Pantelleria for a modern life somewhere else.

We walked through the vineyard around the winery, passed through a greenhouse where an older slumped man was separating raisins from stems, and peered into an old *giardino*, where a pair of centuries-old citrus trees grew side by side. Then, as the sun began to drop behind us, we sat on the small terrace in front of the *dammuso* and sipped the wine from Salvatore's steel vats. We faced eastward, looking down over the deep green valley known as the Piana di Ghirlandia. The only sounds came from evening birds, and, for the first time since I'd landed on the island, there was no wind.

Salvatore brought the first sample in a steel pitcher no bigger than a milk creamer. It was from a vat of his 2007 *passito*. A medium amber-colored wine, it was sweet and floral and delicate. Salvatore said, "Personally, I cannot call it *passito* yet."

The second sample was from 2006: It smelled and tasted like lightly baked apples or pears fresh from the oven. It was the slow oxidation of the wine over time that in effect "cooked" it and brought out new flavors. "This I would call a quasi-*passito*," Salvatore said.

Then came 2005. The fruit here tasted more baked and concentrated, and you could smell and taste earthy aromas. Surely this, I thought, could be called *passito* and I said so to Salvatore. "It's more evolved," he hesitated. "But . . ."

Salvatore disappeared inside his *cantina* again and emerged with yet another sample in the little pitcher. He poured half a glass of what was by far the darkest and most potent wine. It was the color of an old cognac, and it smelled and tasted like the previous sample, only earthier, wilder. I closed my eyes and imagined the sun, the rocks, the wind. From the first glass to the last we'd moved from a lovely soprano to a chorus led by a commanding baritone. Salvatore said that this last sample also came from 2005—from a different plot of vines laced with white calcareous stone. "This we can call *passito*," he said, sitting at last in a wood chair.

Sebastiano left us, and I sat with the Ferrandeses for a while. The man who had been plucking the raisins from their stems came to join us and brought with him some dried grape bunches in a small plastic bag. These raisins were fat, supple, and contained enough moisture and seed and life to remind you of living Muscat. We ate them and sipped the wine while Salvatore spoke about life in this strange isolated place he rarely left.

I drove back to Bukkuram in the dark. The men had cleaned up the winery and the machines and were making a dinner of a simple ham *frittata* (omelet), which we ate together in the dining room. I brought up the problems that Salvatore faced in bottling his wine, and Sebastiano reacted impatiently.

"He needs to organize himself. Why doesn't he organize like

everybody else and invest and get the permits he needs?" he said, derisively.

Organized? I thought. To me the Ferrandeses were nothing if not organized.

"He doesn't want to organize because he is *Pantesco* and to be *Pantesco* is to be . . . " Sebastiano stopped, leaned back in his chair, and held his palms upward—miming a helpless state of resignation.

The insults continued and Francesco piled on. It was a stunning moment. I thought of how northerners looked down on the south, and of how the rest of Italy often looked down at Sicily. So who did Sicilians have to ridicule? The people on the islands at the edges of Sicily's orbit.

I countered Sebastiano, telling him that everything he was saying about the Panteschi could be said by others of the Sicilians.

He opened his eyes wide and shrugged: "Exactly."

THAT NIGHT I AWOKE about four in the morning—mouth dry and feeling restless. I tossed off the bedcovers, got up to drink from a bottle of water, and walked out onto the roof just outside the bedroom door. A half moon shone gauzy in the black sky, the wind swirled from an indefinite direction, and I could hear dogs barking from near and far away. They had felt the disturbance too. Off on the horizon I could see the pulsing of a lighthouse on the Tunisian shore, and out in that direction over the sea I saw small veins of lightning that quietly flashed in the sky. I felt the sudden urge to get back to "land" as soon as possible.

I would be returning to Palermo later that day. After lying awake and waiting for the sun to rise, I got up and found some lukewarm espresso in the kitchen. This morning Angelo and Francesco were out in the greenhouse turning grape bunches, and Sebastiano was working in the winery. His mood had brightened, and—perhaps feeling bad about his remarks about the Panteschi—he said he had someone for me to meet.

The someone was a neighbor and young wine producer who was, according to Sebastiano, "organized." The two of us walked down the street and, behind a modest *dammuso*, found Fabrizio Basile in his small, modern winery. Cats roamed a low wall that separated the *dammuso* terrace from Basile's family vineyards. Basile was born into *passito*, and after years of selling his grapes, in 2006 he began making his own wine named for his Milanese-born wife, Shamira.

At thirty-three Basile bore no resemblance to most *Panteschi contadini*. A husky man with thick hands and broad shoulders, he wore a pink Lacoste shirt, blue jeans, and flip-flops, his hair pulled back in a short ponytail. Basile's mind seemed to be in constant motion, his pale blue eyes sparkling as he talked about *passito*, finance, and the winery machinery he hoped to better adapt to the making of the sweet wine.

He was indeed organized—though he said he had to rely on a fellow producer to bottle his *passito*, which was different than the De Bartoli and Ferrandes *passitos*. Basile used what he called "the old system to make a young wine." He had just released—and had no problem selling—his first vintage of 7,000 bottles of a handcrafted wine that he insisted was easier drinking and less expensive than traditional *passito*.

His first *passito* (2006) was light, floral, and tasted of apples and apricots—a wine that Salvatore Ferrandes would call "not yet" a *passito*. But that didn't matter to Basile, a young man in touch with modern tastes and the drinking habits of the north. The only aspect of modernity that troubled him was the increasing difficulty of finding manual labor.

"The *passito* of our grandparents' day doesn't exist anymore," Basile said without any regret. His grandparents, he said, had drunk a dark brown, cloudy liquid that was higher in alcohol and sugar than anything presently on the island. And another thing: that generation didn't make *passito* for its meditative qualities, but did it as a way of reviving the previous year's dry white wines that had begun oxidizing in their barrels.

"Look at this," Basile said as he shuffled over to a long wood table on which were stacked wooden crates full of fat, red-brown Zibibbo raisins. "All this has to be done by hand. Machines cannot do this."

Basile found a whole grape stem and grabbed roughly at the fruit.

"Machines break the stems," he said, illustrating. His workforce for plucking raisins was old *contadini*, including his eighty-five-year-old grandmother, who worked on a table in front of her television. "They have to be picked one at a time. But young people don't want to do this kind of work. I don't know what we'll do when these old people go."

FROM BUKKURAM, SEBASTIANO AND I headed south along the coast, taking a final tour of the island in my rental car before I headed to the airport. At Scauri we turned inland on the flanks of Mount Gibele. We entered an area of steep terraced vineyards, vast expanses of wild *macchia*, and every so often an abandoned *dammuso* or *giardino arabo*. There were no electric or phone lines, and the roughness of the place was highlighted by the speed at which the sun and shadow seemed to move over the hills that morning.

It was here in Contrada Serraglio that Carole Bouquet, the French actress, fell in love with Pantelleria and bought and renovated her vineyards. The European press had been full of stories to the effect that Bouquet—the former Bond girl who helped save the free world in *For Your Eyes Only* (1981)—was now rescuing abandoned vineyards on Pantelleria and producing her own *passito* with a name worthy of a Bond movie: Sangue d'Oro (Golden Blood).

We stopped in front of the private road that led to Bouquet's property and decided to take a look around, knowing that as the summer season was over, Bouquet was likely at home in Paris or off shooting a film somewhere else. We turned down the road and pulled up to a *dammuso* with a few cars parked on the side. The structure, which looked to be a renovated old fieldworker's house, was perched above a valley of walled vineyards. In front was a small terrace overhung by an iron arbor covered with the large plumes of Pampas grass. The sky had turned gray, but off in the distance the sun shone brightly on an aquamarine slice of the Mediterranean.

"*C'è qualcuno?*" Sebastiano called out by the open front door, asking if anyone was home.

Two women arrived from around back of the house, speaking rapidly in Italian—ignoring us as they seemed to be concluding a conversation. One appeared to be a local businesswoman and the other was Carole Bouquet. Not the young Melina Havelock in *For Your Eyes Only* or the icy, elegant Carole in the Chanel No. 5 advertisements, but a different Carole Bouquet.

This Carole Bouquet wore no makeup over features that nevertheless came together in an unmistakable beauty: the broad high cheekbones, the thin nose, the long, slightly down-turned lips. Her skin was white and unwrinkled behind a pair of rectangular amber-colored eyeglass frames. Her not quite shoulder-length hair was tied in a floppy ponytail. She wore baggy rumpled clothes—flowing white linen top, gray linen pants, and athletic shoes. A thick gold cotton sweater was tied around her waist.

After she finished her business and the other woman went on her way, Bouquet gave us a critical look-over. Sebastiano did the talking —explaining in Italian that he was a son of Marco De Bartoli and I was here on a mission to chronicle Sicilian wine. Bouquet folded her arms as if in thought and looked at our shoes.

Then she declared, in perfect Italian, with the ease and geniality that I've come to expect from rural winemakers, that yes, she would accompany us to her winery down in the village. First, however, she needed to find her land foreman and winemaker, who was somewhere up on the mountain behind us.

The mountain slopes were traversed by a network of lava stone walls that served double duty here as both paths through the vines and windscreens. Bouquet jumped on one of the walls and bounded like a goat up the trail of loose stones.

"Nunzio!" she called out, stopping to look up the mountain. She unwrapped the sweater from around her waist and pulled it over her head. "Nunzio!"

She climbed higher and faster. Up the mountain patches of mist were now blowing just over our heads.

"Nunzio!" she called into the wind.

Sebastiano surveyed the folds of the landscape and spotted a tiny figure a couple of hundred yards away. He pointed the figure out to Bouquet, who waved her hand over her head and called out. Nunzio waved back and made his way toward us.

"*Ma che cosa fa in Pantelleria?*" Sebastiano asked with bemusement. Indeed, what was *she doing here?*

Bouquet laughed. "What language shall we speak? Is English good?" She could shift seamlessly between at least three tongues.

"I don't know what I'm doing in Pantelleria!" She sang out, "I'm crazy. Everything here was abandoned for as much as twenty years."

"I never thought I would make wine, but I started fixing things," she spoke as quickly as the wind. "And then I bought one hectare, then two, then three, then five. And now ten!"

Bouquet, now at fifty-one, had been introduced to Pantelleria thirteen years earlier by her good friend, the actress/model/author Isabella Rossellini. She fell in love with this part of the island and bought the abandoned *dammuso* eight years earlier, when she was married to Gérard Depardieu, the actor and producer of bombastic wines.

"Everybody said you can't buy there—there's no electricity!" Bouquet said. It took five years for her to obtain a construction permit. She'd installed a generator for electricity and moved in part of the year two years earlier.

"So you start fixing things up and then what do you do with the grapes?" she said. Many of her vines were planted in dug-out holes—like the Ferandeses' were. They all had to be tilled by hand—obviously hands other than those of film stars.

Nunzio Gorgone reached us—an elegant man of nearly sixty with weathered skin and stained clothes. Bouquet led the way down, arms flapping as she raced ahead skirting the wild capers along the path.

Sebastiano and I followed her and Nunzio to the winery, which was as aesthetically composed as a Milan boutique. The walls were dramatically painted the amber gold of her *passito*, and the floor was painted blood red. In the small bottling room off to the side were stacked cases of her third vintage, 2007 Sangue d'Oro, that had just been put in bottles.

Nunzio produced a chilled bottle and some glasses. The wine was lighter in color—golden as the name implies—than any of the other handcrafted *passito* I'd seen. Bouquet used her local winemaker, Nunzio, and the famed Piedmont oenologist Donato Lanati (who also consulted for Graci on Etna and Palari in Messina) to make a young, expressive floral *passito*, lightened by a streak of refreshing acidity.

"What I make is a *passito* I like," she said. "It's a *passito* that makes me happy . . . and that reflects the island."

I'd spent the last few days talking with male winemakers who dried their grapes under the plastic of greenhouses. Bouquet insisted that hers be dried in the full elements: the air, the wind, and even the rain. Bouquet spoke as lovingly about Pantelleria's nature as Salvatore Ferrandes had—but with the energy of a cyclone.

"I didn't do it for the money. I'm not making money," she said. "I did it because I loved the land . . . it was the land speaking."

Surely, Carole Bouquet is an actress who is paid to emote. She is paid to put her face on products to seduce men and women into buying. She puts her name on her bottles of Sangue d'Oro. I was doubtful about her influence in Pantelleria. My first impulse would be to think of her as one more dilettante celebrity winemaker. But she was here alone in the middle of nowhere—she had come for the bottling. And more than most accomplished people who take up winemaking later in life, she seemed to really care about the wine she made in collaboration with this land and in this wind. In fact, Bouquet seemed a woman not so much planted in the soil as balanced in the wind. I thought of the way she ran through the vineyards—the way she seemed to move in time with the strange currents on Pantelleria. And I thought the daughter of the wind had come home.

12

A Bridge Too Close

AT THE NORTHEASTERN TIP OF Sicily, Messina curls around the toe of the Italian boot and the seafront of Reggio di Calabria in a way that has teased generations since the time of Julius Caesar. At its narrowest point, the Strait of Messina—separating Sicily from mainland Italy—is less than 2 miles wide, and from Messina you can almost feel the breath of the steep, rugged Aspromonte chain of mountains that rises up from the mainland. For more than two thousand years, emperors, kings, and politicians have talked about bridging the Strait. So far, Sicily and Calabria have remained separated—two lands with their distinct contours, agriculture, traditions, cooking, mafias, wines, and their own long, troubled histories. Now it seems doubtful that Sicily will survive the twenty-first century—or even another decade—as its own *continente*.

In the new millennium, the champion of the Strait of Messina bridge has been a man who by his own account is the world's greatest living leader: the Italian prime minister, Silvio Berlusconi. Where Caesar only dreamed of a bridge, Berlusconi has steamrolled a path for the world's longest suspension structure—with train rails and twelve lanes for motor vehicles fed by billions of euros flowing from the European Union.

The bridge, Berlusconi has said, "will give Sicilians 100 percent status as Italian citizens," a bizarre statement implying that Sicilians have less than whole status.

Work was set to begin sometime in 2010 and last for six years, but this being Italy, one can always hope for dysfunction or scandal. Sicilians are in favor of the bridge—so say the polls—though I imagine many are caught in a Sicilian paradox: being for the bridge *as long as it is not actually constructed* in their lifetimes. I have yet to find one Sicilian who wants the thing built. Of course, I speak mainly with the kind of people who don't put much faith in the Italian government's grandiose industrial designs.

There are many arguments against the bridge. Environmentalists are concerned about the effects on bird migration. Dissenting seismologists warn of the structure's inability to withstand a shock like the 1908 earthquake that leveled Messina and claimed two-thirds of its population. And it is hard to imagine that modern Italy's grandest public works project could not be a boon to Mafia coffers.

But there is a reason even more fundamental. It's a feeling expressed by Salvatore Geraci, the Messina wine producer, when he says: "*Meglio che La Sicilia resta isolata*" ("Better that Sicily stays apart").

In wine, Messina is its own island, represented by a tiny, once near-extinct appellation in the steep hills southwest of town known as Faro (literally, "lighthouse"). There are only a handful producers in Faro—the most formidable being Geraci, a Messina architect whose small winery, Palari, uses what were once his grandparents' vineyards to make what some argue is the most individual and complex red wine in all of Italy.

My first experience with Palari Faro was the first released vintage —a 1994 of less than 5,000 bottles. Alessio Planeta had visitors in the Planeta cellars in Menfi late one afternoon, and I remember the reverent way he pulled out the dusty bottle and opened it. Alessio may oversee production of millions of bottles, but he appreciates micro-production wines and products of the Sicilian soil and sun. After that, I remember the smell: the sort of stinky-meets-the-sublime way the odors rushed out from the glass. There were aromas of animal, and peasant feet walking on a carpet of mushrooms. In other words, French. At the same time, there was balance, acidic elegance, staying power. In this Sicilian cellar it tasted like Burgundy's Nuits-Saint-Georges—though later, on French soil, another bottle tasted as if it were from somewhere in Italy north of the olive line.

That season the Italian wine bible, *Gambero Rosso*, named Palari Faro's 2005 vintage as Italy's "Red of the Year." In speaking about recent vintages the editors hyperbolized: "The only reds of comparable elegance and complexity might be a Chambolle-Musigny or Vosne-Romanée from the Burgundy heartlands."

For eighteen years Geraci had worked in concert with Donato Lanati, who also crafted Carole Bouquet's wines and consulted with Graci on Etna. Among oenologists, Lanati is known as a *terroir* man—his work is about meticulous analysis of grapes in the vineyard rather than winery tricks or additives.

Yet I still found Geraci/Palari's fairytale incredible. How was it possible that an architect with little wine background could turn his attention to his family's unknown vineyards and produce wine this distinct?

I'd arranged to meet Geraci on a weekday morning in late October not far from the freeway exit ramp. From there I would follow him to the Faro hills and his vineyards. In our phone conversations in Italian, Geraci repeatedly downplayed his winery as "small," "nothing," a "garage."

I began to picture Geraci as a serious craftsman who got his hands and feet dirty in his vineyards and winery. He was no doubt a man who *lived* wine, and when he stuck his hand out to greet me it would be rough and the creases would be stained purple from the recent harvest.

Then, after Geraci fixed our meeting point, he said, "I'll be waiting for you—I'll be in my green *Jag-u-ar.*"

Now, I understand that there are winemakers who love beautiful cars—witness Marco De Bartoli. But there did seem to me something a bit on the dandy side in the choice of his ride.

When I pulled up behind the hunter green Jaguar XJ, the man

who stepped out from the driver's seat was nothing like what I'd expected. Geraci was a man of medium height and good looks. He had an easy boyish smile, and his silver hair did a rakish flip on top of his head. He removed a pair of dark, horn-rimmed Ray-Bans, revealing a pair of soft hazel eyes.

The surprise came in the way Geraci was put together: his thoroughly impeccable tailoring. He wore a sky-blue linen suit—a patterned hankie tucked into the jacket pocket. He wore no tie, and the cuffs of his red-and-white-striped shirt were fastened with a pair of lapis links. The shoes were black cherry, tassled loafers. He was probably the best-dressed man this side of Naples, and when he extended his hand it was muscular but manicured. I was now completely confused: not only was this man working wonders in his family vineyards, but he was doing it with the easy style of a Latin lover.

I followed Geraci and his Jag to a parking lot in front of a vegetable stand where we left our cars and met his younger brother, Giampiero, who drove a four-wheel-drive truck. Giampiero wore stained green work pants, heavy boots, and a worn button-down shirt. So here was the muscle in the operation, I figured. We drove into the steep hills—passing the ancient monastery converted to an agronomy school where Giampiero had studied. Giampiero, who I learned was indeed both the foreman over the land and supervisor for the grunt work in the winery, drove silently. He was accustomed, it seemed, to letting his older brother do the talking.

At one point Messina came into view and beyond it the Calabria coast—a dark shadow in the morning haze. The roads grew steeper, narrower, and rougher as we climbed through turns so sharp Giampiero had to put the truck into reverse and restart the climb to finish them. The hills seemed to spread in every direction—colored with prickly pear cacti, light unripe olives, and oranges that were still deep green. Near the small, perched village of Pezzolo we looked out over a valley at the stone terraces that had surrendered to *macchia*.

"The sad story of Sicily," Salvatore exhaled in Italian, and we kept climbing until the road turned to a sandy dirt track that wound through olive groves and vineyards. The leaves of the vines, along with those of the occasional wild cherry or almond tree, were turning gold and brown. A stray mountain ash added an explosion of red. We had climbed so quickly my ears popped.

"In Sicily if you don't have altitude you can't make elegant wine—you make *marmellata*," Salvatore pronounced the word for marmalade neutrally, pretending to reserve judgment. "It is easy in Sicily to make *marmellata*; it is not so easy to make a wine that is complex."

The truck stopped in front of a small iron gate, and we got out. We had climbed about 600 meters above the sea. It was a bright Mediterranean day, and a light breeze mingled the salt air with the smells of Sicilian autumn—a mix of decaying leaves with the new carpet of wildflowers and grasses.

We walked through the gate and into the vineyards, where shaggy *alberello*-shaped vines, each supported by a traditional chestnut post, seemed to be floating in a low jungle of weeds. Along with the two mainstay grapes found in Etna wines—Nerello Mascalese, Nerello Cappuccio—were planted lesser-known Sicilian varietals such as Acitana, Nocera, and Galatena.

The harvest in the vineyard had been completed two weeks earlier, and I struggled to imagine Salvatore picking and loading grapes, which he said he did. The vineyard had none of the groomed sentry-like order of Burgundy. Fruit and nut trees sprouted here and there, and the vines followed the uneven contours of the terraces. It was a vineyard created by people who didn't see themselves as winemakers in the modern sense.

These acres were planted in the 1930s by Geraci's grandparents, who had lived through the Messina earthquake and whose main business was growing citrus for the perfume industry. As a sideline they made a rustic wine that they sold in bulk locally and enjoyed with family members and friends.

Though there is evidence of winemaking in Messina back to antiquity, by the 1980s it was all but dead. At the close of that decade Salvatore was a successful restoration architect who had, not surprisingly, become a collector of fine Burgundy wines. Before he made wine, he invited Lanati to come look at the Geraci family vineyards. "Lanati said, 'You have heroic vines.' He thought I could make a grand wine, but he told me I would have to experiment," Salvatore said.

Salvatore described his winegrowing operation as organic but said he had no desire to be certified as such or to place it on Palari bottles. "When you have the sun and the wind you don't have problems," Salvatore said as he gave an Italian make-it-look-easy shrug. "Here we have natural harmony." Salvatore made it all seem so naturally harmonious, in fact, I had to wonder why he would need an oenologist to helicopter in here to help him make wine. In Eden, after all, shouldn't you just have to collect the grapes and let the wine make itself?

"The natural product of grapes is not wine." Salvatore paused as we reached the southern edge of the ridge, and he peered at me as if he were about to let me in on a secret. "The natural product of grapes is vinegar!" Fair enough: grapes do naturally ferment to wine; after that, if exposed to oxygen, aceto bacteria will take over and turn it to vinegar. I was not as impressed with the science behind his statement as much as its élan—delivered as if Salvatore were saying, "The natural product of silk worms is not Brioni suits."

Still, Geraci insisted that his winemaking use only a small helping of technology. He used yeasts selected and preserved from his own vineyards. After that, Lanati's role was studying grapes to improve vinification. By understanding the vineyard's raw material, the oenologist and winemaker adjusted variables such as the harvest dates, fermentation temperatures, maceration times before pressing, or the amount of yeast to be used. It's largely those elements of timing and technique that make his wine and not the wine of his grandparents.

We walked back to the truck and rode down the creases of the hillside to Villa Geraci. The family villa was an imposing eighteenth-century half-ruin, decorated in a jumble of Sicilian styles for an eclectic, eccentric result. The iron gates at the south side of the villa hung in a stone archway topped by a giant Baroque-looking moustache—a flamboyant touch repeated at the edge of the garden terrace. At the front of the building, a grand double staircase climbed to an impressive arched doorway.

The melodrama of the place comes from its redecoration in the nineteenth century to resemble a medieval castle. Finishing the effect are battlements known as Ghibelline merlons—geometric fish-tail shapes originally invented to protect archers with crossbows. On Villa Geraci, however, the battlements were purely theatrical. Palms stood on the terrace of sand and worn grass, and bougainvillea hugged the walls. The views down the hillsides toward the sea and mainland Italy were nearly perfect—marred only by the villa's position, perched just above the sad jumble of concrete confusion that is the village of Santo Stefano di Briga. Behind the façade, there is a working winery—a series of large rooms permanently open to the elements through window openings or nonexistent walls. In a wing used for bottling, the roof had fallen in and had been only partially replaced. The vaulted cellar, dug into the hillside, was neatly renovated and lined with the new pricey *barriques* made of Troncais forest oak from central France.

Salvatore and I went to the simple office on the ground floor. We sat on opposite sides of his desk next to a large open window. At the top of a pile of papers on his desk, I noticed a book called *The London Cut*—about Savile Row tailoring. Despite his admiration for English suits, Salvatore spoke little of the English language. So we conversed that day in Italian. Salvatore moved some piles of mail around on his desk, sat down, and asked what questions I had of him.

"How old are you?" I asked.

"The ladies don't need to know that." The boyish smile eased across his face. But when I persisted, he grew serious and then annoyed. Finally he said, "You don't need to write this: I am fifty-five, but we can say for the purposes of publication . . . forty-seven."

The interview had gotten off to a bad start. Salvatore seemed ready for it to end. It was time for lunch, he announced. He stood and used his *telefonino* to reserve a table in Messina. He fetched a few bottles to take with us, and Giampiero drove us back to town in his truck. The route we took was an all-too-typical Sicilian juxtaposition of beauty and squalor: the desolateness of Santo Stefano was followed by a spontaneous trash dump, a shepherd grazing his flock on weeds and trash, and the open wound of a cement plant just before we got to the road along the sea.

Downtown Messina, in contrast, is a bright bustling town that was destroyed in the 1908 earthquake and rebuilt thereafter. I followed Salvatore in his Jag to the Piazza Municipio—the city hall plaza and the simple but intimate ten-table Osteria, Le Due Sorelle.

Entering the restaurant with his arms full of bottles, Salvatore exchanged cheek-brushing kisses with the owner Renato Orlando, a slightly older balding man and a reputed lover of wine. He called out to the restaurant's only waitress—a young woman with long black hair and dark eyes—that we required large Burgundy glasses. Salvatore opened the door of the refrigerated wine storage case and slipped the bottles inside.

"I prefer to drink them a little cool, like in Burgundy," he said and added a loving flourish: "Like Romanée Conti."

In the Italian wine press, Burgundian references to Palari Faro have become almost gratuitous. They began even before the wine's first public release by Luigi "Gino" Veronelli, the late legend of Italian wine and gastronomy who compared Geraci-Lanati's first experiments to Domaine de la Romanée Conti—the world's most fabled wine producer with the most revered vineyard and the most expensive wine. (One bottle of some recent vintages were valued about the same as Salvatore's XJ.)

Six large balloon glasses—tapered at the rim—arrived at our table, and Salvatore ceremoniously stuck his nose in each one of them. The first four passed the sniff taste; the last two made his head recoil in a blast of dishwasher smell. Salvatore signaled the waitress to come take them away.

Salvatore stood and went to the wine case to get the first of the bottles for tasting. As he settled back into the chair, he gripped the lapels of his jacket and asked, *"Permesso?"* ("May I?") It was a gentlemanly, theatrical touch, as I was already in shirtsleeves. As Salvatore opened the first bottle, he spoke about his trips to the United States, which he makes several times a year. "When I am in New York . . . " Salvatore made a dramatic gesture sucking air in through his nose, "I breathe! It's the shopping, everything."

We then spoke about the bridge that would cross the Messina Strait. Salvatore began by speaking of the staggering expense of the proposed Messina bridge. "Messina to Palermo is the same distance as Paris to Lyon. It takes one and a half hours by train to go from Paris to Lyon; Messina to Palermo takes four hours," he said. "The whole island of Sicily has only two golf courses and two pleasure ports for boats. What do we need with a bridge?"

I didn't get what golf courses and yacht berths had to do with a bridge. I didn't like the idea of a bridge, but for other reasons: Sicily had retained its soul at least in part because it was removed. It had resisted the worst symptoms of globalization: everywhere becoming like everywhere else. There seemed something troubling, wrong, and arrogantly human about trying to pull Sicily closer to mainland Europe.

Salvatore rinsed a pair of glasses with the first wine, transferring a couple of ounces from one glass to the next, swirling, and finally emptying the wine in a water glass. As he poured the first wine—Palari's base wine called Rosso del Soprano, from his own as well as other purchased grapes outside Faro—Geraci quoted the Sicilian novelist and social critic Leonardo Sciascia, who died around the time the Geracis were making their first wines.

"Sciascia said that to be born, to live, and to die on an island is a particular existence," Salvatore said wistfully. "He called it a condition of noble solitude." We lifted the hefty glasses and smelled and tasted what—at least here in Sicily—seemed vaguely reminiscent of Burgundy. "If you build a bridge, you are no longer an island," Salvatore pointed to the side of his temple, adding, ". . . mentally."

We ate grilled swordfish and vegetables, then drank Salvatore's lauded 2005 Palari Faro. It was ruby red, and what again struck me was the deep earthy pastoral scent. The wine had power and silkiness—it was bigger than my favorite Nerello-based wines from Etna, and it slowly crawled down the sides of the throat where it finally dissolved. It was a wine with character—not a perfectly polished international wine. It was unlike anything else in Sicily and, frankly, was baffling. Was this a wine that was just waiting to be made in Geraci's family vineyards? I thought of the new expensive *barriques* in the winery, and tried to find some evidence of oak abuse. *Barriques* can smother some wines with flavors of roasted vanilla and licorice that are layered on like frosting on a cake. But in this wine, the barrel aging was mellow, well-integrated. It was a wine I liked certainly more than I understood.

Some Sicilian historians like to point out that Messina made wine for Rome during Caesar's day—something that Salvatore dismissed with a shrug. "The history of quality Sicilian wines goes back twenty years when people started using modern methods and oenologists" he said, "Before that Sicily was growing grapes to make wine to add alcohol and color to wines in the north of Italy and France."

"You know," he went on, "Sicily makes more grapes than the Piedmont, Tuscany, and Umbria combined. Eighteen percent goes into wine. What happens to the other 82 percent?" He paused, then answered his own question: "Distillation, concentrated grape must, and bulk wine that goes to northern Italy and France."

When the plates were cleared from the table, Salvatore stood and went to the wine case and got a third bottle of wine—a Palari Faro 2000. As he settled back in his chair, he said, "Veronelli wrote that the French take silver grapes and make gold wine. And that the Italians—particularly in the South—take golden grapes and make silver wine!"

It wasn't difficult to figure out which metal Salvatore Geraci preferred. Yet, even with his gold medal accomplishments, he feared for the future of Sicilian wine.

"There was a time when the future was going to be the Sicilian coast . . . when it was going to be the only coast in the world," Salvatore said. "So what happened? Everyone built on the Sicilian coast and they destroyed it. Now Sicilian wine is coming into fashion. My fear is that in ten years it will be over . . . finished . . . destroyed by too much Merlot, Chardonnay, et cetera, and all that will be left is a few small producers."

Plates of cheese arrived including aged ricotta and raw sheep's *tomma* studded with peppercorns (a cheese which I thought shared some smells of Salvatore's wine). Salvatore rinsed the third pair of glasses and he poured the Faro 2000—a wine more delicate than the last, it seemed tamed by the passage of time.

Salvatore spoke of his personal life. There was a fiancée, a Belgian architect. And there was his wife, also an architect. Salvatore was not divorced. And as he explained the situation, I understood his personal outrage at the bridge project: the woman he described as his soon-to-be-ex-wife (with whom he had two grown daughters) lived not on Sicily but in her native Calabria—just on the other side of the strait. Salvatore had a very good reason for not wanting Sicily connected with the world. He was, after all, a man who needed to breathe.

"*Meglio che La Sicilia resta isolata.*"

As we stood, preparing to leave the restaurant, Salvatore fell into what seemed a very personal conversation with our young waitress. From what I could understand, there was a concern in her private life: her boyfriend or her husband. Salvatore was as attentive as a young priest listening to confession. In the end, he quietly cradled her hand, bent from the waist, and kissed it.

We drove for a bit in the Jag around the center of Messina, and every few yards, someone—pedestrians, guys on motorcycles, other people in cars—seemed to recognize Salvatore and waved. Salvatore stopped the car across the street from the Bar Progresso. He ignored the fact that there were open parking spaces perpendicular to the curb, and instead he left the car in the middle of the street while we crossed to the bar. Salvatore wanted to take me there to experience the local ice cream treat called *spongati*—a smooth light-brown cream flavored with intense espresso and left half-frozen, almost soupy as it was hand-slathered into cones.

We got back in the Jag and rolled slowly in traffic to another café, where we stood at the bar and ordered a pair of espressos. "In hot cups, please," Salvatore called out. The café was chic, and behind the bar were a tall handsome young man and a young woman with black hair, a black outfit sprayed on her slender frame, and a small diamond stud in her Roman nose.

It was afternoon and the bar was busy. People came up to greet Salvatore, to exchange kisses, or talk business. Salvatore glanced in the mirror, cooed something to the woman behind the bar. Our espressos arrived in their hot cups and Salvatore carefully stirred the thick light, speckled froth—*crema*—on top of the coffee. The place had the kind of pulse you can only find in Italian cafés: fueled by the beat of pop radio in the background, the hissing and droning of the espresso machine, and the clinking of porcelain and metal. In an instant, I saw Salvatore in his element, moving to the beat. He was Sicilian. He was worldly. He was continental. As long as the continent kept its distance.

13

Palmento

ON ETNA, ONE PERFECTLY CRYSTALLINE morning in late October, it was difficult to imagine the despair that led my grandfather and so many thousands of others to want to leave this place. I drove to Passopisciaro and climbed through vineyards—each breath felt like an invigorating blast of oxygen. With the fall rains the landscape had been transformed: the vineyard soils had turned black and heavy and were now covered with a spring-like blanket of grasses, wild-flowers, and *ferula*. I looked up to the mid haunches of Etna into a profoundly mountain-blue sky. The changing colors of the vines from green to yellow seemed to vibrate against the backdrop of volcanic stone terraces. Then I looked north, down the mountain toward the Alcantara Valley and the Peloritani Mountains. In those moments it all seemed like Eden.

Suddenly a violent blast erupted from Andrea Franchetti's vines and sent a flurry of wings flapping upwards. Franchetti was now using propane cannons to keep away the magpies and other foraging birds, which had discovered that his were among the last vineyards to get picked and were swarming for breakfast. Franchetti was one of the last harvesters on Etna along with Alberto Aiello Graci and

Frank Cornelissen—all of whom were waiting for the maturing of phenols in the skins and seeds that would add color and aromas to their wine. The idea that there were winemakers now timing their harvests to chase elusive flavors to be put in bottles and later uncorked on foreign shores would surely have been unthinkable in my grandfather's time and remains a mystery to many *contadini* today.

I'd returned to Etna because I was eager to see the end of the harvest and learn how the vintage was turning out. From the airport I'd phoned Marco de Grazia, who like most Etna wine producers had finished his *vendemmia* (harvest) a week earlier. De Grazia spoke on his cell phone from Palermo en route to the continent, enthusing breathlessly about the 2008 vintage.

"It's been an unbelievable year for the grapes," de Grazia gushed. He went on about the qualities of the October sunlight before harvest and the perfection of fruit to such an extent that I imagined de Grazia's grapes begging to be crushed—impatient to show off their attributes in wine. "2008 is turning out to be a vintage like I have never seen!"

I later called Andrea Franchetti and got a much different assessment. "It's been a shitty year," croaked Franchetti, who was in Tuscany in the grip of a flu virus that had lowered his growl a full octave. The phenols, he explained, were half their normal level. The juice produced by the grapes was thin. "It's been a shitty year all over Europe."

I began repeating what de Grazia had told me and he cut me off: "De Grazia is a salesman! I don't give a shit what he thinks!"

De Grazia and Franchetti both seemed the kind of men who create their own worlds and then live in them. They were casual friends. But on that day in October, with de Grazia's grapes finishing fermentation and Franchetti's still on the vine, those worlds couldn't have seemed farther apart. To have any perspective on the harvest, I would have to go to elsewhere.

I joined Alberto Aiello Graci on an almost perfect morning, marred only by a cool swirling wind that smelled of storms, at his winery north of Passopisciaro. At about 600 meters in altitude, the Contrada

Arcuria is a relatively low and gentle slope with vineyards separated by lava veins of *sciara* now covered with wild almond trees, broom, and brambles.

I found the winery grounds littered with construction debris. Inside, Alberto had begun to transform the old winery. The second story with its old *palmento* and a row of large chestnut casks remained encrusted with mold and dust. But now large plateglass windows separated it from the floor below and Alberto's spotless—but nearly empty—new winery. The winery was roughly the size of a school gymnasium with soaring stone arches that held up the roof. Along a long back wall were five new *tini*, upright conical oak casks set on stout wood stands. Each *tino* was of slightly different design and bore manufacturer's imprints from Italy, Austria, and Bulgaria.

I was here because Alberto was a young winemaker still learning his trade, and I considered him forthright and free of illusions. Alberto, wearing a zippered sweater, tall rubber work boots, and jeans, seemed more nervous than I had ever seen him. We crossed the country road into the vineyards, and on the way he explained to me his worries. In Alberto's estimation, the crop in his vineyards was neither the marvel described by de Grazia nor the disaster portrayed by Franchetti, but uneven and difficult to understand. "We won't know until the grapes start fermenting," he said, pushing up the rims of his thick glasses.

Alberto's problem was this: In the long dry spell of summer, many of his vines—particularly the young vines he'd planted here in Arcuria—had shut down their photosynthesis and the grapes stopped maturing. Alberto wanted more time for the fruit to mature, but in waiting there was risk. Rain—predicted as early as that evening—could swell the grapes and burst the skins. In one of his vineyards a late summer hail had already damaged much of the crop.

Alberto wanted ripe grapes but he also needed healthy grapes. On this day a dozen pickers, men and women from young to middle-aged, were harvesting vines planted in *alberello* form but attached to cordon wires rather than chestnut posts—a technique to simplify plowing the vine rows by tractor. What struck me about the work was the slow, deliberate, and focused way it was carried out. The pickers would first clip a small bunch of Nerello grapes, then turn it over in their hands while clipping out any mold-tinted grapes or bare parts of stem. Each, it seemed, got a careful trim.

Between the vine rows were wild plants at knee height. There were white trumpet-shaped flowers of wild peppers, the small yellow blooms of *cavolicello* (Mediterranean cabbage), and the violet blossoms of the minty cooking herb *nepitella*.

Alberto huddled with his vineyard foreman, Nino, a compact man with rounded features, and who, in his forties, had a smile that easily creased his white beard and weathered face. The two men talked about the sections of the vineyard that would be picked that morning. Alberto then darted from one vine row to another, pulling grapes from their clusters. He popped the grapes into his mouth and squeezed drops of juice onto a handheld refractometer—which when held to the sun gave a reading of sugar content. As he did this, the dark eyebrows furrowed to make the only wrinkles in his boyish face.

"When you taste the grapes you taste the wine," Alberto said. "Compared with 2007, I am a bit afraid because of the quality of the tannins. Last year we had more elegant tannins. This year the skins taste tougher, harder."

"Anyway, it is only after the vinification that we will know. We will know everything. Right now . . . I just don't know."

Alberto repeated variations of these phrases as if reciting the Rosary. For most of that morning I followed him up and down the contours of the vineyard, where the soils seemed to change dramatically from black dirt sprouting meadows of weeds to bare stretches of jagged fist-sized stones. Alberto noted that in a vineyard sunken into a small depression, the grapes had more bitter tannins and far less sugar—about 20 percent less—than a vineyard on a ridge above.

"This is Etna," Alberto said both admiring and confounded by the nuances of his own land. "Five meters away and the grapes are totally different."

As we walked back to the others, the weather had shifted. A wind from the east had carried on its breath a cool, damp fog reminiscent

of Lombardy or the Piedmont. Not far from the road, an old truck
trailer squatted amid the vines. Next to it was a concrete pad, the size
of an Italian living room, furnished with scattered plastic chairs and
a table welded together from an old steel door. Sheltering this setup
was a steel frame covered with makeshift layers of now soggy roof
underlayment. As we walked closer I saw inside the trailer where
there were plastic crates filled with provisions, along with a small
refrigerator powered by a wire that was fed through a hole in the
sidewall and attached to a nearby utility pole.

At the edge of this setup, Nino the foreman—wearing a once-red,
baseball-style cap now weathered to illegibility—used a short wood
paddle to fan the charcoal in a pair of small metal barbecue grills. The
smoke dangling in the sudden chill teased one of the most delicious
anticipations I know: the promise of a harvest lunch.

As the coals turned white, Nino filled two steel grilling racks, one
with thick pieces of pancetta and the other with strings of pork sausage. He placed the meat over the coals—the dripping hot fat igniting
small fires, which he smothered with handfuls of coarse salt. The
wind swirled the fatty smoke and the bacon smells, and the pair of
dogs who guarded the vineyard came and hovered close by.

A siren wailed from somewhere up the valley, signaling lunchtime.
About a dozen workers gathered around the trailer and pulled up
empty harvest crates on which they sat. Most everyone, Nino explained, was part of his extended family—cousins, nieces, relations by
marriage. Large rounds of bread were sliced—brown on the outside
and as yellow as cake within. Some of the workers had brought their
own home-baked loaves. A leather-faced man squatting next to me
on a crate offered a piece of a loaf made by his mother. He sliced it
by holding the knife—blade toward himself—and pushing the loaf
against the cutting edge with his thumb.

His mamma's bread was dense and faintly sweet and the most
fragrant of all. We folded the bread around pieces of the meat,
then used it to sop the brown juices from the plastic plates. A jug
of red wine was pulled out and poured into plastic cups—part of
Alberto's production that did not make it into his final bottlings

from the previous year. This reject wine was more rewarding than most Sicilian wines I'd tasted in bottle. It was simple and tart, and it beautifully cleaned away the fatty juices left from the pork.

Nino fed scraps of pancetta to the dogs, who then licked the last drippings from our discarded plates. The cold blanket of winter was not far off. And as the men rolled tobacco into cigarettes and ignited them, I almost wished that I smoked—settling instead for a small cup of coffee poured out of a thermos that was passed from hand to hand.

ANOTHER REASON FOR MY RETURNING to Etna was to spend more time with Salvo Foti. I wanted to learn more from this oenologist who had thoroughly studied Etna, its wines, and its *palmenti* long before the foreigners such as Franchetti or de Grazia had moved in. I met Foti one morning at a café in Passopisciaro, and we drove north and west toward his small vineyard in Contrada Calderara. It had rained that night and this morning the sky remained troubled, Etna hiding itself from view.

Along the road in Foti's truck we passed Alberto's vineyard in Arcuria, and then we passed some traditional rows of *alberello* vines trained on chestnut posts. Foti insisted that this format was essential for Sicilian winegrowing—that it created a harmony of leaf, shade, and exposition perfectly adapted for Sicily's hot, dry summers.

"It is more work," Foti said. "But it is much more beautiful, and a beautiful vineyard is a beautiful wine."

There it was again: the sweeping verbal gesture magnified in the prism of Sicily, the pronouncement so poetic it nullified any arguments before they could take their first breath. The vines, the amphorae, the thousands of years of history, the *palmenti*, the volcano—the beauty and power of it all. In Italy, of course, beauty is next to holiness. Sicily was long the most treasured daughter of the Mediterranean. So who can teach Sicily anything about beauty?

"The *vigneri* who work for me are the sons of *vigneri* and the grandsons of *vigneri*," Foti said. "This is important—that the method of working is in the DNA."

Another pronouncement—that the creation of beauty was hereditary, passed on to the male child in the womb. Foti's gray hair had grown longer in the month since I had seen him last, and he wore a white stubble of beard. I was struck not so much by the sweep of his arguments but by the somber religiosity with which he delivered them. As he drove past a vineyard belonging to de Grazia, Foti spoke about grapes de Grazia had bought from a local grower—a neighbor of Foti's—in a voice that oozed disdain. It seemed a dislike that Foti harbored for all the *stranieri*—at least those who were not his clients.

Foti was born in Catania and spent years of his childhood living with his winemaking grandfather in Passopisciaro. He had so immersed himself in Etna's history and lore that for him winemaking could not be separated from the mountain and the people. He was a man, I figured, who had begun to communicate with Etna's ghosts.

He explained that Calderara, where we were headed, was one of Etna's oldest craters, formed hundreds of millions of years ago. He told of how the *palmento* system had been developed on Etna and was described by Pliny the Elder nearly two thousand years ago; of the abandonment of the terraces in the industrial postwar decades as wine was made more cheaply with modern machines on the plains of western Sicily; and of how nowadays the traditional Sicilian *palmento* was a mere relic—made illegal for commercial use by questionable European sanitary regulations.

He bottled his wines according to the phases of the moon, his winegrowing practices were organic, and he practiced natural minimalist winemaking. But Foti avoided any labels like *"biologico,"* that to him sounded fashionable, foreign, and thereby worthy of contempt.

"For me the vine is a way that we connect, not just with nature but with everything," he said, pulling up a black dirt road toward an iron gate. "Wine is not the end—it is an instrument."

Ah! The gesture, the beauty, the belief. I might have asked Foti what indeed the end was, but I knew the answer involved service to a greater purpose. Divinity.

"There are people who make *the wine of Etna*," Foti said, separating the believers from the heathens, "and there are people who make *their wine* on Etna."

He stopped at the iron gate, behind which was a small house and about an acre of vineyards—the vines divided between those Foti had planted here after buying this land four years earlier and those that had been planted up to a century ago. They were all trained in *alberello* form—each with its own chestnut tutor. Foti kneeled down and pointed to the bases of some new vines. Some were grafted on modern American phylloxera-resistant rootstock and others were ungrafted. Different species of Nerello were mixed together as well, duplicating the older part of the vineyard.

"It is like a village or a city here," Foti said. "Some of the vines are young, some are old, some are more intelligent, and others more stupid."

From this vineyard Foti produced a Nerello blend called Vinupetra—a local way of saying that it was wine grown from stone. But the Foti wine that most interested me was simply called I Vigneri, his "illegal wine."

The story of I Vigneri wine began with an abundance of grapes in the 2005 harvest. Foti and his fellow *vigneri* decided to make an old-time peasant red in an old *palmento*. Of the first 1,000 bottles, about 200 went to an importer in the United States, and another 200 went to Japan; about half was consumed by Foti and friends. Since then, Foti has made the wine regularly, though in some years the quantity was so small it was all drunk by the *vigneri* themselves.

What made the wine "illegal" was this: the old open lava stone and mortar fermentation basins did not conform to twenty-first-century European sanitary regulations, thereby making bottling and selling the stuff commercially prohibited. Yet as with small pleasures in the European countryside, these laws were frequently ignored or circumvented.

"I should say," Foti corrected, "that the wine itself is not illegal. It is the method of making it that is illegal."

Naturally, I wanted to see the *palmento* where this illegal production took place, but when I told Foti so he became evasive. In fact, the location had changed from *palmento* to *palmento* from year to year. One of the *palmenti* was a few miles to the northeast—Foti waved vaguely in the direction, saying that he didn't have the key to the property with him. Another was on the other side of the mountain—too far. Besides, he insisted, there was nothing to see. The harvest was done, and in the *palmento* system the pressing of the grapes all took place within a day or two—so the *palmenti* were now empty. In any case, Foti said, "If I am asked if the wine is made in a *palmento*, I must say 'no!'"

Foti secured the vineyard with a chain and padlock, and we left in his truck. Heading westward up the valley on the road to Randazzo, we passed one abandoned *palmento* after another. For centuries these *palmenti* had been used by sharecroppers of subdivided vineyards to make wine on the spot—the grapes carried on shoulders or on the backs of donkeys.

"I don't understand how a system that has so much history can be made illegal," Foti shook his head. *"Questo per me e stupido,"* he said ("To me this is stupid"), and added in English: "Very, very stupid!"

Most of the vineyards we passed along the Alcantara Valley were organized for mechanization with *spalliera* rows of cordoned vines supported by cement posts, a sight that led Foti to comment, "Why all this big change?"

He quoted from *Il Gattopardo*—the Sicilian paradox laid out by the Prince's nephew Tancredi: "If we want things to stay as they are, things will have to change." Surely, Foti added, change was inevitable. "But," he freed his right hand from the steering wheel and gently tamped down the air between us, *"a poco a poco"* ("little by little").

"I don't want to invent anything," Foti said—an admission that sounded so odd to my American ears. "I want to conserve and make better—*basta*."

Along the road, we passed lava fields from 1981 that had swallowed portions of vineyards, devoured olive groves, and reshaped the contours of the landscape. Some of the *sciara* were littered with tires, household garbage, plastic bottles, and bags—acts of illegal dumping with their own perverse logic: *The mountain dumps on us, so we dump on the mountain.*

Foti stopped on the wide two-lane as it entered Randazzo, just before the medieval town center. He parked and I noticed coming our way a flock of a couple of hundred sheep taking up both lanes of the road. Out in front of the flock was a shepherd, a stocky man no more than forty years old with close-cropped hair, wearing baggy jeans and a red sweatshirt emblazoned with the word BELIEVE. He carried a stick and flapped his lips to make sheep noises: *"brrraaaanh . . . brrraaaanh."* I followed Foti on foot to the local Carabinieri headquarters, where—he informed me—he needed to pay a visit.

I wondered why Foti would have to stop here. Had his illegal winemaking practices landed him in hot minestrone? Had I Vigneri made him a wanted man? We walked into a police station that would have been called modern decades ago, and Foti informed the officer sitting in shirtsleeves behind bullet-proof glass that he had an appointment with the chief. The man disappeared and moments later returned at a side door with a compact middle-aged superior in a tailored blue-and-red-trimmed jacket fastened by a row of four shiny silver buttons. He was Carlo Procopio, from Calabria, who now headed the local Carabinieri station in Randazzo.

Foti and Procopio exchanged kisses on the cheeks. Procopio shook my hand and then led us down the hall to a drab institutional office that had been enlivened by a small collection of Italian military relics and family memorabilia. On the top of a white plaster replica of a Roman column was displayed a historic full-dress double-breasted jacket of the Carabinieri topped with the famous red-and-blue-plumed hat.

Procopio motioned us into our seats while he lowered himself into a leather chair behind a glass-topped desk. He lit a filterless cigarette with a disposable lighter and picked a piece of tobacco from his nicotine-stained teeth. The men chatted about their families, exchanged bits of unimportant news, and three espressos in plastic cups were brought into the room by the officer from the front desk.

Salvo spoke about his harvest—without mentioning his clandestine wine. Procopio then began probing Foti with technical questions about temperature control and the proper conditions for storing wine. Was it a test? Had Foti ran afoul of some other European edict? Why the technical questions? The more I listened, the more I understood the situation. Procopio kept a small wine cellar at home and was concerned about excessive temperatures—in the summer heat the temperature in the cellar had reached 22°C (nearly 72°F). Foti suggested that the maximum temperature should be no more than 18° to 20° (about 64° to 68°F) and recommended adding insulation, perhaps a heat pump. Procopio ground out his cigarette in an ashtray full of butts. We drained our coffees. Then, without having spoken of anything significant, the men stood. Procopio walked us to the entry and said farewell to Foti with another pair of beard-brushing embraces.

Out on the street, the shepherd's flock had gone. Above the din of the traffic, I asked Foti about the meaning of our visit here.

"In Sicily there are two kinds of people who control the territory —there is the *carabinieri* and there are the shepherds. So it is very important to have good relations with the *carabinieri* and the shepherds."

"I am a friend of the *carabinieri* and a friend of the shepherds," Foti smiled, and added in English: "Public relations."

From Randazzo we drove southwest along the road that cuts across Etna's western slope at more than 1,000 meters' elevation. As we crossed into Bronte, the slope of Etna flattened into a long expanse of brown and green *macchia* interspersed with forests that climbed upward to a peak that was still obscured in cloud. There were no black terraces and lava fields, and from this angle Etna seemed an ordinary mountain.

Foti turned up a small, semi-paved road that led us through a stand of chestnut trees now dropping their fruit. He turned again on a dirt road that led through a dense forest of Ilex oaks and finally to a vineyard. Foti stopped the truck and shut off the ignition, informing me that at 1,200 meters, this was the highest vineyard on Mount Etna. It was a vineyard crudely fenced with a patchwork of thin wire and—in one section—a rusty cot frame. In front of the small iron gate lay a pile of sheep shit the size of a Fiat 500.

Foti took out a heavy ring full of keys, unlocked the padlock, and pushed on the gate, which sighed as it opened. He stood there for a moment in the silence and said, "Listen." There was nothing to hear except an occasional twittering and the flapping of small wings overhead. "What peace. Here we are alone: No Franchetti. No de Grazia. No Planeta. No one."

The statement betrayed Foti's complex contradictions. Yet clearly he loved this place in Bronte's Contrada di Nave. He'd discovered it only a few years earlier when he'd been out walking on the mountain with one of his sons. A wild pig, he said, led them here to this place—the vines up to two hundred years old with stout trunks as thick as trees.

The old man he'd bought it from had continued his family's practice of plowing the vineyard by mule and made Foti promise to do the same as a condition of the sale. We walked through a jungle of thick, gnarled vine trunks with shoots that rose to head height. The vineyard had recently been picked to make the second edition of Vinudilice, meaning "wine of Ilex"—a reference to the surrounding forest.

For the last two harvests this vineyard of less than an acre made enough wine to fill only 650 bottles per year—a level of production that could be called "private." Yet more interesting than the confidentiality of the label was the chance blend of grapes that went into the wine. The vineyard mixed deep-black Alicante with white grapes such as Minnella, Carricante, and Grecanico. Thrown into the mix were other red grapes that fall into the *Francisi* category of unknown origins.

Rather than try to select the wine he would make from the vineyard, Foti gathered all the grapes—just as he did for all wines made under his I Vigneri label—de-stemmed and crushed the bunches and left them to ferment all together in wood *tini*. The result was neither a red wine nor a white wine, but a pinkish one.

"The vineyard decided it was rosé," Foti said triumphantly. "I could separate the grapes, but why?" he shrugged. "It's the vineyard that made the wine—not me."

Another grand statement, only more personal, with an edge in his voice and fire in his eyes. Foti's sense of self seemed to be built on the discipline of his ego and—like the shepherds on high—his resoluteness.

We left the vineyard and walked up a trail among Ilex oaks, Foti reflecting on the history of Etna winemaking. The difficult nature of the land meant that it was divided into smaller parcels among *contadini*. Historically, the landlords—mostly aristocratic families and the Church—Foti said—had enjoyed relatively good relations with the *contadini* because they too tended to live on the land and not in far-off Palermo.

The wines that were produced "were not soft, harmonious wines like now. They were completely different," Foti said. "They were *molto* . . . " he clenched his fist to his chest, "hard . . . tannic, acidic, with high alcohol. What was considered quality was a wine that could travel and not turn to vinegar."

What changed everything on Etna was the postwar investment in industrial winemaking and the construction of large cooperatives in the 1960s and 1970s. "Everything was geared to volume," Foti said. "Irrigation, chemicals, mechanization, everything."

"I am not against technology," Foti insisted. "Technology is not bad in itself—it is the way it is used. For example, you can make a knife and use it to cut bread, or you can use a knife to kill someone. It is not the knife that is bad, it is the use."

It seemed a perfect analogy for the Sicilian countryside, where everyone carried a knife. But I wasn't sure how this related to wine. Foti went on explaining that in wine, using refrigeration to control the temperature during fermentation was not a bad thing.

"By using cold you can use less sulfur and that is good. But now there are people who use cold to make ice wine [a sweet wine naturally made in cold northern European climates] in Sicily. They put the grapes in a freezer and people say, 'Ice wine in Sicily, wow!' But what does ice wine have to do with Sicily? And then there are producers of *passito* in Pantelleria who use electric ovens to dry grapes . . . why use the ovens when you have the sun and wind? It makes no sense."

We stopped climbing at the edge of a dense grove of hazelnut trees. Along the trail I'd noted the fencing and the barbed wire everywhere, and I recounted to Foti the problems Franchetti had with shepherds and fires on his land.

"I am sorry that he has problems," Foti said unconvincingly. "But sometimes when people come from the outside they treat people like they are beneath them. You have to talk with people and respect them. Franchetti is here how many days per year? Twenty? And how many days of the year are the shepherds here? All the time. We must respect nature, respect the vines, and respect the people."

There would be little doubt whose side Foti was on. For all his education and travels, he'd remained a local. And that was only the start of his conflicting impulses: he was the intellectual who identified with *contadini*, the oenologist who disputed the methods of modern oenology, the businessman uncomfortable with capitalism, and the purist who advised the rich and famous.

At lunch in a restaurant in Randazzo we sampled some of Foti's wines, and I was most eager to try his "illegal" I Vigneri. We ordered a rare bottle of its 2005 version and drank it with antipasti. The wine was indeed wild, "hard," astringent, and aggressively acidic. It was stunning that a man capable of making soft, seductive wines (his wines for Benanti and other clients had won medals and were avidly collected in Italy) chose to make a wine so raw.

"This is how I believe the wine was," Foti said. But I also saw it as a wine that was Foti in the present: a Sicilian wine that seemed intent to offend polite company. On the back label of the bottle was a citation from his book, *La Montagna di Fuoco (Mountain of Fire)*, the retelling of conversations on wine, culture, and history that Foti had with friends on Etna over a period of days:

Si conosce veramente e intimamente l'uomo attraverso il suo vino . . . credo che ognuno fa il vino che è! (One truly and intimately knows a man by his wine . . . I believe that each makes the wine he is!) Beyond the poetry of the thought, I saw in it a challenge. A simple phrase that damned the sinners and comforted the righteous. Not so much a wine as a call to judgment.

THE NEXT DAY WAS my last in Sicily for some time. I planned to meet a man who worked for the local forest service and had a small vineyard in Passopisciaro from which he made a wine that was a local legend known as Il Vino Cosmico ("The Cosmic Wine").

"Pietro is not entirely of this world," warned Frank Cornelissen, something I took as a strong recommendation coming from Frank, who was himself often considered from another realm.

At five in the evening, as I drove to Passopisciaro, the sun appeared a white obscure disk in a wet sky. At the local café I met Giuseppe Zingali, the Sicilian who had worked for Frank the previous winter but was now a caretaker of others' vineyards. Giuseppe, who had his two-year-old son in a baby carrier in his car, would lead me to Pietro and his cosmic vineyard.

I followed Giuseppe through Arcuria. We turned off the road onto a dirt trail of parallel tire tracks that snaked through the *sciara* of rough boulders scattered with almond trees, wild olives, and *macchia*. We stopped in front of a small stone cabin surrounded by fruit trees and a garden plot that still had the last dying traces of that season's tomatoes and zucchini.

Standing in front of the cabin, Pietro Crimi was thin, medium height, with hazel eyes and smooth skin covered with white-flecked stubble. His most noticeable feature was a healthy head of dark, wavy hair that—combined with a face that is free of any apparent stress—made him look much younger than his fifty-five years. He wore a thick white button-up shirt, baggy brown corduroys tucked into tall brown rubber boots, and a gray canvas hunting vest. Pietro was handsome but as he smiled brightly with his eyes, I noticed that his lips remained puckered inward. Pietro has no teeth.

He invited us into the cabin—one room with a cement floor. There was a cot along the back wall next to a corner fireplace, some tin and wood cabinets, and some wooden folding chairs. On the walls were a few paintings of people and places in the countryside made on canvas and paper, bunches of drying herbs, a rusty antique axe, and a pair of coiled extensions cords. In the center of the room sat one wood table crammed with nuts and pieces of cut bread and bottles in varying states of emptiness, which seemed to contain—or to have contained—red wine.

Pietro picked a small half-smoked cigar off the table and rolled it between his fingers. A bachelor, Pietro lived most of the time in his family house in Randazzo with his aged and ailing mother. But when there was work to be done on the farm in Arcuria, he lived here in the cabin with seven cats and two canine mutts. From behind my head I heard a barely perceptible tapping and turned to see that on one of the cupboards was a gray mole climbing the side of a live trap. "That's a little friend I am going to transfer to another place," Pietro smiled—his mouth widening to an "O."

Pietro led us back around the house, in through another door, and into a tiny cellar no bigger than a one-car garage. The room was filled with an old-fashioned *palmento* that Pietro himself had replicated here twenty years earlier. At the back of the room was a rectangular cement basin about three meters wide by two deep. The mouth of the basin was covered with thick, worn, and purple-stained boards.

Pietro explained how it all worked. Here, each year, Pietro gathered friends for the harvest. The grapes from Pietro's small vineyard were placed on the boards as groups of men, women, and children with rolled-up pant cuffs did a rhythmic barefoot dance in the fruit while someone picked up a guitar and played something gypsy-sounding or Pietro breathed out a melody on his flute. As they danced, the juice dripped down between the boards into the 1,000-liter vat. When the juice stopped flowing, the must was piled into a mound and more boards were placed on it. About a half-dozen of Pietro's merry harvesters lent their weight to the task of pressing—balanced on the boards while holding onto each other or the wood rafters. More purple juice flowed. At the end of the day, all the pressed skins were swept into the vat below to begin fermentation. A day or two later, a thick valve at the bottom of the basin was opened and the fermenting juice spilled out into a smaller vertical vat sunken in the ground. The pomace was squeezed in an old wood basket press, and all the juice was placed in a 700-liter chestnut barrel that Pietro would transport by truck to an old barn stall in Randazzo.

The whole process was, by the standards of modern winemaking, rustic—laughable. Forget temperature control, Pietro didn't even use a thermometer.

In the last light of the day, Pietro walked us out toward his vines. At the side of his house was an orange tree laden with fruit that was now deep green. Further on was a persimmon tree—leaf bare and dangling its yield like small brilliant-red pumpkins. Pietro took a knife from his pocket and cut into the shriveled skins, handing each of us an open fruit with oozing sweet flesh. As we devoured them, he led us to a garden faucet to wash the jammy stickiness from our hands. We walked up the entry road past almond trees and larch and Ilex oaks. The ground burst with color from knee-high red valerian (a flowering herb used for centuries as a natural sedative), yellow *cavolicello* blooms, and wild cyclamens.

Pietro had bought this land nearly thirty years before. The vines were tall, trained along cordon wires strung between concrete posts. The small vineyard had been planted for mechanization, but under Pietro's stewardship had fallen back into being worked by hand and fed only with garden compost. Pietro evidently did not share the same perceptions of *alberello* vines with Foti and his *vigneri*, but he was every bit as much a man formed by Etna and its soil.

Standing amid the vines, we spoke of Il Vino Cosmico. Pietro laughed, twirled the unlit cigar in the air, and explained how the name was coined after one long night of feasting and drinking with friends up on the mountain. On that night, several years earlier, there were about twenty people gathered outdoors by the light of a fire when Pietro stood to speak.

"I had drunk quite a bit," he admitted. "I spoke about the vines, humanity, the sun, the wind . . . Etna," each word spoken with a flourish, rising to a crescendo. In Italian it sounded like this: *"Le viti! L'umanità! Il sole! Il vento! L'Etna!"*

"I spoke about the vines, my wine, and the cosmos, because I do believe there is a correspondence . . . and then I said, 'Il Vino Cosmico.'" Pietro showed that hollowed toothless smile once more and repeated, "Il Vino Cosmico!"

The Sicilian countryside remains still enough that a man can say something in a fit of drunken inspiration that follows him around for life and becomes his epitaph. We walked back to the cabin, feet tamping through the damp earth.

"The origin of wine is to drink normally in family, without all this . . . *raffinatezza*." Pietro waved the cigar hand toward the sky. I had never up until that moment thought of the word "refinement" in the way Pietro was using it—to describe fine wines as novelty. "I find what's happening to wine now all a bit distorted. I see it as something *stupido*."

While Giuseppe's son slept in the car, the three of us went inside Pietro's cabin. Pietro walked over to the fireplace and removed an improvised tin cover that had been placed over the opening. Behind was an assortment of incongruous jugs, bottles, and jars, showing contents of different colors. Pietro searched among them until he pulled out one clear wine bottle filled with a light cherry-colored liquid.

Pietro rarely bottled his wine—most of it went into jugs and was drunk within the year. But here was one of two remaining bottles of his 2006 wine. Il Vino Cosmico. He brought out some tumblers from a cabinet and set them on the table, uncorked the bottle, and poured. We saluted.

I didn't expect much. The wine was fruity and quaffable and dissolved at the back of the throat with a prickly citrus afterburn. There was nothing that made you want to burst forth with comparisons with Burgundy or Barolo, but somehow it made you want to drink more. It was less harsh than Foti's I Vigneri (delivered without the edgy political message) and it was less extracted and ripe than Frank Cornelissen's Rosso del Contadino. But it was from the same family of old Etna wines.

Giuseppe and I cracked walnuts and ate them whole, and I watched as Pietro took some and put them into a little hand-cranked mill that turned the nuts into a powder, which he spooned into his hollow mouth. A black and white cat jumped on his shoulder.

Soon the glasses were empty and refilled. I asked how much alcohol was in the wine and Pietro shrugged. He found a miniature glass hydrometer in a cupboard and dropped it into a tumbler full of wine. It was a strong 14.5 percent.

Giuseppe smiled. "You could drink three bottles of this easily."

I thought of the months I had traveled from one end of Sicily to the other. Of the cellars, vines, helicopters, aristocrats, entrepreneurs, and foreigners. After all that, I'd ended up with a man who at this moment seemed the wisest of all: Saint Francis without even a molar to call his own.

Giuseppe drained another glass and grinned. "The more you drink the better it gets."

He was right. Pietro refilled our glasses again with wine that could never be for sale, because then there wouldn't be enough for Pietro to drink with friends the rest of the year. When the bottle of Il Vino Cosmico was finished, we walked outside. The sky was glowing with a purplish haze, empty. Looking north, the lights of the town of Malvinia, perched on a hillside a mile away, appeared like the only stars in the night.

Pietro lit his cigar stub. He had one more thing he wanted to tell me and it was this: "The fact that we have left one epoch for another so quickly." He cupped the fingers of his free hand, pressed his fingers to the center of his chest. "That is something that bothers me, a lot . . . truly . . . inside."

Sicily and change was an inevitable subject, even in places where it was little changed. Certainly, Sicily seemed to be in a good period. It was free. It was an optimistic part of the twenty-first century. It had young, smart people who little by little were building resorts and spas and golf courses and sophisticated restaurants and making great wines. Yet it seemed to be only a matter of time before—like much of the rest of Italy—it would lose something. I thought of the bridge that would connect Sicily to the Italian boot and the continent and an endless supply of fashion outlets, fast food, and doubt.

Sicily, I thought, is Italy's last stand. In Sicily's heart, she must know this.

16. Andrea Franchetti in Passopisciaro

17. Passopisciaro vineyards in fall

18. Pop star Mick Hucknall (*right*) being
interviewed in his vineyard by Italian television

19. Ciro Biondi in an abandoned *palmento* on Etna

20. Sebastiano De Bartoli on Pantelleria

21. Salvatore Ferrandes in his grape-
drying greenhouse on Pantelleria

22. Carole Bouquet among her
vineyards on Pantelleria

23. Salvatore Geraci of Palari

24. An abandoned *palmento* on Etna

25. Alberto Aiello Graci

26. Nino, the foreman at Graci

27. Salvo Foti

28. Pietro Crimi in the *palmento* where
he makes his cosmic wine

29. Making ricotta on Etna

30. Giovanni Scarfone of Bonavita

A New Year

14

New Wine

THE THIRD SUNDAY OF MARCH 2009 was set as the date when the
2008 Etna vintage would reveal itself—at least to Sicily and a slice of
the Italian wine trade and press. The second edition of *Le Contrade
dell'Etna* would unfold at Andrea Franchetti's Passopisciaro winery,
with producers from all over the mountain showing off their wines.
Mass wine tastings—the kind where professionals gather to swirl,
sniff, spit, take notes—aren't generally my kind of thing. The businesslike routine sends my blood sinking to my feet, and after about
fifteen or twenty mouthfuls of wine I find it hard to taste much of
anything—let alone get pleasure from the experience.

Still, I'd become fond of Etna and felt close to some of its winemakers; I'd seen the vineyards play out in all their seasons and didn't
want to miss the final act. On Friday afternoon, two days before the
gathering, I drove up the mountain to Sandro's bar. A cold rain was
falling, and by the time I arrived in Solicchiata, the Friday night tasting
was under way. I filled up on sausages and homemade pizza at the
bar and caught up on news of the regulars: Frank, Alberto, Pippo the
mechanic, Brandon the retired American Navy technician who had
been based in Catania and never left. I learned that Frank and Alberto

would not be producing wines from their five-acre vineyard at 1,000 meters in the Barbabecchi *contrada* (from which Alberto planned to make his "Nicole Kidman" *cru*). This high-elevation vineyard had been the last they were planning to harvest, but before the grapes had a chance to reach maturity someone else had taken the washed-out rugged trail up the mountain and done the harvest themselves. In other words, the year's crop had been *stolen*.

"We're still in Sicily," Frank said with a weary grin. "In early November they were the only grapes left on the vines. So some people probably just came along and said, 'Look here's some grapes that haven't been picked. Let's take them.'" As a result he and Alberto would be putting up more fences—not just to keep out rabbits or stray cattle or sheep, but Sicilians who perhaps disagreed with waiting until November for the wine harvest.

Those next few nights I spent in Sandro's *casetta*—a little house in the vineyards and olive groves west of Passopisciaro that he and his wife, Lucia, rented out by the day. The place was sealed up tight with a padlocked door and steel window shutters that were barred from inside. It was a charming bungalow: one large room with a couch, fireplace, and kitchen; the dishes, pots, and pans were all neatly arranged in their drawers, and the cabinets stocked with pasta and canned tomatoes and spices. There was a small bedroom and bath off the main room, and, up a set of wood stairs, a sleeping loft under the exposed roof beams.

That very day was the first day of spring, a time when I'd expected gentle breezes, sunshine, and the music of songbirds. Yet that night it felt as damp and wintry as it had at Mr. Purello's apartment more than a year earlier. In Sandro's place, heat was supplied by one source: the fireplace that had been crammed with olive branches ready to be lit and was eager to consume the pile of firewood stacked in the corner by the like-new stereo with turntable. The concept of warmth was complicated in that I was wearing light cotton clothes (which, I was told, would have been appropriate the week before when everyone was running around in shirtsleeves) and Alitalia had left my suitcase—and my sweaters and parka—behind in Rome. Though

Rome to Catania was little more than an hour's flight, I knew that my bag was now in the hands of Italian bureaucracy. Getting anything to Catania and then up the road to Solicchiata would take a couple of days. So all weekend I stoked the fire. That first night I piled blankets on the upstairs mattress and went to sleep with the shadows of flames dancing on the ceiling.

The next morning, I awoke early to add some logs to the smoldering coals and ran up the stairs to fall back into bed. After a shower, timed to the mood of the fifty-liter hot water tank, I dried off while standing as close as I could to the hearth without grilling my flesh. A wind from the west was blowing cold and wet, covering Etna's north face and the Alcantara Valley in mist. After breakfast of a hot cappuccino and a marmalade-filled cornetto (the sweet Italian version of a croissant) while standing at Sandro's bar, I headed off for my first wine of the day at Azienda Terre di Trente.

While it may sound like a wine operation that's been there forever, Terre di Trente was in fact part of the newest of Etna's new wave, where the international art set met the volcano. I drove through Linguaglossa, followed another car the wrong way down a one-way street, splashed through a running stream, idled through a flock of sheep, and then arrived at the lush, steep amphitheater of the Contrada Mollarella vineyards.

Trente is Trente Hargrove—the female African American part of the couple with her partner, the Belgian art dealer Filip Kesteloot. Tall and fit with flowing dreadlocks and a warm, soft handshake and smile, Trente greeted me at the door of the renovated *palmento* with a glass of wine. The place was done in great taste—from the mammoth modern Spanish oil painting of nudes over the fireplace to a great gather-round kitchen, to the living room with artifacts and instruments from South Asia, to the sleek bathroom with the double shower. There was no winery here. The pair farmed their grapes organically with the help of a local vineyard man, and then brought them to Marco de Grazia's winery, where they were vinified and bottled under their own label.

Filip was up on the terraces somewhere above the *palmento*, using a chain saw to clear brush for some new vine plantings. Trente sat with perfect posture on a plump sofa and told her abbreviated life story. She was born in Bridgeport, Connecticut, a decade before I was, yet she could pass for someone twenty years younger than her age. Given that calculus, I wondered if Filip—who has boyish looks and appeared about my age—might be old enough to be my father.

The story of how Trente landed on the north face of Etna begins, "I was living in Pakistan . . . " and from there it becomes a tangle of places and coincidences. As a youth in Manhattan she studied music and art in high school and later got her real estate broker's license. At one point there was the marriage to an Italian diplomat—a Sicilian—hence the diplomatic move to Pakistan. In Pakistan, Trente told, she developed herbal treatments, co-founded the country's first woman-owned business, wrote anti-aging tracts, and played the sitar. She was, she said, working on a formula for an herbal equivalent of Viagra when her husband left her and headed to Brussels. Because she was in Pakistan on her husband's visa, his departure meant she had to leave the country immediately—so she followed her husband to Brussels to sue for divorce. To pay her divorce costs she sold an Erté sculpture to the only dealer around qualified for such a transaction—it was Filip's gallery.

After their relationship blossomed they might have lived happily as Brussels art dealers, except they had decided to buy a vacation home in Sicily. But the deal fell through, and one day in October 2003 they were lost in a rainstorm on Etna and fell upon de Grazia's winery. Marco offered them a cup of tea. He told them about a property with about five acres of vineyards that he knew of, but they were not interested. Then—Trente gave me a wide-eyed look as she recounted this part—a man showed up at Marco's door and had the same last name as her ex-husband. That simple fact changed everything and convinced her they needed to look at this property and what was then the rat-infested pile of stones of an abandoned *palmento*.

It would be easy to cynically mock this kind of story—to interpret it as seekers weaving coincidence out of air. But after experiencing the seasons of Sicily, I was somewhat sympathetic. I had my own share of personal odd experiences in which fate seemed to have played no small role. Adding to the sense of destiny, Trente also likes to point out that their terrain is divided, as is their couple, into "ebony and ivory": half the vineyard is white calcareous soil, and the other half—on the other side of the stream—black volcanic earth.

When Filip returned to the house, wet from the rain that had begun to fall and covered in dust, he explained how he had first seen wine as a sort of novel accessory to his gallery. "We bought a lot of wine and champagne for the gallery anyway, so I figured why not make something we could give away." Now, several years down that road, they were producing a red wine sold in Europe that was a somewhat brighter version of de Grazia's.

SUNDAY MORNING—THE DAY OF *Le Contrade* and the third day into spring—I opened the front door of the *casetta* to a sight that took my mind a few moments to comprehend. The front terrace of the house and the nearby olive groves and vines were covered in a blanket of several of inches of snow that was falling from a heavy sky.

About an hour later, I edged slowly down the hill—the thigh-high weeds and spring wildflowers were bent and wilting in the cold. I drove toward Passopisciaro and then turned down the road to Solicchiata, which was covered with a slushy soup. Through the fogged windshield I noticed the morning's second odd sight, which took a few seconds to process: standing by the road in the snow was a hooded monk in Franciscan habit. A wooden cross dangled from the rope belt slung around his waist, and his feet were bare and raw in a pair of leather sandals that looked as though they had been made a thousand years ago. He was facing with his right hand outstretched—the thumb extended heavenward. In summary: here was a Franciscan monk hitchhiking on a snowy day in spring.

I stopped the car and rolled down the window, explaining in Italian that I was going to Solicchiata. "Not Linguaglossa?" He responded in Italian with a funny accent I couldn't pin down. Was it some sort of mountain Sicilian dialect? No, I shrugged. While Solicchiata was only a couple of minutes away, Linguaglossa was at least another twenty minutes down the road in these miserable driving conditions. I put the car in gear and started down the road. I drove about eighty yards, and then I looked in the rearview mirror and saw the robed figure standing there. It then hit me like a thunderbolt: I had not only just seen a Franciscan monk hitchhiking on a snowy day in spring, but I had blown him off!

I stepped on the brakes, stopped the car, put it in reverse, and backed down the road to where I'd been a minute earlier. "Linguaglossa—okay!" I said. He looked at me. Was that the look of satisfaction men of the order get when they save a soul? He was tall enough that he had to duck into the car. We conversed a bit in Italian, and I listened attentively to that weird accent.

"Lei parla Inglese?" I ventured.

It turned out that Brother Alessio, as he introduced himself, not only spoke English but was from Massachusetts. That strange accent was pure New England! He was living in a monastery in the Alcantara Valley and hitchhiking his way to Mass in Acireale on the southwest side of the mountain, about fifty minutes away. He had just spent his first winter in Sicily. He was about forty years old and had a light beard. I don't remember his face because my eyes were on the road, but I do remember his voice—the familiar, friendly New England chatter as he told me about his work in Sicily as a writer, documenting the lives of Catholic saints.

I told him that I was a writer as well—that I wrote about wine. And other things.

"How good a job is that?!" he said.

We spent nearly a half hour in that car together, talking about people and wine.

"None of the locals around here buy wine," Alessio said. "They all seem to make their own or have someone in the family who makes it. When I ask them about buying wine they all tell me, 'The other wines are watered down,' or 'They have chemicals.' They don't trust it."

As we approached Linguaglossa, I asked Brother Alessio if his feet ever got cold. "Oh yes!" he said, and mentioned something about penance. I turned up the heat to the floorboards. I left him on a bustling corner where he was sure to find another lift. As he left me he said, "May God bless you for this act of charity." I would need that blessing later the next week—when I negotiated a hairpin turn going in opposition to traffic on a one-way street by the coast.

I drove back through the slush to Solicchiata and Sandro's bar, where I met with a group that was heading up the mountain. The driving was done by Brandon, the Bronx native who lived, it seemed, for wine and women. Every time I had met him over the course of a year he seemed to be acquiring more of the former and losing one of the latter. "I just broke up with my girlfriend" usually entered into the conversation in the first five minutes. It was hard to keep track, though Brandon informed me that the last breakup was with a Sicilian geologist whom he had asked to return the pearl necklace he'd given her. Brandon reported that she had obliged—but only after dipping the pearls in corrosive acid.

Franchetti's winery was engulfed in a blizzard. Snowflakes the size of fat local Nocellara olives dropped to the ground and formed a soup with the mud puddles. Large white tents were wrapped around the back of the winery—a temporary dining room to feed the lunchtime masses. Inside the winery bottling room—cleared for the occasion—about fifty wine producers lined the perimeter where they displayed and offered tastes of their latest bottlings along with vintages still in barrel and some older ones.

From about ten in the morning until the last rays of light that afternoon, the room was packed with a rotating crowd of several hundred people. There was a lot of drinking and talking but very little spitting. There were the people who looked like they parachuted in from Rome or Milan—the men in pinstripes and soft loafers and the women in skirts and boots with heels as tall as railroad spikes. There were the Tuscan winemakers with properties on Etna who looked the part of Italian gentleman and gentlewoman farmers. There was Dr. Giuseppe Benanti, the pharmaceuticals executive, and his sons from the Benanti winery with a range of white Carricante-based wines that grew more complex and delicious with age. Ciro Biondi, in a tweedy jacket, with his English wife, Stephanie Pollock, poured samples of an intriguing, smoky 2008 Outis Bianco that blended many of the grapes I'd seen in Biondi's vineyards: Carricante, Catarratto, Minnella, Muscatella, and Bianca di Candia. But this vintage also had a higher content of Malvasia—grapes that came from a vineyard that had previously been used by Ciro's father to make his own wine.

There were the young winemakers local to the region, like Giuseppe Russo and Alberto Aiello Graci. And there were the exotic *stranieri* couples: Trente and Filip, Frank and Aki (who was now showing her pregnancy and was expecting to deliver in summer after their wedding in July). It had not been long ago that all the winemakers in Sicily putting wine into bottles could have fit in this room. Now it contained barely half the winemakers on Etna. There were delicious wines and woody wines and weird wines, lively wines, dead wines, and wines that still fizzed in the bottle. One Scandinavian woman oenologist working for a Tuscan winemaker claimed to have bottled the vinous equivalent of "pure lava."

Roaming around the edges of the crowd—usually pursued by colleagues, friends, or journalists—was Franchetti, the beaming maestro who had made this all possible. Franchetti had a boyish mismatched look: a flannel shirt and fire engine red sweater covered by a gray wool blazer. How, I wondered, had the 2008 vintage—which Franchetti pronounced just a couple of months ago as thin and shitty—turned out?

Oh, it wasn't so bad after all, Franchetti was saying. In fact, he told me, "The wines can be tougher, tighter." He was talking of moving to earlier harvests and lighter wines—completely changing the course of his winemaking. "In Tuscany I went to one extreme in the other direction. Now I am going to turn the wheel the other way."

What had happened to convert Andrea Franchetti from a Nerello skeptic to a proponent of austerity? Was it his artistic streak? A response to the marketplace? Or his mood of the day? No doubt it had something to do with his winemaker, Anna Martins, who spent much time on Etna that year working, observing, and tasting. I would like to think that Franchetti—a man who went to Etna to mold the vineyards in his style—ended up being changed by the mountain.

The most enduring memory of the day came in late morning. I had found my way to one of the small stone sheds behind the winery. There, in the cold and damp, a pair of local young *contadini* had set up a large gas burner with a stew pot propped over the flame. They were heating the morning's sheep milk and stirring it with a wood spoon the length of a yardstick. There was a small crowd of about a dozen people—as many as would fit in this tiny shed, plus a trail of others outside—waiting with white plates and large soup spoons. There was that distinct smell of milk touching hot metal, but in this case the milk had a whole other dimension of animal life. To start the curdling of the cheese, the men added water in which they had soaked fig branches. The milk swirled and solidified until it was deemed thick enough to serve. This ricotta, something between liquid and cheese, was ladled into the white outstretched plates. It was more intimate and comforting than any food I have ever tasted.

MY LAST MORNING ON ETNA, I went to open the metal door of the casetta to see how high the snow had mounted. As the door cracked open I was blinded not by another blizzard but by the sheen of a warm, bright morning sun. The snow among the olives and vines had melted, and a breeze from the north had chased away any clouds. The Peloritani Mountains formed a snow-capped white chain that sparkled in the light.

I was headed to Messina, accompanied by the wine writer and Rome wine wholesaler Tiziana Gallo. Tiziana had a career as a lawyer before she'd fallen for wine a decade earlier and became an advocate of Italy's natural wine movement. In Messina we met a young winemaker by the name of Giovanni Scarfone, who was producing Faro wines on family plots perched above the village of Faro Superiore—overlooking Messina and the Strait.

Like Salvatore Geraci of Palari, Giovanni was one of just a handful of Faro producers. There the similarities ended. While Geraci was established, Giovanni was working on his third vintage. While Geraci was seasoned, manicured, loquacious, and operatic, Giovanni was twenty-nine, youthful, and raw with a quiet demeanor and expressive eyes. He was rail thin, wore a black leather jacket and jeans, and had long sideburns and untamed curly black hair that stood atop a long, slightly rutted face.

Giovanni drove us into the hills in a van with his girlfriend, Santina, a light-haired mother of three with a gentle smile and sad-looking eyes that turned downward at the corners. We stopped at his family home—a two-story 1960s-era apartment block where Giovanni lived with his parents and made wine with his father, Carmelo, in a cramped white-tiled basement. The wine was released under the label Bonavita; the first vintage of 2006 produced only 3,000 bottles, which quickly sold out in Italy at about half the price of Palari.

Behind the house on a pitted dirt road was the ruin of a grand two-story *palmento*: the outer masonry was peeling away to reveal irregular thin bricks, and a corner of the building had been shaved away by vehicles that did not quite make a tricky turn in the road. Now, blocking the front arched stone doorway, was the rusting shell of a Fiat 500 firmly in the jaws of giant brambles.

Giovanni, whose only memories of the *palmento* were just as it was that day, drove us further into the hills. We stopped in front of a padlocked gate and walked along a path lined with prickly pear cacti, tall cypresses, oaks and maritime pines. We came to a clearing and saw a vineyard. The patchwork plots of cordoned vines (which Giovanni insisted were better adapted than *alberello*-shaped vines to this maritime-influenced tip of the island) were carpeted with wild flowers and fava plants sprouting from porous tufa-like earth. The vine rows extended to a point a couple of hundreds yards to the north where the land seemed to melt into a horizon of blue sea. We were at edge of the Messina peninsula facing north, the Messina Strait and the horizon of Calabria now behind us.

Giovanni and his father, a retired bank clerk, worked five acres of vines themselves plus some acres of olive groves—their only fertilizer provided by the nitrogen-fixing fava plants and the nearby chickens in a coop on the hillside. This vineyard had been passed down from Giovanni's great-grandfather—one of the family's only survivors of the 1908 Messina earthquake. It was a rare thing to see at this edge of Sicily, where so many farms and vineyards had been abandoned decades ago and left to the wild grasses.

Like so many places in Sicily and the Italian Mezzogiorno, Messina and its outlying lands had been defined by natural disaster: the earthquake shook for less than a minute in the predawn, but it destroyed more than 90 percent of the city's buildings and killed more than 100,000 people. A century later, Messina was rebuilt into a modern city with a thriving port and bustling boulevards. But the countryside has never healed.

"So many people died in the earthquake that people had to come from other places to work the land. But there wasn't really anyone who cared about it," Giovanni said, adding, so as not to be presumptuous, "this is what I have always heard from my grandfather and father."

"That is why, we say, that the Messinese are not *citizens* of Messina, they are *residents*. They are people who happen to live here, but they are all people from elsewhere."

After the earthquake many survivors fled their horrible memories for a new start. Following two world wars, there was a proliferation of government jobs in town—easy money that seemed to flow into Sicily as part of the reconstruction of the Italian Mezzogiorno. Cultivation slowed, and the hillsides became bedroom communities for functionaries and their progeny.

"It's hard to make my friends understand why I am working the land in the country," Giovanni said. He had grown up watching his father work the vineyards in his spare time—selling grapes or making wine for the family. He considered this legacy a great gift, and at twenty he decided he would become a winemaker and went north to study agronomy. "They prefer to be doing something simpler—that makes more money—like a lawyer."

We walked back to the van, Santina pulling the tops of wild fennel plants that she placed in a plastic bag. The four of us headed to lunch in Messina with bottles of Bonavita's first two vintages—a softer, simpler, and more subtle Faro than Geraci's.

We spoke of many things—particularly about his generation that had mastered the art of virtual communication. Giovanni was on Facebook, but he preferred face contact—"to speak to people eye to eye." "Only in this way," he said, "is it possible to understand the emotion of the person."

Once a year, he invited his friends from town to join in the harvest for a day or two. They worked, they ate together, and the next morning they were back at their desks. These young city dwellers loved what came out of the Sicilian countryside and its traditions. Or, rather, "they like *the idea*," Giovanni corrected. "But it's putting it into practice that is hard."

"I am pessimistic," he said softly. "We lack the culture of agriculture . . . it interests no one."

I headed down the coast that afternoon with a different feeling. I had come to Sicily to explore its wines but ended up discovering many other things—among them that there are still people like Giovanni, who have a deep sense of place that has taken me years to understand. It was a thought, or rather, an emotion that seemed to crystallize for me that day in Messina: the way each generation cultivates the land and reaches out across time. The simple act of trimming a vine not only changes the life of the plant but also leaves an imprint for future generations. This is communion that, with some hope, will continue long after we return to livid dust.

I Vini

ADDRESSES OF FEATURED WINEMAKERS BY REGION

ETNA

Azienda Vinicola Benanti
Via Garibaldi, 475
95029 Viagrande
+39 095 7893438
www.vinicolabenanti.it

Vini Biondi
Corso Sicilia, 20
95039 Trecastagni
+39 392 8191538
www.vinibiondi.it

Il Cantante
Via Cavour, 42
95010 Sant'Alfio
+39 095 968203
www.ilcantante.com

Azienda Agricola Frank Cornelissen
Via Nazionale 281
95030 Solicchiata
+39 0942 986315

I Vigneri di Salvo Foti
Via Tamburino Merlini
95044 Mineo
+39 0933 982942
www.salvofoti.it

Graci
Contrada Arcuria, Passopisciaro
95012 Castiglione di Sicilia
+39 3487 016773
www.graci.eu

Passopisciaro
Via S. Spirito, Passopisciaro
95030 Castiglione di Sicilia
+39 0578 267110
www.passopisciaro.com

Girolamo Russo
Via Regina Margherita, 78
95012 Passopisciaro
www.girolamorusso.it
+39 328 3840247

Tenuta delle Terre Nere
Contrada Calderara
95036 Randazzo
+39 095 924002

Azienda Terre di Trente
Contrada Mollarella
95015 Linguaglossa
+39 340 3075433
www.terreditrente.com

ISPICA

Antica Azienda Agraria Curto
Via Galilei, 4
97014 Ispica
+39 0932 950161
www.curto.it

Riofavara
Contrada Favara
97014 Ispica
+39 0932 705130
www.riofavara.it

MARSALA

Marco De Bartoli
Contrada Fornara Samperi
91025 Marsala
+39 0923 962093
www.marcodebartoli.com

Carlo Pellegrino & C.
Via del Fante, 39
91025 Marsala
+39 0923 719911
www.carlopellegrino.it

MENFI

Aziende Agricole Planeta
Contrada Dispensa
92013 Menfi
+39 0925 80009
www.planeta.it

MESSINA

Bonavita
Contrada Corso
Faro Superiore
98158 Messina
+39 090 2932106
www.bonavitafaro.it

Azienda Agricola Palari
98137 S. Stefano di Briga
+39 090 630194
www.palari.it

PALERMO (PROVINCE)

Coop Placido Rizzotto-Libera Terra
Via Porta Palermo, 132
San Giuseppe Jato
+39 091 8577655
www.cantinacentopassi.it

Tasca d'Almerita
Tenuta Regaleali
90020 Sclafani Bagni
+39 091 6459711
www.tascadalmerita.it

PANTELLERIA

Fabrizio Basile
Contrada Bukkuram
91017 Pantelleria
+39 0923 917205

Azienda Agricola Ferrandes
Via del Fante, 8
Tracino
91017 Pantelleria

Serraglio di Carole Bouquet
Strada Ponte Rekale Nica'
91017 Pantelleria
+39 092 3916885

VITTORIA

Azienda Agricola COS
SP 3
97019 Vittoria
+39 0932 876145
www.cosvittoria.it

Azienda Agricola Arianna Occhipinti
Via dei Mille, 55
97019 Vittoria
+39 339 7383580
www.agricolaocchipinti.it

In the At Table series

*The Food and Cooking of
Eastern Europe*
Lesley Chamberlain
With a new introduction
by the author

The Food and Cooking of Russia
Lesley Chamberlain
With a new introduction
by the author

The World on a Plate
*A Tour through the History of
America's Ethnic Cuisine*
Joel Denker

Jewish American Food Culture
Jonathan Deutsch and
Rachel D. Saks

The Recipe Reader
Narratives, Contexts, Traditions
Edited by Janet Floyd and
Laurel Forster

Masters of American Cookery
*M. F. K. Fisher, James Beard,
Craig Claiborne, Julia Child*
Betty Fussell
With a preface by the author

My Kitchen Wars
A Memoir
Betty Fussell
With a new introduction
by Laura Shapiro

Good Things
Jane Grigson

Jane Grigson's Fruit Book
Jane Grigson
With a new introduction
by Sara Dickerman

Jane Grigson's Vegetable Book
Jane Grigson
With a new introduction
by Amy Sherman

Dining with Marcel Proust
*A Practical Guide to French
Cuisine of the Belle Epoque*
Shirley King
Foreword by James Beard

Pampille's Table
*Recipes and Writings from the French
Countryside from Marthe Daudet's*
Les Bons Plats de France
Translated and adapted
by Shirley King

Moveable Feasts
The History, Science, and Lore of Food
Gregory McNamee

To order or obtain more
information on these or other
University of Nebraska Press titles,
visit www.nebraskapress.unl.edu.